THE COURT AND

LOCAL LAW ENFORCEMENT

The Court and
Local Law Enforcement

THE IMPACT OF *MIRANDA*

Neal A. Milner

 SAGE PUBLICATIONS
Beverly Hills, California

For information address:

Sage Publications, Inc.
275 South Beverly Drive
Beverly Hills, California 90212

Printed in the United States of America

Library of Congress Catalog Card No.: 76-127991

Standard Book Number: 8039-0075-9

First Printing

TO *Joy*

PREFACE

Anyone who has ever attempted research requiring both library and field work will attest to the fact that a large number of cooperative and insightful people are necessary to implement the project's goals. My research was no exception. I briefly thank all those who assisted me; their help was invaluable. I take ultimate responsibility, of course, for the research·findings and conclusions.

The police chiefs in each of the four Wisconsin cities were particularly helpful. Without their cooperation I could not have submitted questionnaires to the rest of the department. Nor could I have gained valuable insights about police behavior which I acquired traveling with on-duty detectives. The chiefs are Elmer Madsen (Green Bay), Le Roy Jenkins (Racine), Wilbur Emery (Madison), and J. Leo Buchmann (Kenosha). I extend special acknowledgment to all the state and local officials who consented to be interviewed. Most of them, however, must remain anonymous.

Here a word is necessary about the degree of anonymity in this study. Although local officials are usually not quoted by name, the cities themselves are clearly identified. There are two reasons for this partial anonymity. First, much important material about the political cultures of these cities comes from a recently published book about them. Thus it would be difficult to conceal their identity and still give proper credit to information sources. Second, in my opinion, scholars too often use anonymity as a check against criticism of their work. I would rather risk such criticism in the interest of frankness, especially since the subject matter should have important public significance.

I would also like to thank various colleagues who read the manuscript. Particular appreciation must go to David Fellman and John Gardiner for their thorough reading and insightful comments. Others who helpfully saw all or parts of the work are Norman Adler, Robert Alford, Bradley Canon, Edward Greenberg, and Joel Grossman. Frederick W. Kramer and Barry Gaberman helped me compile the data.

My thanks are also due to Sage Publications and the Law and Society Association for allowing me to use some material previously published in *Law and Society Review*.

I would also like to thank Cheryl Jones and Beverly Youtz, both of whom typed the manuscript. Grinnell College generously paid for expenses associated with final preparation of the manuscript.

My wife Joy was exceedingly thoughtful, understanding, and patient during the preparation of this book. The dedication only partially repays my debt to her.

N. M.

Grinnell, Iowa
November, 1969

CONTENTS

Contents

Chapter 1

THE IMPACT OF
COURT DECISIONS

At the height of a speech castigating the United States Supreme Court's *Mallory* decision—a decision which reversed the conviction of an accused rapist on the grounds that he was detained illegally by police—Senator William Jenner exclaimed, "How many more . . . girls will be raped in 1957 because the Supreme Court was so zealous a protector of Andrew Mallory's rights as an individual?" [1] At first glance this statement might be dismissed as another intemperate exaggeration by a man who was not known either for his temperance or for his adoration of the Warren Court. Yet, on second thought, he raises an interesting question which neither the antagonists—nor in fact the defenders of the Court's decision—can answer with certainty. It is indeed easy for protagonists to accuse Jenner of oversimplifying the issue with his claim that there is a direct causal relation between sexual perversion and Court decisions. When pressed, however, the Court's defenders cannot really offer a good description or explanation of the effects of the *Mallory* decision, or for that matter any other similar decision.

What follows is an attempt not to answer Senator Jenner's precise question but rather to develop a method of more systematically answering the *type* of question he asked. More specifically, this book attempts to assess the impact that the United States Supreme Court's *Miranda v. Arizona* decision had on four Wisconsin police departments during the first fourteen months after the decision. The cities are Racine, Madison, Green Bay and Kenosha. Although such impact research has been hailed as "the second important breakthrough in the modern study of the Supreme Court," [2] it is disconcerting to discover that most theories employed to study the consequences of Court decisions are not all that much better developed than Senator Jenner's rationale.[3] While offering no all-encompassing general theory, this study does attempt to clarify the meaning of such hitherto vague terms as "impact" and "compliance." Furthermore, and probably more significantly in terms of theory-building, it attempts to show how certain social and political variables are related to the impact of a policy. Thus, four concepts must immediately be clarified: policy, impact, compliance, and socio-political variables.

Public Policy and Its Consequences

Supreme Court Justices, like other policy makers, have certain preferences which they desire to be implemented. They attempt to use their power to bring about behavior which implements these preferences. The Court opinion is a means of declaring the Justice's intentions about these aims, and it can also be used to communicate to some degree the means with which policies must be implemented. Not all Court opinions are equally clear about the Justices' goals and the actions required to implement policies based on these goals, but the basic components of policy-making—(1) intent, (2) a desired line of action to implement this intent, and (3) a line of action which the implementers *actually* adopt—are characteristic of the relationship between the Supreme Court and those whom the Court desires to affect.[4] What makes such policy public policy is its adoption by "authorities," that is, by those who engage in the daily affairs of a political system, are recognized by most members of the system as having responsibility in these matters, and whose actions are normally accepted as binding.[5]

Let us think of the implications of Senator Jenner's statements in terms of the components of public policy. The Senator implied that whatever the Court's intent in making the *Mallory* decision, the consequences of the decision were not what the Court had intended (assuming that he did not think the Court wanted to encourage rape). With the procedures it required to implement its intent, the Court brought about consequences which were different and, in the Senator's opinion, far more dastardly than it had desired.

His implications suggest that it is important to investigate the difference between the initial decisions made by a policy-making body and the consequences of these decisions.[6] We must sensitize ourselves to the fact that the consequences of public policy might not turn out to be the anticipated ones (a statement that would seemingly be self-evident had not social scientists tacitly ignored for so long the importance of this fact),[7] and that one way to evaluate the consequences of a policy is by comparing them to the goals of the public policy maker.

In this book I use the term "outputs" to refer to Supreme Court decisions. "Impact" refers to the consequences of policy output. This is not exactly the same as Easton's commonly used term, "outcome," which refers to the secondary and tertiary—but not the initial—consequences of policy output.[8] There is no reason to assume that even the initial change will be the type desired by the policy maker. Thus, outcome and impact are used interchangeably in this study.

Something else is important about Senator Jenner's short statement. It suggests that his methods of analysis greatly limit the type of conclusions he can reach. He concentrated on a single event and assumed that the most important consequences of the decision were found in this event. One must avoid this. The *Miranda* decision may indeed hamper the police, but concentration only upon this possibility limits the likelihood of seeing other more subtle but nonetheless important changes. One must avoid treating an anticipated highly important event as though it were certain to occur.[9]

The questions asked in assessing impact are closely related to the analyst's perceptions of, and probably his values about, the subject of his analysis. This is certainly true in Senator Jenner's case. Yet all social scientists make certain assumptions in their choice of problems, the emphasis placed on various aspects of their analysis, and the resources used to solve these intellectual problems.[10] Consequently, both *what* to evaluate and *how* to evaluate it become important questions. This book focuses on impact exercised on an organization, namely police departments. Certainly *Miranda* may have important consequences for attorneys, judges, or suspects, and any one of these could also be valid and useful areas of study.

I used two checks against the pitfall of anticipating the consequences. First, preliminary interviews were non-structured so that many perceptions of impact were initially obtained. Police perceptions are compared with other perceptions. Second, in addition to presenting the analyst's view of the consequences, this approach attempts, in Van Dyke's words,[11] to

> identify the actors who are relevant to it . . . [to] describe, analyze, and perhaps appraise the perceptions that the actors have of their environment, the motivations or purpose or values or belief systems of the actors, [and] the arguments they employ.

An impact study should look at who was affected, how people think they were affected and, to a lesser extent, the reasons they give to explain or defend their perceptions and attitudes about this effect.[12]

An evaluation of the consequences of public policy requires that careful attention be paid to the "hard" indicators used to measure impact. It is easier to deny that measurement of the rate of a serious sex crime is a valid indicator of impact than it is to develop rational criteria for choosing other indicators. The choice of indicators, which, after all, is closely associated with the choice of questions that one asks, is also closely associated with one's own value preferences.[13]

There are several factors which limit the usefulness of crime statistics in assessing impact. Statistics for various types of crime are indiscriminately lumped together. The indicators which are commonly used to measure police efficiency do not accurately reflect all —or even the most common—police activities. The latter characteristic is particularly limiting, because one of our primary interests is the impact of the *Miranda* decision on the workload of the police. Finally, some useful data are not even gathered.

Crime statistics which are furnished by the police through the FBI's *Uniform Crime Reports* are virtually the sole source of measurement of the police criminal-apprehension workload. These data purport to measure the extent of serious crime in America and the success which the police have had in solving these crimes. Many crimes, however, are never reported or are reported inaccurately.[14] Because the seven crimes that form the basis for the index of "serious" crime are very different from each other, and increase at considerably different rates, this index is misleading when it is used to discuss the extent of serious crime in America.[15]

The clearance rate, the most frequently used indicator of police efficiency, assesses only the percentage of crimes cleared by arrest. This indicator has two serious weaknesses. First, there is no necessary relationship between arresting a person and his ultimate conviction. Nevertheless, police efficiency is measured by this rate and not by an indicator which would better evaluate the quality of the police department's case against a suspect upon arrest.[16] It would be invaluable to have statistics which measured the ratio of cases "cleared" by confessions to those in which a person is ultimately found guilty or pleads guilty in court. Second, society requires that the police carry out other activities in addition to arrests. The process of arrest is only one exercise of social control or conflict resolution, and perhaps a relatively unimportant one at that.[17] The clearance rate is at best a partial indicator of police efficiency.

Clearance statistics were devised by the police for their own purposes. Since police departments perceive that the public usually evaluates law enforcement activities by means of crime and clearance rates, they repeatedly use these figures to assess the impact of Court decisions. The social scientist might want to ask entirely different questions about policy impact and make entirely different assumptions, and may be disappointed that an organization simply does not have the data he would find most useful. As a corollary he is also less willing to accept the validity or reliability of existing measures.[18]

In assessing the impact of *Miranda* there is no way to establish a cause-and-effect relationship between the Court's interrogation policy and crime or arrest rates. There are also no standard indicators which can be used to assess other possible consequences, such as the relationship between police and other organizations in the criminal justice process. No existing statistics even measure the change in the number of confessions obtained prior to and after the decision.[19]

Because of the weaknesses of police workload measures and because these measures are nevertheless considered to be important by police officials, this study approaches their usage with a considerable degree of ambivalence. Because of their perceived importance, crime and clearance rates were investigated in each of four communities, but at the same time keeping in mind the limitations of these measures. Interviews, mail-back questionnaires, and participant-observation were also used to investigate other possible consequences or perceived consequences (see Appendix A).

There is even less agreement about the standards that should be used to measure compliance. Supreme Court decisions may invoke a whole range of responses, and it is inaccurate to dichotomize this behavior as "compliance" or "non-compliance." Such a dichotomy suggests that there is only one approved response to a Court decision and that this response is clearly understood.[20] When the responses involve behavior related to a policy output but not directly litigated in the Court, the compliance/non-compliance division becomes even more misleading. Edward Barrett shows how these complexities apply to police behavior:[21]

> No one disputes the simple proposition that the police must obey the law. The difficulty arises because in many areas there is wide disagreement about what the law is that the police must obey—and even wider disagreement about what rules governing police are consistent with adequate law enforcement under modern conditions.

There is thus no single standard of compliance, particularly in regard to the complexities of police-court relations. Social perceptions of what the law is and how it should be obeyed affect a range of behavior that can be called compliance.[22] While policy output assessment requires a relatively general study of the consequences, assessment of compliance requires the evaluation of behavior *in terms of standards perceived by relevant participants in the process.* Many standards could be chosen, but those used here are based upon the goals either expressed or implied in the *Miranda* decision's majority opinion. Court opinions might not accurately reflect a Justice's motives, goals or policy preferences, but, regardless of their accuracy, they state or imply that certain constraints and directions should be followed by those who must implement the policy output.[23] To measure compliance, police behavior can be compared to the behavior that the majority of Justices seemed to desire and sanction in the *Miranda* opinion. If police behavior does not measure up to these standards, we must ask the following questions: Why did this inconsistency exist? Were the police aware of the inconsistency? Were other standards more frequently used by the police as a frame of reference?

Socio-political Variables

Policy output is the independent variable in this study. The dependent variable is the *impact* of policy output. Other impact studies offer little guidance about intervening variables which affect the process of implementing Court policy.[24] The degree of police professionalization and the extent to which groups participate in the police decision-making process are considered to be the two crucial intervening variables. Their importance results from the relationship of these characteristics to some important aspects of the Court's interrogation policy.

It should be clear that the previously discussed methods for studying impact lend themselves to the study of innovation. Certainly the Supreme Court Justices often intend to bring about innovation and thus often advocate means of achieving such intent. If these are the intentions, then the indicators which are used to measure policy impact—that is, the change related to the implementation of a policy—can also reflect response to desired innovation. Indeed, when we discuss the impact of *Miranda*, we are really discussing the consequences of a decision which quite explicitly attempted to bring about important and basic innovations in law enforcement procedures.

The *Miranda* decision and the Court's recent interrogation policy reflect an attempt to bring about innovations in police behavior, often by bureaucratizing police procedures. *Miranda* furnishes the police with an explicit set of formal rules which are to be used prior to and during all custodial interrogations (see Chapter 2 for further details). Professionalization and participation are important variables because they are both closely related to amenability to innovation and to reactions to bureaucratization.

Although social scientists have shown that some forms of professionalization are related to community innovation, no studies have systematically related police professionalization to response to innovation.[25] This is surprising, because the dominant theme of police reformers has been that police professionalization increases the amenability to innovation policies. Empirical tests of these propositions are lacking, and indeed there is some evidence to suggest that professionalization may *limit* police acceptance of innovations involving police-community relations policies.[26]

James Q. Wilson's studies of police behavior stand alone in their systematic consideration of the effects of professionalization. Although his conclusions will not be specifically tested here, they are valuable because they clearly show the relationship between professionalization and important differences in police behavior. For example, professionalized departments are more likely to arrest and formally process juveniles.[27] Moreover, police departments in cities with professionalized "good government" requirements are more likely to have legalistic police forces that make more arrests for larceny and drunken driving, while departments in the less professionalized, partisan mayor-council cities have higher arrest rates for disorderly conduct.[28] Wilson convincingly shows that such behavior is related to the political culture of the communities.

To summarize briefly, many have suggested—or at least implied —that police professionalization is related to innovation. Though this hypothesis has not been tested, its importance is suggested by two factors. First, innovation and professionalization have been related in non-police studies. Second, and most important, the professionalization of police departments not only seems related to local government professionalization but also to differences in law enforcement behavior.

On the basis of their study of the four Wisconsin cities also analyzed here, Alford and Scoble showed that the degree of bureaucratization and participation in a community is closely related to a community's response regarding innovation and further bureaucratization.[29] Cities with the highest degree of each of these two variables are most likely to adopt new policies at an earlier date and to have a greater number of programs related to these policies. Cities with low levels of bureaucratization and participation are least likely to manifest these characteristics.[30] Highly bureaucratized cities with a high level of participation are most likely to use formal channels of influence and to place greater reliance on formal procedures. Community norms regarding these two variables are closely related to the norms which groups and organizations involved in governmental decision-making manifest. The political culture of a community (roughly defined as the existence of public norms about participation and bureaucratization) is clearly related to the bureaucratic and participatory characteristics of local governmental organizations.[31]

Since the present study focuses on police departments, bureaucratization and participation are used primarily to analyze police departments and the groups that impinge on police decision-making. The concept of professionalization is used instead of bureaucratization. Admittedly there is some distinction between the two. Unlike bureaucratization, professionalization refers more to the existence of technically trained, quite autonomous experts. The distinction, however, is not crucial in this case. The concept of police professionalization is commonly used in a manner which makes it very similar to bureaucratization.[32] Another reason the distinction between bureaucratization and professionalization is not important is that, in governmental organizations in cities the size of the four Wisconsin communities, professionalization and bureaucratization seem to develop simultaneously and are closely related.[33] A more thorough comparison of the communities on the basis of the two variables is found in Chapter 4.

Only one further brief, but important, comment about the importance of these two variables is necessary here. In addition to the previously suggested relationship between professionalization, participation, and *Miranda's* consequences, the impact of that decision could have another important effect. As we shall see in the next chapter, the majority opinion in the *Miranda* case encourages police to become more professionalized and more amenable to outside groups. Thus in addition to the possibility that existing levels of these two variables affect *Miranda's* consequences, there is also the reverse possibility that *Miranda's* consequences affect these variables. Both of these alternatives are investigated here.

Conclusion

The impact of Supreme Court policy, like any other policy output, is studied by evaluating policy consequences. An assessessment of impact requires a look at "hard" measures as well as at relevant actors' perceptions of, and attitudes about, the meaning and impact of policy and the process which communicates information about this meaning. Their behavior, as well as their rationalizations or explanations for this behavior, is investigated. In order to facilitate a comparative study of policy consequences, two socio-political variables—professionalization and participation—are considered intervening variables which are related to differences in impact. These variables are particularly relevant to an analysis of *Miranda* because they are related to differences in response to innovation and bureaucratization.

In the next chapter we examine the development of the Court's police interrogation policies. Court-police relations are set in an historical perspective. Chapter 3 takes a general look at criminal justice policy-making in Wisconsin and the role various people played in the process relating to police response to *Miranda*. In Chapter 4, we make a brief but important comparison of the cities according to the degree of police professionalization and participation. Chapters 5-8 are community case studies which both evaluate the relationship between professionalization, participation, and *Miranda's* consequences and show to what extent *Miranda* affected existing professionalization and participation levels. Interrogation behavior is not specifically discussed in these four chapters but is instead analyzed comparatively in Chapter 10. This follows another comparative analysis (Chapter 9), of the relationship between the two variables and *Miranda* consequences other than interrogation behavior changes.

NOTES

1. Quoted in Walter F. Murphy, *Congress and the Court* (Chicago: University of Chicago Press: 1965), 155. The case referred to is *Mallory v. U.S.*, 354 U.S. 449 (1967).

2. Theodore L. Becker, "Editor's Introduction," in Theodore L. Becker (ed.), *The Impact of Supreme Court Decisions* (New York: Oxford, 1969). 2.

3. There are at least two noteworthy exceptions: William Muir, *Prayer in the Public Schools: Law and Attitude Change* (Chicago: University of Chicago, 1968); Richard M. Johnson, *The Dynamics of Compliance: Supreme Court Decision-making from a New Perspective* (Evanston, Ill.: Northwestern, 1967).

4. Austin Ranney, "The Study of Policy Content: A Framework for Choice," in Austin Ranney (ed.), *Political Science and Public Policy* (Chicago: Markham, 1968), 7. Wells and Grossman correctly point out that most conceptualizations of judicial policy-making overemphasize the judge's motives and the interpersonal relationships between the judges. Wells and Grossman view policy-making as a problem-solving endeavor or enterprise, a concept which connotes not only determination of a course of action by deciding among competing considerations of social advantage but also the *implementation* of that action. This is a most acceptable viewpoint. See Richard S. Wells and Joel B. Grossman, "The Concept of Judicial Policy-Making." *Journal of Public Law* 15 (1966), 286–307.

5. David Easton, *A Systems Analysis of Political Life* (New York: Wiley, 1965), 212.

6. Easton calls these initial decisions "outputs." He calls the consequences traceable to the output, "however long the train of causation," the "outcome." Such a distinction is not very clear. Nowhere does Easton explain how to tell the difference between initial and other traceable change. Moreover, he is not clear about the extent to which these consequences are determined by the perceptions of participants in the policy process and the extent to which they are determined by other indicators. For example, was the perceived increase in the number of rapes an outcome of the *Mallory* decision because the Senator said so? If not, what other criteria must be used to assess impact? *Ibid.*, 351–52.

7. For some reasons see Ranney, *op. cit.*, 9–13.

8. Easton, *op. cit.*, 351.

9. For a general discussion of these pitfalls, see Raymond Bauer, "Detection and Anticipation of Impact," in Raymond Bauer (ed.), *Social Indicators* (Cambridge, Mass.: MIT, 1966), 17–18.

10. Abraham Kaplan, *Conduct of Inquiry* (San Francisco: Chandler, 1964), 381–84.

11. Vernon Van Dyke, "Process and Policy as Focal Concepts," in Ranney (ed.), *op. cit.*, 29.

12. For an interesting study which more thoroughly examines explanation and defense of attitude change, see Muir, *op. cit.*

13. See Albert D. Biederman, "Social Indicators and Goals," in Bauer (ed.), *op. cit.*, 91–97, for a discussion of our increasing dependence upon indicators.

14. The following are the most relevant of the extensive literature on crime statistics: Harry Shulman, "The Measures of Crime in the United States." *Journal of Criminal Law, Criminology and Police Science* 57 (1966), 483–92; President's Commission on Law Enforcement and the Administration of Justice, *An Assessment of Crime* (Washington: U.S. Government Printing Office, 1967). A more extensive listing of such articles appears in the bibliography.

15. A recent governmental publication regarding the development of social indicators continues to use these seven crimes to measure serious crimes but it does criticize lumping the seven together. U.S. Department of Health, Education, and Welfare, *Toward a Social Report* (Washington: U.S. Government Printing Office, 1969), 55–64. See also David J. Pittman and William F. Hardy, "Uniform Crime Reporting: Some Suggested Improvements." *Sociology and Social Research* 46 (1962), 139. For an interesting attempt to deal with the pitfalls of crime statistics see John A. Gardiner, *Traffic and the Police* (Cambridge, Mass.: Harvard University, 1969), 5–13.

16. Jerome H. Skolnick, *Justice Without Trial* (New York: Wiley, 1966), 164–66.

17. James Q. Wilson, *Varieties of Police Behavior* (Cambridge, Mass.: Harvard University, 1969), 84–89. Donald J. Newman "The Effect of Accommodations in Justice Administration on Criminal Statistics." *Sociology and Social Research* 46 (1962), 780–790.

18. "Many of our statistics on social problems are merely a byproduct of the informational requirements of routine management. This byproduct process does not usually produce the information that we most need for policy or scholarly purposes, and it means that our supply of statistics has an accidental or an unbalanced character." *Toward a Social Report*, 96.

19. A recent attempt was made to investigate crime in society by using information in addition to the standard indicators. See *Ibid.*, 58–60.

20. Johnson, *op. cit.*, 23.

21. Edward C. Barrett, "Police Practices and the Law from Arrest to Trial." *California Law Review* 50 (1962), 13.

22. Samuel Krislov, "The Parameters of Power: Patterns of Compliance and Opposition to Supreme Court Decisions," unpublished paper delivered to American Political Science Association, New York, 1963, 11.

23. Martin Shapiro, *The Supreme Court and Administrative Agencies* (New York: Free Press, 1968), 36, 38-39. Becker, *op. cit.*, 4.

24. Dolbeare suggests that the difference in public attitudes toward the Supreme Court and other courts, as well as the propensity of the people to use the courts, might constitute socio-political variables which are related to significant differences in impact at the state level. He shows that these differences exist, but does not use them to assess impact. Kenneth Dolbeare, "The Supreme Court and the States: From Abstract Doctrine to Local Behavioral Conformity," in Becker (ed.), *op. cit.*, 206–213.

25. For a study of community innovation which discusses professionalization, see Robert L. Crain, Elihu Katz, and Donald B. Rosenthal, *The Politics of Community Conflict* (Indianapolis: Bobbs Merrill, 1969), 171–176, 240–41.

26. Bruce J. Terris, "The Role of the Police." *Annals* 374 (1967) 58–69. Neal Milner, "Professionalism, Pluralism, and Police Reform," in Edward S. Greenberg, Neal Milner, and David J. Olson (eds.), *Black Politics—The Inevitability of Conflict-Readings* (New York: Holt, Rinehart & Winston, forthcoming).

27. Wilson, *op. cit.*; James Q. Wilson, "The Police and the Delinquent in Two Cities," in James Q. Wilson (ed.), *City Politics and Public Policy* (New York: Wiley, 1968), 173–96.

28. Wilson, *Varieties of Police Behavior.*

29. Robert R. Alford with the collaboration of Harry M. Scoble, *Bureaucracy and Participation: Political Cultures in Four Wisconsin Cities* (Chicago: Rand McNally, 1969). Bureaucratization refers to the degree of development of specialized agencies to carry out governmental functions. Participation refers to the extent to which groups and individuals impinge upon the decision-making process. *Ibid.*, chapter II.

30. Alford and Scoble tried to choose issues whose decisions required limited involvement with the government and politics outside of the city. Thus local factors could be seen more clearly.

31. *Ibid.*, 154.

32. Neal Milner, "Comparative Analysis of Patterns of Compliance with Supreme Court Decisions: *Miranda* and the Police in Four Communities." *Law and Society Review* 4 (August, 1970). For a discussion of the implications of this view of professionalization, see Skolnick, *op. cit.*, 235–39.

33. Alford with Scoble. *op. cit.*, 18. Professionalization is directly related to three of their five indicators of bureaucratization. *Ibid.*, 120.

Chapter 2

INTERROGATION POLICY
AND THE POLICE

The impact of a court policy greatly depends upon the types of cues policy implementers receive about the policy and its intent. Such cues can come from many sources, ranging from direct reading of a court opinion to a conversation with a buddy in a squad car. In this chapter we shall take a somewhat historical look at the types of information the Court has furnished concerning its intent in regulating police interrogation procedure. More specifically, we shall investigate the nature of the Justices' goals, the consistency and clarity of these goals, and the reactions of law-enforcement organizations upon whom goal implementation ultimately depended. In Chapter 3 cues from other sources will be considered.

It has become conventional wisdom to talk of court-police relations in terms of the conflict between United States Supreme Court decisions and law enforcement preferences. Presumably, as this conflict increased, police departments grew less likely to implement policies or to comply with the mandates of the Court. The consequences of the Court's policy, then, would be greatly affected by this conflict and the resulting degree of non-compliance. Thus one must delve more closely into the nature of this conflict in order to assess accurately the consequences of Court policy, since this conflict may be just as important as the lack of clarity of court decisions or ambiguity of court policy.

Some have said that there is a rather simple explanation for the disagreement between the Court and the police. The Bill of Rights and even the Fourteenth Amendment were established before the municipal police force came into existence in America. Since there were no publicly financed police departments, the present police interrogation problem was irrelevant to eighteenth- and much of nineteenth-century England. The state did not marshal its power against a suspect until the trial stage and the majority of trials were prosecuted by private individuals.[1] This historical explanation, however, is at best a partial one. In other areas, the Court has certainly been able to develop rationale for decisions involving problems which did not exist when the Constitution was framed.

A more important reason for the conflict can be attributed to what without much oversimplification can be called a difference in court-police perspectives. The Court posits requirements based on the Rule of Law which emphasizes individual rights and the legitimacy and necessity of constraints upon law enforcement officials. Police departments, however, are bureaucracies that are required to maintain order. They operate in a milieu which emphasizes efficiency and social control, and consequently they develop an ideology which emphasizes order, efficiency, and initiative. An acceptance of the Rule of Law requires recognition that it is legitimate to impair such efficiency and initiative. Members of the law enforcement occupation have been reluctant to grant this recognition.[2]

It is particularly important to understand that this is not simply a case of an "ornery," lazy cop who would rather beat or otherwise coerce prisoners than do the necessary leg work to get a conviction. On the contrary, police perceive somewhat correctly that institutional and societal sanctions exist to reward police for behavior which is inconsistent with the Rule of Law. The rewards for a "good pinch," that is, an important arrest, have traditionally been greater than the rewards for paying primary attention to Court-imposed job constraints. Police do not use illegal methods merely because courts place restrictions on police procedures. Value systems may exist which, for reasons quite independent of court decisions, sanction such behavior. Some aspects of police brutality, *e.g.* condoning rough treatment for sex offenders, have no relationship to the difficulty of getting evidence in such cases.[3]

On the surface, there already appear ample reasons to anticipate a difference between policy output and outcome. Goal conflict and value differences are important factors related to resistance to change.

There is also another important reason the difference can be anticipated. The Supreme Court has never been able to get consistently
reliable, first-hand information about police interrogation behavior.
Although police officers are probably the most important definers
of what Skolnick calls "the operative legality" of criminal law, police
work is extremely secluded, decentralized, and unsupervised.[4]

Characteristically the interrogation process has always been
fraught with such secrecy. Without reliable information it is difficult
to gain an understanding of the dynamics of police interrogation behavior. Thus in the process of making interrogation policy the Court
encountered a built-in obstacle which limited it from either accurately evaluating behavior or from evaluating the consequences of its
own decisions.[5] This problem was clearly reflected in the Court's interrogation decisions prior to *Miranda.*

The Justices were often divided in their interpretation of seemingly straightforward, mundane facts.[6] Opinions emphasized vague
but broad themes like the "totality of circumstances" or "special circumstances" rule which held that the validity of a confession would
depend upon specific conditions, such as the suspect's age, intelli-
gence, experience, and tactics of police officers.[7] This rule did not
give the police much guidance about the relative importance of each
circumstance in the interrogation process. In addition there was certainly little consensus among the Justices about the long-range aims
of Court interrogation policy.[8]

This more sophisticated, socio-psychological explanation of the
court-police conflict is, for our purposes, incomplete because it tells
little about the dynamics of the conflict. How has this conflict
changed? Why, if at all, did the change occur? What effects do such
changes have on the consequences of policy? This approach must be
put in an historical context. What follows is an attempt to answer
these questions by looking at Court interrogation policy and police
responses to them. It is by no means a complete examination since,
for the most part, police-court relations are discussed apart from
other important events and activities which may have affected this
relationship.

In brief, this chapter will show that, despite certain Court cue-
giving activities which could have exacerbated the police-court conflict and thus could presumably have increased non-compliance, such

conflict was absent throughout most of the history of the Supreme Court's attempts to regulate police interrogation. The conflict was absent primarily because the Court's decisions avoided the crux of the issue, the differences in the perspective and goals of advocates of the Rule of Law and those of law-enforcement officials whose milieu emphasized efficiency, order and control.

Interrogation Policy and Police Response Prior to Escobedo and Miranda

Despite the amenability of this milieu to conflict, there was relatively little law enforcement response to early Supreme Court opinions which attempted to regulate police interrogation behavior. Police-court conflict was minimal mainly because the behavior which the Court attempted to regulate appeared to be quite atypical. The first interrogation case decided on the basis of the Fourteenth Amendment was the only case in which the Justices invalidated a confession on the grounds that physical coercion had been used to obtain it.[9] In that case even the lawyers representing the state did not deny that the prisoner had been beaten. Most likely, the decision had been a freak case that slipped through the state judicial process. Both Mississippi (where the case originated) and other states had previously overturned convictions based on confessions gained by violence.[10] In other United States Supreme Court cases the police were at least accused of physical coercion, but their decisions did not seem to have much effect. From 1926-1945 there were 106 state supreme court cases in which it was alleged that torture or physical violence led to confession. Forty-eight of these convictions were reversed in the state court. There was no noticeable increase in the number of such cases during the years the Supreme Court made its decisions involving similar allegations.[11]

The Justices constantly agreed to accept only facts that were not disputed either by the suspect or by the interrogators and, as a result, usually deferred to the trial-court interpretation of the facts.[12] Consequently, if the police disputed a suspect's claim that he was physically coerced, the Justices typically did not accept the claim. But even cases concerned with other types of police interrogation procedure usually involved police behavior that was atypical and bizarre.[13] In one case, for example, young, ignorant sharecroppers were questioned almost non-stop for five days while under the constant threat of mob violence.[14]

In terms of our rough definition of public policy, police response was limited because the intent of the Court was limited. The Court never seriously considered implementing protection against coerced confessions by requiring counsel at interrogation if the suspect so desired. In the early cases, the Court did not even confront the possibility that the interrogation process *per se* was coercive and that all confessions were inherently coerced. There were, of course, serious disputes over facts and an increasing number of dissenting opinions, but, for the most part, the broader consequences of the Supreme Court interrogation policy were never really discussed. There was further evidence of the lack of perceived broader implications: *Amicus curiae* briefs were filed in only three of the interrogation decisions prior to 1964.[15] None of these briefs was filed by a law-enforcement organization. Police statistical procedures reflected no increase in attempts to keep accurate data which could be used as indicators of the importance of confessions for conviction. As late as 1964, police officials in thirteen states were asked merely to *estimate* the percentage of cases where interrogation produced a confession. The range varied from 12 to 89 percent, probably suggesting lack of concern about keeping such data as much as differences in police practices.[16]

The United States Supreme Court did not seem to be an important source of guidance to state supreme court decision-making regarding interrogation policy. From January, 1961, to May, 1962, state appellate decisions regarding coerced confessions seldom referred to U.S. Supreme Court precedents. Of seventy-four such decisions, only seventeen mentioned any of these precedents. There was no geographic pattern found among the courts which used the precedents and the ones which did not.[17]

The above analysis might somewhat underestimate the response to certain interrogation decisions. It does, however, correctly suggest that, despite differences in the perspective of the police and the Court, conflict was avoided because of the limited intent of much of the Court's interrogation policy. The Court did not seem to be too concerned with declaring its intent to the typical police department since it was assumed that such departments did not manifest unacceptable interrogation behavior. When the conflict did develop, it clearly resulted because of perceptions, both on the part of the Justices and police officials, that the Court now attempted to regulate more representative interrogation behavior.

A closer look at a few of these more controversial cases supports the contention that the consequences of the Court decisions were perceived to grow as basic police assumptions about typical interrogation behavior were questioned. In the *Ashcraft* case, decided in 1944, the suspect was questioned non-stop for thirty-eight hours.[18] He was not an indigent and was evidently a reasonably intelligent, middle-aged man. Once again all the Justices agreed that only the undisputed facts should be considered, eliminating consideration of the prisoner's contention that he had been struck. The only issue was whether the prolonged interrogation *per se* invalidated the confession. Writing for the majority, Justice Black said that consideration only of undisputed facts is necessary to concentrate on the "inescapable consequence of secret inquisitorial practices." [19] Despite their stating a theme ("undisputed facts") which, on the surface, gave the local authorities much leeway, the majority found, however, that on the basis of these facts the confession was indeed coerced. The thirty-eight hour interrogation "is so inherently coercive that its very existence is irreconcilable with the possession of mental freedom by a lone suspect against whom its full coercive force is brought to bear." [20]

An acceptance of Black's viewpoint on the inherent coerciveness of confessions certainly would have broadened the intent of Court interrogation policy, because it suggested that all interrogations were inherently coercive. Justice Jackson's vigorous dissent in this case is interesting because he worried about the implications of Black's view. He felt that suspects varied greatly in their reactions to interrogation and that the Court could not possibly establish a practical standard which could take all such variations into consideration. Behind this criticism lay Jackson's unwillingness to accept the view that interrogations themselves were inherently coercive. The prisoner's confession should be overturned only if he lost his freedom of choice. Furthermore, Jackson made the first attempt to introduce the police perspective into the discussion. In all previous cases, he insisted, the state received the presumption of regularity in the procedures of its local police departments. Furthermore, confessions were possibly acceptable even if the police had abused their power. In his words,

"We have no power to discipline the police or law enforcement officers of the State of Tennessee nor to reverse its convictions in retribution for conduct which we may personally disapprove." [21]

Although there is no evidence of significant nationwide police response to the *Ashcraft* decision, the decision is important because it clearly showed how the issue of the inherent coerciveness of all interrogation could easily be closely intertwined with the amount of discretion granted to local police departments. The roots of the basic conflict between common police procedures and the Rule of Law are found in this case.

The *Mallory* decision best exemplified the relationship between perceived Court intent and police response.[22] Ironically the formal decision did not at all involve most local police. It pertained to use of a federal rule of criminal procedure, and the only metropolitan police force directly affected was that of the District of Columbia. In this case, the Court invalidated a confession solely because the police did not bring the suspect before a magistrate "without unnecessary delay," a stipulation of the Federal Rules of Criminal Procedure. With but one dissent, the Court had ruled the same way on the basis of virtually the same federal rule some fifteen years earlier.[23] The limited intent of the Court seemed clear because, despite dissents by Justices Black and Douglas,[24] the remainder of the Justices had explicitly refused to invalidate confessions obtained by local non-federal police during similar incarcerations.[25]

Nevertheless, unlike virtually all other previously discussed confession cases, there was an intensely hostile reaction to the *Mallory* decision. Writing in *Police* magazine, the Washington, D.C., police chief insisted that the decision aided Communism. "It is . . . all too true," he exclaimed, "that the majority of the Court unwittingly serves the cause of those who seek to create impotence in the administration of justice as one means to their ideological end." [26] The International Association of Chiefs of Police severely criticized the decision. Despite the explicit limits of the *Mallory* decision, this group was particularly frightened by the *potential* implications such a decision might have for both state and federal law enforcement.[27] Concern with potential consequence was also manifested by several local prosecutors who refused to prosecute certain cases because they "knew" *Mallory* precluded acceptance of the confessions obtained for their cases.[28] In the summer of 1957, only a few months after the decision, a special subcommittee of the House Judiciary Committee was appointed to study the *Mallory* case. At its hearings the decisions were again intensely criticized as purveyors of destruction of law enforcement, and Congress narrowly missed passing a bill which would have limited the effects of the *Mallory* decision.[29]

Why the sudden interest and concern about the Court's confession decisions? The timing of the decision was one important factor. It occurred at a time when the Court had recently ruled to prohibit *de jure* segregation, and to protect the rights of some alleged Communists against the tirades of the McCarthy era. Communism, integrationism, and protection of the rights of a suspected criminal were all intertwined according to the most vigorous opponents of the Warren Court. As one Southern anti-court newspaper so aptly put it, "The dope peddlers are smiling, and so is Uncle Nikita." [30] Opposition grew more intense on the basis of these unifying bonds. The decision was made in a political climate which seemed conducive to criticism of Court decisions. Yet there was a far more important reason for this perhaps unanticipated reaction to a Court decision which in a formal sense barely, if at all, broadened the intent of Court interrogation policy.

It was stated earlier that most states refused to tolerate coerced confessions long before the Supreme Court became involved with the problem. Since the changes the Court had made in its definition of coercion were both small and inconsistent, no state had been greatly affected. The *Mallory* decision, though it did not require counsel at interrogation, may have helped to effectuate the right to counsel by ensuring that at an early stage the magistrate give advice about the right to have an attorney. No state required the presence of counsel at the police station, and at the time no state or local police had to follow rules which were as stringent as the *Mallory* procedure.[31] According to a sociologist who is also an ex-police officer, the decision was perceived as a threat "to eliminate a traditional police *modus operandi* for solving cases—extended interrogation of suspects prior to arraignment." [32] This combination of perceptions of the political environment and possibilities of constraints on typical police behavior made the *Mallory* decision especially salient and worrisome to police officials.

Consensus on the Court over interrogation questions began to deteriorate after the *Mallory* decision. Despite an important attempt by Justice Frankfurter to bring the Court together on this question,[33] by 1961 the basic and pervasive divisions on the Court were obvious. The Justices' incremental style of decision-making, however, continued somewhat to mask the implications of these differences. They continued to accept the vague but flexible "totality of circumstances" theme as their basic criteria for evaluating confessions. They made no hard and fast rules requiring advisement of rights or presence of lawyers. The necessity for such procedures continued to depend upon the circumstances. Both Chief Justice Warren and Justice Douglas, who were among the increasingly more vocal minority which began to distrust the entire interrogation process, nevertheless accepted the totality of circumstances rationale, and indeed used it to invalidate confessions even in cases where counsel was denied and incarceration was illegal.[34] Douglas, with Black, usually wrote concurring opinions in these situations, although in one case which included these two circumstances—so divisive to the Court—Douglas did decide on the basis of other facts.[35] The basic issues of counsel and inherent coercion were judiciously avoided.

Despite this effort to achieve consensus on a basic theme, the Justices had greater difficulty agreeing on the meaning of the facts. On the surface, members of the Court continued to accept the proposition that the reliability of information concerning actions in the interrogation room required the Court to accept only facts acknowledged by both the state and the individual. But in fact, there were many disputes about these so-called "undisputed facts." The Justices often disagreed over the extent of independent review they could give to the local trial court's interpretation of the facts. Furthermore, even if consensus was reached on this issue, the Justices often disagreed over the extent of independent review they could give to the local trial court's interpretation of the facts. Even if consensus were reached on this issue, the Justices still quite often interpreted the facts in entirely different ways. As Justice Frankfurter so realistically noted, the totality of circumstances theme was not a consistent rule, but rather broad, often inconsistent and ambiguous, precisely because the Justices could not agree on the meaning of the facts applicable to the theme. Precedents were not consistently built one upon the other because the facts and their interpretation were diverse enough to preclude such consistency.

Though not plainly or uniformly, the perspectives of the Court shifted. Originally, the Justices excluded only clearly implicating statements made under circumstances where a reasonably fit innocent man could have falsely confessed. The perspective then shifted to center upon the accused as a person who, regardless of guilt or innocence, had basic rights. The Court began to inquire whether the individual was aware of these rights and whether he had the opportunity to use them.[36] The breadth of these shifts was limited for two reasons. First, the change in perspective was by no means a constant, unilateral movement accepted by all Justices. Second, the Court's rhetoric may have in fact concealed such changes. The Justices did not agree on the intent of Court interrogation policy. Their decisions, consequently, reflected a hedging quite characteristic of a decision-making body uncertain of its goals. The Court was rather ambiguous in its declaration of interrogation policy, and was not a very helpful source of information. Others perceived clarity at surprising times, as when law enforcement officials thought that in the *Mallory* case the Justices attempted to communicate a radically different line of action concerning interrogation policy, but this intent was not implemented.

The Court's opinions reflected very little substantive information about police behavior. Occasionally, the Justices mentioned the danger of the third degree or of police noncompliance, while the Justices who were less likely to invalidate confessions discussed the general importance of allowing the police to do their job. As the Court became more concerned with the inherent coerciveness of the interrogation itself, and with police behavior regardless of the suspect's characteristics, some Justices, notably Frankfurter and Douglas, began to cite police textbooks.[37] But these were usually only briefly mentioned, and the Justices opposing the rulings never questioned the validity of the use of textbooks as evidence of actual police behavior. This communications problem was not as yet serious because there was still little reason for the Court to know about typical interrogation techniques. The bulk of these techniques was still at least tacitly accepted.

Local discretion predominated both at the court and police level. The trial judge and, most significantly, the police officer exercised much control over the raw material which would be accepted by appellate courts. The Supreme Court made only small, often inconsistent changes which, for the most part, had not as yet put this Court in direct conflict with the police perspective. The possibilities of such conflict had been mentioned by various Justices, including Jackson, the young Harlan, Warren, and Frankfurter. The control of information about misconduct, however, remained essentially in the hands of the police, and Court guidance regarding other police procedures remained unclear. But the conflict in the Court and the differing perspectives of the Justices had become quite apparent.

The Escobedo Decision

Prior to the *Escobedo* decision there were some further signs that the majority of Justices sought to regulate and constrain more typical police interrogation behavior. In ruling that a man's confession was invalid because he was not allowed to call either his wife or his attorney until after he confessed, five Justices seemed to make a point of ignoring the totality of circumstances theme. The prisoner's isolation plus the refusal to allow him to see his attorney were considered to be reason enough for invalidation regardless of the circumstances.[38] The Court, however, remained divided over the issue of an attorney's proper role in the interrogation process. This conflict increased when the majority of Justices ruled that a confession obtained after an indictment had been made was invalid because the defendant confessed in the absence of counsel.[39] The ruling had nothing directly to do with typical pre-indictment interrogation procedures, but Byron White, one of the dissenting Justices, saw such implications in the decision: [40]

> The reason given for the result here—the admissions were obtained in the absence of counsel—would seem equally pertinent to statements obtained at any time after the right to counsel attaches, whether there has been an indictment or not; to admissions made prior to arraignment, at least where the defendant has counsel or asks for it; to the fruits of admission improperly obtained under the new rule; to criminal proceedings in state courts; and to defendants long since convicted upon evidence including such admissions.

He felt that the majority of the Justices had unquestionably set their goals at constraining common, previously acceptable police behavior by requiring police to permit the presence of counsel at the interrogation.

In the *Escobedo* decision the Court made its policy position on the question of counsel more, though not completely, clear.[41] The interrogation of Danny Escobedo involved no physical beating. No extraordinarily bizarre psychological ploys were used, and the suspect was not forced to undergo a long period of physical isolation. He simply was not advised of his rights to remain silent, and, most importantly, was refused permission to see his own attorney prior to completion of interrogation. The majority of Justices, in overturning Escobedo's conviction, again hedged. The totality of circumstances theme was maintained, but it was quite obvious that under almost no circumstances could a suspect be denied counsel during interrogation if he had requested to see his own attorney.[42]

The explicit refusal of a request for counsel was a sign that, though the suspect had not yet been indicted, the investigation was no longer a general investigation of an unsolved crime. The majority opinion gave little consideration to the general issue of inherent coerciveness. The majority also made little effort to refute the contention that serious consequences would result from its decision. Justice Goldberg admitted that the interrogation stage was important—indeed critical—for police, but, he insisted, the very importance of this stage made the protection of counsel all the more necessary.[43] The dissenters were far less willing to dismiss the broader consequences of this decision. Justice Harlan called the decision "most ill-conceived," and worried that "it seriously and unjustifiably fetters perfectly legitimate methods of criminal law enforcement." [44]

The majority went out of its way to avoid the establishment of an absolute right to counsel. Yet the standards implicit in the Court's ruling were by far the most stringent ever placed upon police officials. Nevertheless, the Court remained unclear about both the extent of this stringency and the extent of retroactivity of the new rules.

The decision created greater trepidation and hostility among police officials. Although the rhetoric of Justice Goldberg's opinion stressed that the decision was merely another small, incremental change consistent with past standards, police-prosecutor officials did not limit their interpretations to this rhetoric alone. Similar to their reactions regarding the *Mallory* decision, these people saw far-reaching implications in the decision. They felt that the Court no longer followed the goal of eliminating only involuntary confessions. Police officials definitely saw the decision as a threat to the use of common, previously accepted, and very crucial police procedures. A sampling of police comments about the decision shows how *Escobedo* more than any previous decision raised basic value conflicts. The Court was accused of unduly hampering police behavior which was both legitimate and necessary to prevent crime. Quite explicit in some of this reasoning was the notion that the police should operate under the same rules as the criminal. The legitimacy of the Rule of Law as a constraint on interrogation behavior was not often recognized.[45]

The Miranda Decision

Like *Escobedo* the real significance in the *Miranda* case and its accompanying cases again lay in the lack of any unique, out-of-the-ordinary police behavior. But unlike Danny Escobedo, none of these suspects had requested counsel. Chief Justice Warren, who wrote the majority opinion, admitted that the record showed "no overt physical coercion or potential psychological ploys." [46] Ernesto Miranda was simply a slightly schizophrenic, ignorant, petty criminal who had experienced trouble with the law before (sexual perversion) and was now accused of rape. In short, he was the type of suspect police quite commonly encounter. Consequently, they reacted the way police officers quite commonly react. Without informing him that he could have counsel, they questioned him in an interrogation room. He was indigent and never asked for counsel. If he had been informed of his right to remain silent—and the point was moot—this information was furnished in a perfunctory manner. He initially gave an oral confession, and after only two hours of interrogation furnished the police with a written confession.[47] The Court had chosen to rule on a case that lacked even the most subtly coercive circumstances found in the *Escobedo* decision. No longer were the Justices making decisions on the basis of relatively isolated police behavior, and no longer were they regulating procedures usually taken care of by the state courts.

The number of people involved in *amicus* briefs reflected the perceptions of the broadened intent of the Court's confession policy. The noted law professor Telford Taylor wrote one *amicus curiae* brief urging acceptance of the confession. This brief was signed by attorneys general from 28 states, Puerto Rico, and the Virgin Islands. The National District Attorneys Association also filed an *amicus* brief urging the acceptance of the confession. The American Civil Liberties Union, which until *Escobedo* had not filed an *amicus* on this subject, filed another such brief urging invalidation of the confession in *Miranda*.[48]

The Justices faced three basic alternatives for deciding this case. They could (1) refuse to invalidate the confession. This alternative seemed unlikely because at no time since 1958 had the Court agreed to hear a confession case and then accept a challenged confession as valid.[49] They could (2) abolish the special circumstances theme as a criterion for judging a confession. Finally, they could (3) expand the use of this old theme to include the circumstances found in ordinary interrogations. But, regardless of the rationale chosen, the Justices were forced to come to grips with the task of defining more clearly the new goals seemingly adopted by the Court majority in *Escobedo*. The seriousness of the *inherently* coercive circumstances of the interrogation room along with the absence of counsel—the two issues upon which the Justices had increasingly split and which directly involved the basic police-court conflict—were especially important in this case because no other circumstances were very special or unique.

Acting to invalidate the confession, Chief Justice Warren, speaking for four other Justices, presented new procedures which *all* interrogations had to follow. They included the following: [50]

> 1. The person in custody must, prior to interrogation, be informed of his right to remain silent, and that anything he says may be held against him in Court and that even if he begins to talk, he may stop the interrogation at any time.
> 2. He must be clearly informed that he has the right to counsel and to have counsel present during interrogation.
> 3. He must be told that if he is indigent, an attorney may be appointed to be present at his interrogation if the suspect so desires.
> 4. Any waiver of these rights on the part of the suspect must be clearly and intelligently done. A heavy burden falls on the state to prove that the waiver was done in this manner.

Thus the majority of the Justices for the first time clearly stated that under all circumstances an interrogation is inherently coercive, and that counsel is necessary to protect an individual from this coercion. A distrust of confessions was evident in this statement by the Chief Justice: [51]

> To respect the inviolability of the human personality, our accusatory system of criminal justice demands that the government seeking to punish an individual produce the evidence against him by its own independent labors, rather than by the cruel, simple expedient of compelling it from his own mouth.

The majority clearly intended to regulate the behavior of the average police officer. The Court's intent stressed the Rule of Law, but the Chief Justice also tried to reconcile police and Court goals. The goals of the *Miranda* majority can be summarized as follows:

> 1. To discourage whenever possible the use of confessions, *all* of which are obtained under circumstances which *inherently* lead to coercion of the suspects.
> 2. To make certain that all suspects are informed of their right to remain silent and their right to have an attorney present to protect this right, even if the suspect could not afford to hire his own lawyer.
> 3. To improve the quality of police officers so that the officers would be able to perform their jobs effectively while still operating under the norms of due process.
> 4. To allay police anxieties by specifically stating that, despite these new constraints created by the Court, interrogation can still at times continue to be a legitimate and effective weapon.

The majority was, of course, mostly concerned directly with implementing the goals which placed constraints on the use of interrogations and which afforded all suspects protection against the inherent coerciveness of the interrogation situation. Though this general intent seemed to be communicated quite clearly, the Court was vague about which specific methods should be adopted to comply with these new procedures. There was no question that the new interrogation procedures entailed more than a perfunctory warning. This warning should not be "simply a preliminary ritual to existing means of interrogation." [52] As an "absolute prerequisite" to overcoming the inherent coerciveness of the interrogation process, it thus had to be given in "unequivocal terms." [53] The majority, however, offered nothing more precise about the methods to be used. In fact the Chief Justice implied that, because of the lack of agreement about methods, his general, flexible approach to the problem was essential. Otherwise, adherence to any particular solution might create "a constitutional straitjacket which will handicap sound efforts at reform." [54]

Implicit in the Court's discussion of procedure was the goal of developing police officers who relied on techniques other than interrogation. The aim of the interrogation process was considered to be nothing less than impairment of rational judgment.[55] Police reliance on this technique encouraged laziness and loss of both zeal and interest in enforcement of the law and the Constitution. Again this discussion did not apply merely to the brutal police officer whose existence the Chief Justice felt was "sufficiently widespread to be the object of concern," [56] but to the run-of-the-mill officer in the average department as well. As with the previously discussed goals, the Justices were not clear on implementation. The *Miranda* opinion was not a treatise on procedures for police reform. Nonetheless, the majority certainly desired that law enforcement organizations develop new procedures and sanctions which would deemphasize the importance of interrogations.[57]

The majority Justices seemed aware that an increasingly sensitive law-enforcement profession could interpret the *Miranda* decision as a manifestation of a loss of faith in American police. Consequently, a tangential but important goal of the Court involved an attempt to ease the police-court conflict. The Chief Justice insisted that "in announcing these principles we are not unmindful of the burdens law enforcement officers must bear, often under trying circumstances." [58] He emphasized that very important forms of police investigatory behavior were still allowed, and specifically stated the following behavior as acceptable.[59]

> 1. When an individual is in custody on probable cause, police may gather evidence against him.
> 2. This investigation may include inquiry of persons not under restraint, presumably without warning these people of their rights.
> 3. The questioning of persons at the scene of a crime is still allowed.
> 4. Spontaneous, voluntary confessions which are given, for example, by a person who walks into a police station and claims that he desires to confess, are still acceptable.

The Chief Justice also sensed another problem. He viewed the new interrogation process as one in which the suspect's attorney would participate actively in the interaction between officer and suspect. He sensed the anxiety that might develop on the part of the police in anticipating the participation of an outsider—and an un-friendly outsider at that—in the interrogation process. He attempted to console the police by explaining to them that this attorney was merely doing an essential job, just as the police were doing: [60]

> An attorney may advise his client not to talk to police until he had an opportunity to investigate the case, or he may wish to be present with his client during any police questioning. In doing so an attorney is merely exercising the good professional judge-ment he has been taught. This is not cause for considering an attorney a menace to law enforcement. He is merely carrying out what he is sworn to do under his oath—to protect to the extent of his ability the rights of his client.

The Court desired to lessen the value and goal conflict by convinc-ing the police that *Miranda's* constraints were limited and that ac-ceptance of some of these constraints was not tantamount to severe impairment in the fight against crime.

Unlike earlier decisions involving interrogation, the *Miranda* de-cision was broad in its intent and wide in its scope. This decision raised all the basic police-court problems, including the informational ones. Because the Court was no longer discussing atypical police behavior, it sought information about common interrogation procedures. Be-cause of the lack of first-hand communication about these procedures, the majority depended upon police manuals as its source of such in-formation. They assumed that the manuals reflected actual police behavior. These manuals reflected what the majority considered to be coercive behavior.[61]

Conclusion

In terms of public policy, the *Miranda* decision attempted to communicate that the Court intended to regulate everyday police in-terrogation behavior. Interrogations were now considered inherently coercive and lawyers were needed to afford suspects protection from such coercion. The majority planned to modify police behavior in order to deemphasize dependence upon self-incriminatory statements. This intent was to be implemented by the use of a regularized pro-cedure which would be required prior to *all* custodial interrogations regardless of the circumstances. The majority was vague about much of the implementation process. They did not clarify the standards for an intelligent and competent waiver. Confusion remained over the precise stage at which the accused must be advised of his rights. The opinion failed to give precise standards for the determining of the voluntariness of a confession. Finally, the Court did not decide on the validity of using *non*-testimonial evidence at trial if that evidence was the fruit of a statement made during prohibited interrogation. (The Court did, however, quickly clarify one important point when it ruled that *Miranda* would not apply retroactively.)[62]

It is clear that the Court's new policy went straight to the heart of the difference in police-court perspectives. Furthermore, the Court majority in *Miranda* seemed to recognize this and implicitly suggested that more professional police who were also amenable to advice from those outside the department could best adopt this innovation. In the following chapter we shall investigate the extent to which cue-givers in Wisconsin emphasize the theme of professionalization and participation. We shall also identify the most important sources of criminal justice information in Wisconsin and see how they were affected by *Miranda*.

NOTES

1. *Yale Law Journal,* Comment. 73 (1963), 934–1048; Vernon Fox, "Sociological and Political Aspects of Police Administration." *Sociology and Social Research* 5 (1966), 39–48.

2. Jerome H. Skolnick, *Justice Without Trial* (New York: Wiley, 1966).

3. Arthur J. Niederhoffer, *Behind the Shield* (Garden City, N.Y.: Doubleday, 1967), 153–155; William Westley, "Violence and the Police." *American Journal of Sociology* 59 (1953), 34–41.

4. Skolnick, *op. cit.,* 14. James Q. Wilson, *Varieties of Police Behavior* (Cambridge, Mass.: Harvard, 1968).

5. Bernard Weisberg, "Police Interrogation of Arrested Persons: A Skeptical View." *Journal of Criminal Law, Criminology and Police Science* 52 (1962), 44.

6. For example, *Lisenba v. California,* 314 U.S. 241 (1941); *Haley v. Ohio,* 332 U.S. 596 (1948). A more complete listing of U.S. Supreme Court cases can be found in the bibliography.

7. For the best discussion of the development and usage of the "totality of circumstances" theme, see Justice Frankfurter's concurring opinion in *Culombe v. Connecticut,* 367 U.S. 568 (1961).

8. The interrogation decisions furnish an excellent example of the incrementalist model of Supreme Court decision-making. Compare Martin Shapiro, "Stability and Change in Judiacial Decision-Making: Incrementalism or Stare Decisis?" *Law in Transition Quarterly* 2 (1966), 134-57. Skolnick suggests that a failure to recognize the Court's ambiguity concerning fact interpretation and goal elucidation leads one to overestimate the regularity with which laws are implemented. Note that he discusses this in the context of a study of police behavior. Skolnick, *op. cit.,* 26-27.

9. *Brown v. Mississippi,* 297 U.S. 278 (1936).

10. Wilfred J. Ritz, "Twenty-five Years of State Criminal Confession Cases in the U.S. Supreme Court." *Washington and Lee Law Review* 37 (1962).

11. Data from Charles T. McCormick, "Some Problems and Developments in the Admissibility of Confessions." *Texas Law Review* 24 (1946), 244 n. 28. Many acts of coercion may go completely unreported. See Arnold Trebach, *The Rationing of Justice* (New Brunswick: Rutgers University, 1964), 43-53.

12. For example, *Lyons v. Oklahoma,* 322 U.S. 596 (1944).

13. *Chambers v. Florida,* 309 U.S. 227 (1939); *Canty v. Alabama,*

309 U.S. 629 (1939); *White v. Texas*, 310 U.S. 530 (1939); *Vernon v. Alabama*, 313 U.S. 547 (1940).

14. *Chambers v. Florida*, 309 U.S. 227 (1939).

15. The three cases for which *amici* were filed were *Lyons v. Oklahoma*, 322 U.S. 596 (1944) (American Civil Liberties Union); *Culombe v. Connecticut*, 367 U.S. 567 (1961) (Connecticut Association for the Mentally Retarded); and *Crooker v. California*, 357 U.S. 433 (1958) (American Civil Liberties Union, Southern California).

16. David ∙J. Sterling, "Police Interrogation and the Psychology of Confession." *Journal of Public Law* 14 (1965), 47-48.

17. H. Frank Way, Jr., "The Supreme Court and State Coerced Confessions." *Journal of Public Law* 12 (1963), 65-66.

18. *Ashcraft v. Tennessee*, 322 U.S. 143 (1944).

19. *Ibid.* at 152.

20. *Ibid.* at 154.

21. *Ibid.* at 158.

22. *Mallory v. U.S.*, 354 U.S. 449 (1957).

23. *McNabb v. U.S.*, 318 U.S. 332 (1943).

24. *Watts v. Indiana*, 330 U.S. 49, 55-56 (1949); *Gallegos v. Nebraska*, 342 U.S. 55, 73-75 (1951).

25. In addition to the cases cited in the note above, see *Brown v. Allen*, 344 U.S. 443 (1952); *Fikes v. Alabama*, 352 U.S. 191 (1957).

26. Edgar Scott, "The Mallory Decision and the Vanishing Rights of Crime Victims." *Police* (1960), 62.

27. Walter F. Murphy, *Congress and the Court* (Chicago: University of Chicago, 1965), 119.

28. "News and Announcements." *Police* 3 (1958), 75.

29. Murphy, *op. cit.*, 176-79, 195, 206-07, 219-20.

30. *Ibid.*, 129.

31. *Yale Law Journal*, Comment. 73 (1963), 1011-1015. See also Henry B. Rothblatt and Emma A. Rothblatt, "Police Interrogation: Right to Counsel and Prompt Arraignments." *Brooklyn Law Review* 27 (1960), 42-44.

32. Niederhoffer, *op. cit.*, 156.

33. *Culombe v. Connecticut*, 367 U.S. 568 (1961).

34. *Blackburn v. Alabama*, 361 U.S. 199 (1960); *Rogers v. Richmond* 365 U.S. 534 (1961).

35. *Reck v. Pate*, 367 U.S. 433 (1961).

36. Karl F. Warden, "Miranda: Some History, Some Observations Some Reflections." *Vanderbilt Law Review* 20 (1966), 47.

37. *Culombe v. Connecticut*, 367 U.S. 568 n. 4, 572, 580 (1961); *Reck v. Pate*, 367 U.S. 433, 438, (1961).

38. *Haynes v. Washington*, 373 U.S. 503 (1963).

39. *Massiah v. U.S.*, 377 U.S. 201 (1964).

40. *Ibid.*, at 208.

41. *Escobedo v. Illinois*, 378 U.S. 478 (1964).

42. *Ibid.*, at 479, 491-92.

43. *Ibid.*, at 488.

44. *Ibid.*, at 493. See also Justice Stewart's comments in *Ibid.* at 495.

45. *New York Times*, September 10, 1965, p. 1. See also the comments by a New York City police commissioner who stated that the decision was "impractical" because it forced police "to use the Marquis of Queensbury rules while permitting the criminal "to butt and gouge" (*New York Times*, May 14, 1965, p. 29). For other comments see *New York Times*, September 11, 1965, p. 3; March 21, 1965, p. 61; Samuel Chapman, "Functional Problems Facing Law Enforcement Stemming from Supreme Court Decisions." *Police* 11 (1966), 45.

46. *Miranda v. Arizona*, 384 U.S. 436, 457 (1966).

47. The other cases combined with *Miranda* were *Vignera v. New York*, *Stewart v. California*, and *Westover v. U.S.* All except *Westover* involved almost entirely similar circumstances. In *Westover* the suspect had been questioned by local officials without counsel or warning. He did not immediately confess and was turned over to the FBI. They gave him a proper warning, but he confessed to the local crime as well as the federal crime. Thus, one of the issues was whether the later "confessions" involving the local crime was so influenced by the coerciveness of the initial local interrogation that it would be invalid. The case hinged on the interpretation of *Miranda* because if *Miranda's* circumstances were coercive, the initial circumstances in *Westover* also would be.

48. *Miranda* at 438-39. It is interesting to compare this to the *Gideon* case which also involved a special circumstances rule, but only in regard to the Fourteenth Amendment right to counsel at the trial stage. In *Gideon*, no *amicus* briefs were filed in favor of the state's case while twenty-two attorneys general signed such a brief urging the Court to rule that *Gideon* was entitled to an attorney. This alone is an interesting commentary on the perceived differences of the impacts of these two decisions. See *Gideon v. Wainwright*, 372 U.S. 335 (1963).

49. The last cases were *Crooker v. California*, 357 U.S. 433 (1958) and *Cicenia v. Lagay*, 357 U.S. 504 (1958).

50. *Miranda* at 444-45, 467-76.

51. *Ibid.*, at 460.

52. *Ibid.*, at 476.

53. *Ibid.*, at 468.

54. *Ibid.*, at 467, 444, 476.

55. *Ibid.* at 448, 450, 451, 455 n. 24. See also Walter Schaefer, *The Suspect and Society* (Evanston, Ill.: Northwestern, 1967), 17.

56. *Miranda* at 447.

57. The fact that five Justices were willing to require the *Miranda* stipulations, without waiting for evidence from the burgeoning studies of the interrogation process which occurred after *Escobedo*, further suggested that they would accept no reform which in any way limited the efficacy of the *Miranda* procedures. For a discussion of these reforms see

New York Times, April 30, 1966, p. 13; April 2, 1966, p. 60; June 3, 1966, p. 41. See also *"Amicus Curiae* Brief of National District Attorneys Association," *Miranda v. Arizona*, 384 U.S. 436; *"Amicus Curiae,* State of New York," *Miranda v. Arizona*, 384, U.S. 436, p. 24.

58. *Miranda* at 481.

59. *Ibid.*, at 477-78.

60. *Ibid.*, at 480-81.

61. *Ibid.*, at 448. The dissenters castigated this assumption more than anything else in the opinion. (See *Ibid.* at 449-50, 499, 530.) The National District Attorneys Association attempted to introduce a wealth of empirical evidence about interrogation behavior. Despite this Association's contention that those data "speak for themselves," the development and presentation of the data reflect a composite of good intentions, lack of methodological sophistication, and poor organization. See *"Amicus Curiae* Brief of National District Attorneys Association," *op. cit.,* especially the appendix.

62. *Johnson v. New Jersey*, 384 U.S. 719 (1966).

Chapter 3

LAW ENFORCEMENT POLICY-MAKING
IN WISCONSIN

The *Miranda* decision can be viewed as an attempt to regularize and formalize common police procedures and to facilitate the development of police departments which not only can understand the proposed changes but also adjust to them. One cannot assume that this intent was clearly presented to local law enforcement officials. The Court itself failed to answer some important questions. Other participants in the process of making public policy and affecting its consequences may have their own values and perceptions of the decisions. They may also be subject to pressure different from the Court's. Also, as Johnson has said, "the formal legal channels through which decisions are transmitted are not necessarily neutral ones which would insure the application of a rule substantially similar to that enunciated by the Supreme Court." [1]

People who have no formal connection with the judiciary may be a more important source of information than any judicial authority. It is somewhat misleading to classify sources as either formal or extra-legal because such a classification seems to imply that formal sources are necessarily authoritative.[2] The authoritativeness of a source of information depends upon the informal and formal sanctions accompanying the source, its clarity and its legitimacy. These are greatly determined by the political milieu in which a policy outcome is developed. In Wisconsin professionalization, bureaucratization, and group impingement were issues characterizing this milieu.

The earlier analysis of Supreme Court interrogation policy suggested that for many years the Court was indeed not a very important source of information. Others, including the state and local courts and the police themselves, were the important developers and interpreters of interrogation policy. As this changed, the conflict between police and Court perspectives became more visible. In this chapter, we take a closer look at the process of interrogation policy-making. Four questions are considered: (1) What is the milieu in which interrogation policy is made? (2) Who was important in this process? (3) What strategies were used? and (4) How did the *Miranda* decision affect the milieu, the persons involved, and the strategies used?

THE CONTEXT

Law enforcement in Wisconsin traditionally has been locally controlled. Except for highly specialized agencies like the state crime laboratory, and a limited number of special agents in the attorney general's office, there presently is virtually no statewide agency with criminal law jurisdiction. Law enforcement agencies are controlled by county or village boards, or by police and fire commissions, all of which guard their local autonomy quite jealously.[3] This pattern of local autonomy generally typifies law enforcement in the United States.[4]

Such decentralization can also be found in local judicial systems. Although local courts have uniform jurisdiction in matters such as probate, there is in fact quite a difference among various county courts as to the way they handle criminal and other civil matters. Wisconsin counties show a great variance in the percentage of criminal cases heard by their circuit courts.[5] Wisconsin district attorneys, like almost any local prosecutors, have virtually complete discretion over bringing charges against a suspect.[6]

As early as 1915 five members of the state legislature were concerned with providing greater degrees of statewide supervision over local law enforcement. Prior to the establishment of a state crime laboratory in 1947, numerous bills had been introduced to establish scientific crime detection institutions. This sort of bill was strongly opposed at the local level. In a 1948 study, the executive secretary of the Wisconsin Legislative Council recommended that the state create a Department of Public Safety which would have expanded statewide law enforcement, including the crime laboratory, the fire marshall's office, and various revenue-inspection divisions. None of the three bills passed.[7] The introduction of these bills actually may have been an attempt to minimize the powers of the crime laboratory by associating its development with the growth of state police.[8] This would have limited police officials' acceptance of the crime laboratory.

Since 1948 there have been some significant increases in state involvement in local law enforcement. The crime laboratory has greatly expanded its facilities. The state attorney general's office created a criminal investigation division, the first of its kind in Wisconsin history. Only recently a massive state reorganization bill placed the crime laboratory, arson investigation, and criminal investigators of the beverage and cigarette tax division of the state department of taxation into a single Department of Justice headed by the attorney general.[9] Yet these developments actually gave the state only a little more control over local law-enforcement activities. The use of the crime laboratory was—and still is—optional. For various strategic and personal reasons, many law-enforcement officials still choose to use other facilities, such as the FBI laboratory in Washington, D.C. The Wisconsin attorney general's criminal investigation unit was created almost solely to cope with an organized crime problem which became increasingly serious after a series of gangland-style murders, unsolved by local police.[10] This small investigating force, however, can exert little control over everyday law enforcement activities. Even in its own domain of organized crime it has not always been successful in convincing either state officials or local police that such crime existed in Wisconsin.[11]

It might already be apparent that the state exerts little formal control or supervision over police training procedures and standards. In 1957, the state's lower house passed a bill authorizing the crime laboratory to prepare and conduct police information and training programs. No vote was taken in the upper house, and the measure died. Outside training sources do have some importance. About 64 percent of Wisconsin law enforcement agency heads claimed that they have sent officers outside their own agency for some training. This included virtually all of the larger police forces.[12] Agency heads did not stipulate how often men were sent or how many, but this figure shows that many small departments receive virtually no outside sources of information about police procedures. The state vocational school system offered local training programs, but the local departmental leaders have great discretion in determining the curriculum. In short, they initially decide what the important subjects are.

Recent governors and attorneys general have shown an interest in increasing state involvement in local law enforcement. In 1965 the governor established the Governor's Commission on Law Enforcement. Even before the first meeting the head of the Commission emphasized the need for better police training procedures. Fears about inadequate training led to the Commission's formation, and consequently much of the $121,000 in federal grants received by the Commission was to be used to develop a curriculum for a pilot police education program. Both the governor and the executive director of the Commission emphasized the need for more centralized coordination of police activities. At the request of this Governor's Commission, legislators introduced a bill to establish a Law Enforcement Standards Council. The purpose of this council was to establish minimum educational standards for law enforcement, to offer financial aid, and to consult with local units of government about maintenance of these standards.[13] The legislature took no immediate action.

The Attorney General's Conference on Law Enforcement was established for a dual purpose. One purpose was to offer law enforcement officers another opportunity to meet as a group to discuss their problems with experts. According to an assistant attorney general who supervised a recent conference, one of the primary reasons for its inception was the rapid change in the field of criminal law.[14] One year after *Miranda*, statewide standards still had not been established. Neither of these commissions had developed any binding standards. Training still remained at the discretion of the local police departments.

There are others, in addition to the local police, who offer some training programs. State police and sheriffs' associations conduct training institutes, though they are optional. The University of Wisconsin Extension Division increased the number of short courses for law enforcement officials. The FBI offers the most extensive programs for local law enforcement. Its most famous, the National FBI Police Academy, caters primarily to the elite or the most promising officers; therefore relatively few attend its training sessions. Since the Academy's inception in 1935, Wisconsin has graduated less than one hundred officers, approximately thirty of whom are now, or have been, chiefs. The graduates include the present police chiefs of Racine and Madison, two of the four cities we shall investigate.[15] One of the purposes of the academy is to teach its students how to train others. In addition the FBI furnished a mass of material relating to local police training programs and training manpower at no charge to local departments. The use of these programs also depends solely upon the discretion of the local law-enforcement director.

The tradition of decentralization and local control was a significant factor in limiting the extent of centralization, consistency, and general bureaucratization which could be implemented by sources outside the community. Its importance was reflected in the rhetoric and strategies of people who attempted to influence the process of implementing *Miranda*. Though by no means the only important stimuli, the *Escobedo* and *Miranda* decisions were key factors in increasing the attempts at centralization and formalization of police training procedures. As put by one newspaper which strongly supported the need for greater training supervision, the training would be particularly valuable "in explaining the *why* of such decisions," *i.e.*, to give more guidance "in helping young men understand the history and development of police function in a democracy, of criminal law in a changing society and other relevant subjects." [16] Despite suggestions for greater centralized authority, most of the sources of these suggestions continued to have only an informal, extra-legal advisory power. Thus, there was no real hierarchy through which binding directives regarding the implementation of the *Miranda* decision could flow. As we shall see, the *Miranda* decision brought about no change in this formal structure. Thus we must pay careful attention to the tactics used by key decision-makers to implement the *Miranda* decisions because the dissemination of information does not depend upon any statewide network of hierarchical authority.

Participants in the Enforcement of Law

THE STATE SUPREME COURT

In its consideration of police interrogation issues, the Wisconsin State Supreme Court was certainly affected by the factions which stressed decentralization and local discretion. On the basis of the earlier analysis of the relations between the United States Supreme

Court and police departments, one might conclude that the highest state appellate courts assumed important policy-making roles regarding interrogation policy. In Wisconsin this was seldom the case.

An investigation of the Wisconsin State Supreme Court must keep in mind the differences between this court and the United States Supreme Court. The state court has little discretion over the types of cases it may hear. Consequently, the state judges probably encounter more mundane cases. For example, many of the police interrogation cases heard by the Wisconsin court raised the confession issue only as an afterthought in appeals concentrating on other issues. While the United States Supreme Court can often limit the issues it will consider on appeal, the state court must usually rule on all the issues raised. United States Supreme Court Justices often choose to hear cases precisely because conflict among the Justices exists, while many more of the state court cases are quite ordinary and without conflict. This may be an important reason why state court justices dissent far less frequently than their confreres on the highest Court.

For over one hundred years the state Supreme Court had ruled on cases involving the problem of allegedly coerced confessions.[17] Some were mundane. For example, one suspect challenged the validity of a confession made after he himself sent for the sheriff in order to confess. The sheriff told him to think it over, and came back about two hours later to take the confession. We might guess that the United States Supreme Court would have denied *certiorari* in such a case. The State Supreme Court wrote a formal opinion.[18]

In some ways the Wisconsin state court has handled the confession problem with methods similar to those used by the high court. It has constantly faced the problem of obtaining reliable information about confession procedures. To solve this problem the justices have given much discretion to trial courts and have accepted only facts undisputed by the police.[19] The state court has also faced the problem of determining the burden of proving which information was reliable. Like the United States Supreme Court, the state court prior to *Miranda* had clearly placed this burden on the state.[20] The state court did seem more equivocal about this. Some justices at one time took the position that the court must assume the defendant knew his rights and would have to prove otherwise. Though this hard line was infrequently followed, the court has not always been willing to give the benefit of a vague record to the defendant. The reluctance was apparent even after the state court ruled that a confession is involuntary if there is reasonable doubt about the circumstances under which it was obtained.[21]

Furthermore, like the United States Supreme Court, the state court has heard only one case where physical coercion was undisputed. The state justices were as horrified as were the United States Supreme Court Justices in their only case of undisputed violence.[22]

The Wisconsin court, however, was not bound too closely by some other Unted States Supreme Court practices. The Wisconsin court had used a standard slightly different from the voluntary-involuntary theme sometimes used by the United States Supreme Court. The ultimate test of a Wisconsin confession was "not whether it was voluntary or was induced by threats or promises or physical violence but whether it was obtained under such circumstances as to be testimonially untrustworthy." [23] This theme was just as vague and ambiguous as the U.S. Supreme Court's criteria for voluntariness, but it was different. It put more of a burden on the suspect. In state cases involving a trustworthiness standard, United States Supreme Court cases were not cited as guiding precedent. The state justices ultimately attempted to use a totality of circumstances theme to determine trustworthiness. The suspect's education,[24] his past experiences with the law,[25] and the action of the law enforcement officer,[26] were all circumstances to be considered. None alone was always sufficient to invalidate a confession. A law enforcement officer's failure to advise a suspect of his rights was not automatically grounds for invalidation. This, too, depended on the circumstances. In fact, the state court took a peculiar position which, on the one hand, came close to insisting that police should advise a suspect of his rights, but yet refused to impose sanctions upon interrogators for failure to so advise.[27]

The state court ignored another important issue after their brethren in Washington became involved with it. Before 1963 the need for counsel during interrogation was virtually never discussed. The State Supreme Court, unlike the United States Supreme Court, showed no signs of adopting *Miranda* standards prior to *Miranda* or *Escobedo*. The advantages of counsel were not discussed, and, in regard to another greatly divisive issue facing the United States Supreme Court Justices, the Wisconsin court squarely ruled that illegal incarceration *per se* was not sufficient to invalidate a confession.[28] The *McNabb* and *Mallory* decisions were mentioned to show that they applied only to federal law-enforcement officials. The state court, while recognizing the possibilities of mental as well as physical coercion, displayed little concern with the premise that all interrogation was inherently coercive.[29]

One year prior to *Escobedo*, a State Supreme Court opinion suggested that the state justices were becoming more concerned with the federal standard for voluntariness of confessions. The facts of this case were again quite ordinary. A woman was apprehended on a charge of killing her husband. Though exceedingly distraught, she made no statement on the way to headquarters and neither confirmed nor denied her guilt. She was questioned for a little over three hours until midnight. At that time she called her father, who warned her not to say anything and said he would get a lawyer. She confessed before the attorney arrived. Later she insisted that the interrogator had promised her a lighter sentence if she confessed. He denied this, but admitted that he repeatedly told her to disregard her father's advice to remain silent and wait for an attorney.

In this case the justices showed greater concern with federal standards. The majority opinion cited virtually all of the United States Supreme Court confession cases. The opinion used these cases to show that the test for voluntariness had become broader than merely one of trustworthiness versus untrustworthiness. The confession was invalidated because of the lateness of the hour, the suspect's lack of sleep, but, most important, *because the police had encouraged the suspect to disregard the advice of her father*. In short, a suspect had some basic rights regardless of his or her characteristics.[30]

For the first time a Wisconsin justice objected to his colleagues' interpretations of U.S. Supreme Court interrogation opinions. Justice Wilke, in a concurring opinion, worried that the state high court, like the United States Supreme Court, was moving into areas fraught with even more than the usual ambiguities of interrogation situations. Very much influenced by Justice Frankfurter's opinion in the *Culombe* case,[31] Justice Wilke reiterated the need to develop uniformity in this difficult area. He attempted to apply Frankfurter's methods of investigating a confession. Furthermore, for the first time, a Wisconsin justice explicitly took issue with the use of certain criteria to determine a confession's validity. He would not accept the majority's inference that interrogation after a request for counsel was itself enough to make a confession involuntary.

Both the issue of counsel and the use of federal precedents had now become more visible, although the conflict over these issues certainly was more restrained than the conflict in the United States Supreme Court. Because of *Escobedo* and *Miranda*, the counsel issue as well as the attempt to use federal standards appeared more frequently in the court's opinions.

It should be noted that criminal law generally became a more important part of the court's workload. During the 1963 term of the state court, criminal-law cases composed 9.7 percent of all cases decided by means of a formal opinion. Criminal law ranked sixth among ten subjects in number of cases considered by the court. A year later the percentage was 11.9 percent, with a rank of fourth. By the 1965 term, which ended in August, 1966, the percentage had risen to 16.8, and criminal law was now the subject most frequently encountered by the court.[32] One must remember that the state justices lack discretion in choosing which cases to hear. Thus, perhaps, other participants in the judicial process had sensed that developments made the state court more hospitable to appeals concerning criminal law issues.

The above percentages actually underestimate the increase, because almost all of the court's unpublished opinions dealt with criminal law subjects. The unpublished opinion has been used by the Wisconsin Supreme Court for many years for cases where, in the justices' view, only a limited explanation was necessary. Many of these cases involved little more than interpretation of specific fact situations. The court explicitly states that these opinions have "no value as precedents in other cases." They are called "unpublished opinions" though the opinions are written and are available in the office of the clerk of the State Supreme Court. Table 3-1 uses these informal opinions to offer some evidence of the impact of *Miranda* and *Escobedo*.

In 1965, the first full year after *Escobedo*, the majority (60 percent) of confession cases, where a confession was challenged, cited *Escobedo*. In 1966, the number of challenged confessions declined substantially. However, all the informal opinions concerning coerced confessions cited *Escobedo*. The court ruled against the suspect in all of these cases. In 1966, both *Escobedo* and *Miranda* were each

Table 3-1. "Unpublished" Opinions—Wisconsin Supreme Court

Year	Total Number	Percent of Total Involving Confessions	Percent of Confession Cases Mentioning Escobedo
1965	31	32 (10)	60 (6)
1966	26	19 (5)	100 (5)
1967[a]	71	18 (13)	7 (1)[b]

a. Through July 31, 1967.
b. Of the 1967 cases, only one mentioned *Miranda*.

mentioned only once. There was nevertheless a corresponding increase in the percentage of cases where a confession was challenged, but where neither *Miranda* nor *Escobedo* was mentioned in the opinions. (In 1966 no such opinions appear; in 1967, 12 of 13 confession opinions did not mention these two decisions.)

The following tentative conclusions can be made on the basis of an analysis of these informal opinions:

1. The state court had not broadly interpreted *Escobedo*. This explains the declining number of appeals on *Escobedo* issues.
2. *Miranda* as yet had had little effect on the appellate process. In fact, from April to July, 1967, the percentage of cases involving confessions decreased, and *Miranda* was not mentioned in any opinions.
3. Attorneys and jailhouse lawyers who understood the prospective application of *Miranda* perceived that the justices might nevertheless be more alert toward confession procedures in general, hence the increase in the percentage of opinions which do not challenge confessions either on *Escobedo* or *Miranda* grounds. This conclusion could be limited because of the previously mentioned decline in confessions from April through July, 1967. Furthermore, the opinions may have merely ignored these Supreme Court cases.

We must look at the post-*Escobedo* formal opinions to investigate these conclusions more thoroughly. In a number of formal opinions, the state court clearly refused to anticipate the United States Supreme Court by interpreting *Escobedo* broadly. For example, one suspect who had never requested counsel challenged his confession because he had never been advised of his rights. The court in a unanimous *per curiam* opinion admitted that the plaintiff sought a broad interpretation of *Escobedo*. This interpretation, according to the opinion, would invalidate a confession obtained either in the absence of counsel (provided there was no waiver of counsel) or in the absence of police officers informing him of his right to be silent.[33] According to the opinion, "a careful study of *Escobedo* convinces us that it did not lay down such sweeping strictures." [34]

Thus the police received virtually no new guidelines as a result of the state court's interpretation of *Escobedo*. There was still no hard and fast rule requiring police to advise a suspect of his rights to remain silent. Caution was the watchword of the justices, and the court was "unwilling to add another step" until the United States Supreme Court required it.[35] In this same opinion the justices recognized the state court's possible role as a source of guidance in criminal justice administration. The court insisted, however, that, until further rationale was furnished for requiring police to advise a suspect, and further guidance was offered on methods of assigning counsel at arrest, the state court would not require new police procedures.[36]

In yet another case, the court was even more willing to allow police to exercise important interrogation policy options. Following his arrest, a suspect was not brought before a magistrate for 55 hours. He made an informal request for counsel. His attorney, however, was not allowed to see the suspect immediately. The police captain's words to the attorney were reminiscent of those heard by Danny Escobedo's attorney in a Chicago police station: "My business as a policeman and investigator, sir, is to get the job done as I know it. I know I couldn't do it if he did confer with an attorney." [37] The court was again unanimous. The trial judge's determination of voluntariness was accepted. Police officers were still not required to inform a suspect of his right to counsel. He was now entitled to see his own counsel, but the court refused to apply *Escobedo* retrospectively. Unwilling to anticipate the Supreme Court's *broadening* of the suspect's rights at interrogation, the state court was nevertheless willing to anticipate the ruling which *limited* the extent of these anticipated changes.[38]

Relatively little need be said about the decisions made soon after *Miranda*. Since *Miranda* was not applied retroactively, the court dismissed the *Miranda* rule as rationale for invalidating any confessions of a man tried prior to *Miranda*, on the grounds that the same old totality of circumstances problem would be encountered.[39] And the court reiterated the difficulties in interpreting the credibility of information. The trial court's conclusions still carried the greatest weight.[40] Furthermore, the justices continued to show more tolerance toward the nuances which occurred during incarceration than did at least some of their brethren in Washington. Illegal detention alone continued to be insufficient to invalidate a confession obtained prior to *Miranda*.[41] They did warn that arrest on Sunday or a holiday would no longer justify lengthy detention. But the clarity of even these limited guidelines was blurred by the following statement: "We do not mean to infer that the police cannot hold an individual in custody for purposes of interrogation, but the period must not be unreasonable under all the circumstances present."[42] An old rule was thus reiterated with little clarification other than a veiled threat that prompt arraignment required the availability of proper facilities seven days a week.

The court decided only one case which may be classified as part of the new era of confession cases where trial occurred after *Miranda*. A 31-year-old man who had been a special sheriff's deputy for several years was charged and found guilty of having sexual intercourse with a child. Prior to his arrest the police informed the suspect by telephone that the girl had implicated him. He thereupon called his attorney who instructed him to be quiet. Two days later two detectives went to the suspect's place of employment and asked to see him. The man was given permission to telephone his lawyer, and subsequently agreed to come down to the police station voluntarily. A detective who had previously worked with the ex-deputy accompanied him to the station in the suspect's own car. He confessed in the car although the detective had asked him no questions. Not until he reached the station was he advised of his rights. While waiting for his attorney, the suspect again volunteered information without questions from the police.[43]

The court accepted the confession. In some ways, the court's opinion might have eased police anxieties. It specifically quoted *Miranda* to show that a person may still give an acceptable confession without being advised of his rights, provided he was not prodded. In addition, the ruling showed that police can use *some* initiative, *e.g.*, ask a suspect to come voluntarily to the station, without advising him of his rights. One of the detectives had contended that upon initial contact at the offender's place of employment he purposely did not advise the suspect because he did not want to implicate the suspect in front of others. The court accepted this rationale. Thus, at least under some circumstances, immediate advisement of rights was not regarded as mandatory.

Yet the most perplexing questions from a police viewpoint were not answered. The court offered no guidelines about the *stage* at which a suspect is in custody. Because of the circumstances of the case the court could merely advise: [44]

> While a defendant being taken down for questioning might be considered 'in custody,' *here we have a former law enforcement officer familiar with police procedures, who did not consider himself in custody.*

Furthermore, the most perplexing problem, determining the criteria for an intelligent waiver, was not raised.

In sum, the state court has played a relatively minor role in offering the police guidelines to implement the *Miranda* procedures. In one respect this resulted from the nature of the appellate process. The court cannot set guidelines until *after* police procedures have been challenged. The *Miranda* decision was still too recent to allow for many of these challenges. Yet in another way the court's earlier strategy itself had definitely limited its guidance function. After *Escobedo*, and despite expectations that *Escobedo* would be broadened, the justices showed a strong reluctance to anticipate a broad interpretation of that decision. In the short run the justices may have been following the venerable maxims of judicial restraint. They also may have felt that such an interpretation was most sympathetic to law enforcement. Yet with its refusal to offer these guidelines the court certainly offered the police little help in adapting to the *Miranda* guidelines.

In a formal sense the Wisconsin Court lay in an intermediate position between the local police official and the Justices in Washington and might indeed have a certain amount of supervision over police activities. Initially, however, it offered little information about the type of supervision to be expected.

THE ATTORNEY GENERAL'S OFFICE

The attorney general exercised virtually no continuous, formal control over local law enforcement, but he performed one function which kept some staff members closely attuned to the problems of local justice. As the chief legal representative of the state, the attorney general represents the state in all appellate proceedings which concern criminal law. The investigatory work necessary to perform this function brings some staff members into close contact with police and prosecutors.[45] Although presently these criminal-law cases are handled by any one of two or three assistants, for many years one man alone handled all of them. Because of his contact with police officials and because of his expertise, this man became an important source of information for police officials who had questions about law-enforcement procedures.

Before 1965, the flow of legal information in Wisconsin was unsystematic. It depended upon requests from local authorities. In 1965 there was a definite formalizing of the information process. At the request of the Wisconsin State Police Chiefs' Association, the attorney general began to write regular articles in the association's periodical. These articles, entitled "Police and the Law," were meant to give police officers information, particularly about new developments in the laws of arrest and searches and seizures. In fact, the first article was concerned with a then recent Wisconsin coerced confession case. In this article the attorney general encouraged the police to inform all suspects of their rights.[46]

The attorney general's information function was also amplified in another way. Some of the attorney general's staff (usually law students working part-time) began to prepare memoranda which were included in the confidential law enforcement bulletins distributed by the state crime laboratory. At least one copy regularly went to every police department in the state. It is impossible to analyze these 1965 memoranda accurately because all but one of them are out of print and unavailable to the author. In all, nineteen memoranda were not available. Of the eight existing ones written before the *Miranda* decision, five discussed confessions or other arrest problems. Two were noteworthy because they encouraged procedures subsequently adopted in *Miranda*. The first memorandum explicitly suggested that police advise suspects of their right to remain silent.[47]

Another encouraged the adoption of the pre-arraignment procedures proposed by the American Law Institute.[48]

Prior to the *Miranada* decision, the attorney general himself took other action. One month before *Miranda* he encouraged greater "professionalism" and legal training for the police. In his view recent court decisions had emphasized the need for law enforcement officers to use discretion more intelligently.[49] As a result, he initiated an annual conference of law enforcement officers to facilitate the mutual flow of information and—according to one of the organizers of the conference—to offer the police an opportunity for "catharsis" in regard to their more complex problems.[50]

Because of the lack of sanctions to force the police to accept his views, the attorney general attempted to gain acceptance by fulfilling a need for information. Moreover, he offered the police a legitimate channel for release of their objections. The *Miranda* decision, however, brought no changes in the structure of the attorney general's organization. No new staff members were added, but changes did take place. These changes are best understood in light of the attorney general's past informal involvement.

The attorney general unequivocally supported the *Miranda* decision. He made quite an effort to publicize both his views and the rationale for them. He continued to use the facilities of law enforcement conferences as a means to ease police anxieties. At a five-county law enforcement conference he stated that *Miranda* was helpful because the opinion gave the police more information and guidelines, and thus removed the ambiguities which had developed through the years. The attorney general also expressed confidence in law enforcement's ability to "meet the challenge presented by the Supreme Court without compromising our responsibilities in protecting our communities." [51]

In addition, the attorney general's staff continued to use the memorandum as a source of information. Within three weeks after the decision, all police departments had received a memorandum about *Miranda*. This document outlined the decision, and directly quoted the portion of the Chief Justice's opinion which explicitly listed the new procedures. It also emphasized the necessity of compliance, it pledged to use all powers of the attorney general's office to assist police, it encouraged officers to make more effort to gather evidence *before* taking a suspect into custody, and it warned the police to keep clear records of waivers. Finally, it emphasized that a person could still be questioned without advisement provided that he was not a suspect.[52] More departments than usual received extra copies of the memorandum, but there were no records showing which departments made requests for extra copies.[53]

The attorney general's office also issued other memoranda aimed at changing matters related to *Miranda*. From July 1, 1966, through April 15, 1967, a total of thirteen memoranda were issued by that office. Five dealt explicitly with confessions, and two others were concerned with other arrest procedures. The first four memoranda written after *Miranda* considered specific problems of interrogation or illegal detention. Two of these four discussed the application of *Miranda* to other procedures, such as obtaining blood samples and questioning juveniles.[54] Each stressed that *Miranda* did not preclude certain important police procedures, while cautioning the police to be cognizant of future changes.

The attorney general thus attempted to improve his position as a source of information in order to get the police to adopt the new procedures. Like the state court, he, too, could not be considered a direct supervisor of everyday law enforcement activities. Nevertheless, he made a strong effort to get police officials to look toward his office for information. The dissemination of this information entailed the most systematic effort by a state organization to present such data quickly. It is doubtful that the attorney general or his staff believed they could change many police officials' basic attitudes of approval or disapproval, but he attempted to minimize the extent of possible conflict between law enforcement policy and United States Supreme Court decisions. In addition, his staff tried to increase the channels of information available to police and to offer a greater opportunity for catharsis.

THE STATE CRIME LABORATORY

The state crime laboratory is another organization which has virtually no control over everyday law enforcement activities, but which tries to impinge upon local police policy-making. Like the attorney general's office, the crime laboratory primarily serves as a source of expertise. Though the laboratory was not established for the purposes of police education, it quickly assumed this function, as is manifest in its monthly bulletins. Its mobile unit serves as a traveling classroom, and the agency has issued a detailed manual describing means of collecting and identifying evidence.[55]

No changes in the education facilities or procedures have occurred since *Miranda*. This was not because of the lack of interest on the part of the director, who recently told some state legislators that their policies on police training were thirty years behind other states. The director complained vigorously that the manual on evidence was out of circulation and available only in a few departments. The staff hoped to make a limited version available to every police officer, but no money had ever been appropriated for this project.[56]

Changes in the procedures used to evaluate evidence did occur. According to the director, the workload of the laboratory increased after *Miranda*, but it had been constantly increasing prior to the decision. The director anticipated, however, that because of *Miranda* police officials would have to be more concerned with collection and evaluation of physical evidence. He felt that his organization was too understaffed to handle the greater amount of evidence which would have to be evaluated as a result of this greater concern. To limit this problem, he adopted formal, written procedures that established a case hierarchy. In a memorandum to police departments he stated that evidence involving any murder, aggravated assault, or sex crime, especially against children, would be given first priority by the laboratory. Next in order would come crimes allegedly committed by persons already in custody.[57] This priority list existed informally prior to the memorandum, but the explicit attempt to regularize and formalize these procedures showed that the workload problem had increased.

Thus the lack of resources to increase its staff limited the agency's ability to implement further its function as an educator. Though it is too early to make definite conclusions, police officials may now find access to the crime laboratory's evidence-evaluating facilities a greater problem than it was prior to the *Miranda* decision.

LAW ENFORCEMENT ORGANIZATIONS

The Wisconsin State Police Chiefs' Association and other similar law-enforcement organizations were not important sources of information on the *Miranda* decision. Of all law enforcement organizations the FBI continued to be the most important source of such information. The basic structure of the FBI education organization was not changed after *Miranda*. The bureau continued to offer its services to police officials. Inspector Dwight J. Dalbey, the FBI's police education expert in Washington, D.C., presented a short course on the decision to large gatherings of usually upper-echelon police officials. He presided over such a gathering in Milwaukee. Local FBI agents lectured to police officials in their respective communities. Inspector Dalbey's published lectures on the subject served as a guide to these local lectures, which were extensively used in Wisconsin.

Because of the importance and pervasiveness of FBI activities, we shall review the inspector's published lectures. (One member of the state attorney general's staff, in a tone suggesting the lectures were considered in law enforcement to be the last word in education, referred to the document as "The Speech.") It would be inaccurate to presume that each local agent delivered the lectures in the manner desired by the national office. Yet the document's use as a model makes further investigation worthwhile.[58] No attempt will be made to analyze thoroughly the legal rationale and precedents cited by the bureau. Instead we shall be concerned with the bureau's perspective about the decision's implications.

Much of the lecture entailed a relatively straightforward account of the procedures established by *Miranda*. The style was similar to that of the state attorney general's *Miranda* memorandum. Methods of recording waivers and furnishing the warning were primarily discussed. It covered the objectives of the decision and Chief Justice Warren's contention that the Court did not desire to eliminate the use of confessions, as well as the minority's contention that in fact the Court *did* eliminate them. The lectures also emphasized that the implications of the Court's decision were as yet unclear. Law enforcement officials were encouraged both to watch for clarification and to obey existing decisions even if the implications were not clear. In addition, the police were encouraged to adopt "more professional and systematic methods of criminal investigation,"[59] and similarly encouraged to put more emphasis on interviewing witnesses and gathering evidence. The lecture stated optimistically, "With total use of truly professional methods of criminal investigation it may prove quite possible to achieve effective law enforcement within the terms of the *Miranda* decision."[60]

In some subtle ways, the FBI's attempt at encouraging acceptance of *Miranda* was severely limited. No real attempt was made to inform the police that the decision may be evidence of the need to re-evaluate the role of the police in a democratic society. The legitimacy of the Rule of Law as a job constraint was never discussed. The discussion of the possible impact of the decision, although quite fair, failed to include any of these broader issues. Portions of the lectures showed a definite unwillingness to accept what lawyers would call the "spirit" of the decision. The supplement, for example, concentrated upon a discussion of the means for avoiding situations where warnings are required. A portion of the supplement made this clear: [61]

> Particular caution is necessary if the interrogation of a criminal suspect *in a law enforcement office* is to be kept *noncustodial* so that the *Miranda* warning and waiver procedure need not be followed. The invitation to the office should be handled in such a way that it clearly *is* an invitation, not a command, order, or arrest. A true invitation can be extended by mail, telephone or friend. The officer can personally contact the suspect and accompany him to the office if he is willing to go. . . . Once the invited suspect reaches the law enforcement office, the conditions of the interrogation should be kept as *noncustodial* as possible. Allow him all available courtesies, such as permission to use the telephone. If the facilities are suitable, conduct the interrogation in some semi-public place such as a desk in the corner of the police department lobby, or in a large room where other desks are occupied by police clerical personnel in the performance of their regular duties.

Although it encouraged the police to take no chances and to anticipate broader interpretations of this confusing area, on the sensitive subject of custodial interrogation the FBI stressed ways to maintain old procedures. The emphasis definitely was on avoiding the necessity of giving the warning. Though the distinction between custodial and non-custodial interrogation was emphasized, the word "suspect" is used with little restraint or clarity. The lectures were well documented with legal citations. Yet, as the discussion of the state Supreme Court showed, legal decisions in this area can easily ignore anticipated changes.

Professionalization and Participation, Rhetoric and Reform

The influence of most state officials and other non-local organizations concerned with the police and *Miranda* depended upon the degree to which they could convince the police that their information was legitimate and useful. Most important, statewide officials who were directly involved with the administration of justice approved of the decision, but played no continuously significant role in attempting to get the police to accept their views.[62] There was no organized statewide opposition to the decision.

Professionalization and amenability to group influence were commonly stressed as means of coping with the *Miranda* decision. Implicit in the strategies of the state officials was an attempt to facilitate standardization and formalization of police procedures by encouraging development of professionalized police departments. Consequently they also stressed the important informational functions which law-enforcement groups could carry out. Typical were the comments of the United States Attorney for the western district of Wisconsin: [63]

> It is high time that we enlarge the capacity of the police[man]. He deserves better tools and training. He must receive more pay. He must receive sustained assistance from the forces of knowledge—the bar, the business community, the university.

It was clear to state officials that the *Miranda* decision was another force which limited the utility of local police discretion and local control over police standards and practices.

The attorney general was quite conscious of the obstacles that local control could place in the way of desired police reform. In his discussions of reform he was quite careful to emphasize that he desired to maintain law enforcement control at the local level.[64]

The FBI, perhaps the only organization which consistently impinged upon local police, also stressed professionalization. In fact, more than any other organization or individual, the bureau stressed the need to develop more bureaucratized procedures in gathering criminal investigation data and maintaining records.

Prior to *Miranda*, professionalization and group participation were both important issues in police reform. Reform measures were closely intertwined with attempts at higher police standards and greater consistency. These measures could only lead to greater centralization of law enforcement activities. *Miranda* increased the pressure for police reform and as a consequence the issues of professionalization and of the impingement of outside groups on the decision-making process also became more visible. Because local police departments continued to exercise great discretion, local factors should be important variables in assessing *Miranda's* impact. The fact that law enforcement policy-making in Wisconsin has traditionally involved questions of group impingement, bureaucratization and professionalization is further evidence of the importance of these variables in investigating police response to *Miranda*. The remaining chapters weigh *Miranda's* impact in these terms.

NOTES

1. Richard M. Johnson, *The Dynamics of Compliance* (Evanston, Ill.: Northwestern, 1967), 62-63.

2. Compare *Ibid.*, chapters 5-6.

3. J. M. Hunger and E. Jackamonis, "Law Enforcement in Wisconsin." Unpublished ms, 1964, 6.

4. Daniel Bell, *End of Ideology* (Glencoe, Ill.: Free Press, 1960), 145.

5. Wisconsin Taxpayers' Alliance, "What Is the Judicial Council?" (Madison: Wisconsin's Taxpayers' Alliance, 1954), 5.

6. Phillip Haberman, *Law Enforcement in Wisconsin* (Madison: Wisconsin Legislative Council, 1948), 63-66. See also Herbert Jacob, "Politics and Criminal Prosecution in New Orleans," in Kenneth N. Vines and Herbert Jacob, "Studies in Judicial Politics." *Tulane Studies in Political Science* 8 (1962) 77-88; Dallin H. Oaks and Warren Lehman, *A Criminal Justice System and the Indigent: A Study of Chicago and Cook County* (Chicago: University of Chicago, 1968), 28-30.

7. P. Robbins, "State Criminal Investigation Agencies." 1962. Legislative Reference Library, Madison, Wisconsin.

8. Interview with Charles W. Wilson, Director State Crime Laboratory, May 9, 1967.

9. Wisconsin State Legislature, 1967, Senate Bill 55, p. 17. This is popularly known as the "Kellett Bill."

10. Executive Office Release 63-473, Governor John Reynolds, September 12, 1963.

11. "Organized Crime in Wisconsin" (Madison: Office of Attorney General, 1966), 2. John Wyngaard, "State Government Moving Into Law Enforcement Field." *Green Bay Press Gazette*, September 3, 1963. All subsequent newspaper citations without dates are from the "Law Enforcement" clipping file in the S.ate Legislative Reference Library, Madison, Wisconsin.

12. Hunger and Jakamonis, *op. cit.*, 27.

13. See *Milwaukee Journal*, December 6, 1965; *La Crosse Tribune*, July 31, 1966; and 1967 State Legislature Senate Bill 215.

14. Interview with Thomas A. Lockyear, Assistant Attorney General, July 13, 1967.

15. "The N A Man." *Wisconsin Police Chief* 4 (1966), 13-14. The chief of Green Bay, another of the four cities, was an ex-FBI agent. Green Bay did not send a man to the Academy until 1963.

16. *Milwaukee Journal*, February 2, 1967. Emphasis is in the original.

17. *Shoeffler v. State*, 3 Wis. 823 (1854). *Keenan v. State*, 8 Wis.

132 (1858). Other early cases were *Yanke v. State*, 51 Wis. 464, 8 N.W. 276 (1881); *Glass v. State*, 50 Wis. 218, 6 N.W. 500 (1880).

18. *State v. Smith*, 201 Wis. 8, 229 N.W. 51 (1920). In recent years the Court has adopted the use of informal unpublished opinions which are used to decide many of the more mundane criminal appeals and petitions for write of *habeas corpus*. The Court states explicitly that they are not to be cited as precedent.

19. *Shephard v. State*, 88 Wis. 185, 59 N.W. 449 (1894); *Conner v. State*, 95 Wis. 70, 69 N.W. 981 (1897); *Lang v. State*, 178 Wis. 114, 189 N.W. 558 (1922); *Pulaski v. State*, 24 Wis. 2d 450, 29 N.W. 2d 204 (1964). Unlike their Washington brethren, no Wisconsin justice has used a dissent to question such fact interpretations.

20. *Bronston v. State*, 17 Wis. 2d 627, 97 N.W. 2d 504 (1959).

21. *Shoeffler v. State*, 3 Wis. 823 (1854); *State v. Whatley*, 210 Wis. 157, 245 N.W. 93 (1933). See also *Farino v. State*, 207 Wis. 374, 381, 234 N.W. 366, 369 (1931).

22. *Lang v. State*, 178 Wis. 114, 189 N.W. 558 (1922). The Wisconsin justice accused the police officers of forgetting that they lived in the twentieth century and of adopting methods which may have been approved in seventeenth-century England. 178 Wis. 114, 122, 189 N.W. 558, 562. Compare *Chambers v. Florida*, 309 U.S. 227 (1940).

23. *Kiefer v. State*, 258 Wis. 47, 53, 44 N.W. 2d 537, 540-41 (1950). See also *State v. Stortecky*, 273 Wis. 362, 376, 77 N.W. 2d 721, 729 (1928); *State v. La Pean*, 247 Wis. 302, 19 N.W. 2d. 289 (1945).

24. *State v. Goodchild*, 272 Wis. 181, 74 N.W. 2d 624 (1956); *Holt v. State*, 17 Wis. 2d 468, 117 N.W. 2d 626 (1962).

25. *Pulaski v. State*, 24 Wis. 2d 450, 29 N.W. 2d 204 (1964).

26. *State v. Whatley*, 210 Wis. 157, 245 N.W. 93 (1933); *Link v. State*, 217 Wis. 582, 259 N.W. 428, 261 N.W. 416 (1935); *Pulaski v. State*, 24 Wis. 2d 450, 29 N.W. 2d 204 (1964); *Bianchi v. State*, 169 Wis. 75, 171 N.W. 639 (1919); *Flamme v. State*, 171 Wis. 501, 177 N.W. 596 (1920).

27. For the best statement of this position, see *Bianchi v. State*, 169 Wis. 75, 95, 171 N.W. 639, 649 (1919). See also *State v. Whatley*, 210 Wis. 157, 245 N.W. 93 (1933); *State v. Stortecky*, 273 Wis. 362, 77 N.W. 2d 721 (1958); *Bronston v. State*, 17 Wis. 2d 627, 97 N.W. 2d 304, (1959).

28. *Bronston v. State*, 17 Wis. 2d 627, 640, 97 N.W. 2d 504, 511 (1959).

29. *State v. Stortecky*, 273 Wis. 362, 375, 77 N.W. 2d 121, 728 (1958); *State v. Francisco*, 257 Wis. 247, 252, 43 N.W. 21, 38, 40 (1950); *Tarasinski v. State*, 146 Wis. 508, 513, 131 N.W. 889, 890 (1911); *Hintz v. State*, 125 Wis. 405, 104 N.W. 110 (1905).

30. *Hoyt v. State*, 21 Wis. 2d 284, 124 N.W. 2d 47 (1963).

31. *Culombe v. Connecticut*, 367 U.S. 568 (1961).

32. Wisconsin Judicial Council, *1965 Biennial Report* (Madison:

Wisconsin Judicial Council, 1965). See also the *1967 Biennial Report*, 3.

33. *Browne v. State*, 24 Wis. 2d 491, 511f, 129 N.W. 2d 169 (1964).

34. *Ibid.* See also *State ex rel. Goodchild v. Burke*, 27 Wis. 2d 244, 133 N.W. 2d 455 (1966).

35. *Neuenfeldt v. State*, 29 Wis. 2d 20, 25, 138 N.W. 2d 252, 255 (1965). In this case Justice Hallows admitted the accuracy of Justice White's pessimistic *Escobedo* dissent, which predicted a *Miranda*-type decision, but refused to rule in a manner consistent with the *Miranda*-type decision he predicted.

36. 29 Wis. 2d 20, 27-28, 138 N.W. 2d 252, 256.

37. *State ex. rel. Van Ermen v. Burke*, 30 Wis. 2d 324, 335, 143 N.W. 2d 737, 752 (1966).

38. 30 Wis. 2d 324, 336, 143, N.W. 2d 737, 742. In a case decided that same year the state court showed its unwillingness to apply retrospectively a Wisconsin decision when it would have greatly upset police practice. See *State ex. rel. La Follette v. Raskin*, 30 Wis., 2d 39, 139 N.W. 2d 667 (1966). The question was whether to apply retrospectively a decision which required a magistrate to issue all warrants. See *State ex rel. White v. Simpson*, 28 Wis. 2d 590, 137 N.W. 2d 390 (1965).

39. *Reimers v. State*, 31 Wis. 2d 80, 146 N.W. 2d 466 (1966). *State v. Carter*, 33 Wis. 2d 80, 146 N.W. 2d 466 (1966).

40. *State v. Carter*, 33 Wis. 2d 80, 146 N.W. 2d 466 (1966).

41. *Reimers v. State*, 31 Wis. 2d 457, 143 N.W. 2d 525. See also *Phillips v. State*, 29 Wis. 2d 521, 139 N.W. 2d 41 (1966).

42. *Reimers v. State*, 31 Wis. 2d 457, 143 N.W. 2d 425, 435.

43. *State v. Miller*, 35 Wis. 2d 454, 151 N.W. 2d 157 (1967).

44. 35 Wis. 2d 454, 469, 151 N.W. 2d 157, 164. Italics are added.

45. See generally Wisconsin Legislative Council, *Law Enforcement in Wisconsin* (Madison: Wisconsin Legislative Council, 1948).

46. Bronson LaFollette, "Police and the Law." *Wisconsin Police Chief* 3 (July-August, 1965), 5-7.

47. "Special Memorandum #1," *Wisconsin Law Enforcement Bulletin*, May 1, 1965, hereinafter cited "Special Memorandum."

48. "Special Memorandum #24," April 15, 1966.

49. *Wisconsin State Journal*, May 14, 1966.

50. Interview with Thomas A. Lockyear, July 13, 1967.

51. "Attorney General's Office Release, 66-137," Bronson L. LaFollette, July 12, 1966. These views were again publicized in *Capital Times*, July 21, 1966.

52. "Special Memorandum #29," July 1, 1966.

53. Interview with Charles W. Wilson, May 9, 1967.

54. "Special Memorandum #31," August 1, 1966; "Special Memorandum #32," August 15, 1966.

55. Wisconsin Taxpayers' Alliance, "Crime Detection" (Madison: Wisconsin Taxpayers' Alliance, 1954).

56. Possibly, the tension that existed between certain local police

officials and the director of the crime laboratory results partially from his attempts at impingement upon local control. Many had feared the establishment of the laboratory as a threat to local discretion in police activities.

57. Interview with Charles W. Wilson, May 9, 1967.

58. The following information, unless otherwise cited, comes from "Police Interrogation—the Miranda Rule" (Washington: FBI National Academy, May, 1967) or from the supplement (July, 1967). Hereinafter they will be cited as "Police Interrogation" and "Police Interrogation Supplement" respectively.

59. "Police Interrogation," p. 8.

60. *Ibid.*, p. 9.

61. "Police Interrogation Supplement," pp. 9-10. Emphasis is in the original.

62. The state public defender, the president of the state bar association, as well as the United States Attorney for the Western District of Wisconsin all favored the ruling. See *Wisconsin State Journal* (Madison), June 30, 1966, and August 11, 1966; *Capital Times* (Madison), June 30, 1966; *Milwaukee Journal*, January 29, 1967. The Chief Justice of the State Supreme Court initially approved of the decision, but in the midst of an unsuccessful campaign for reelection he hedged on this position. *Capital Times*, June 14, 1966, and October 1, 1966; *Wisconsin State Journal*, November 17, 1966.

63. *Wisconsin State Journal*, August 11, 1966.

64. "Attorney General's Office Release, 17-45," Bronson L. La-Follette, February 27, 1967. *Ibid.*, 66-249, November 3, 1966; *Milwaukee Journal*, February 28, 1967.

Chapter 4

FOUR CITIES AND THE POLICE

A Comparative Profile

Madison, Racine, Kenosha, and Green Bay are the central cities of the four standard metropolitan statistical areas of Wisconsin outside of Milwaukee. Their 1960 population varied in size from 63,000 (Green Bay) to 127,000 (Madison). Since 1960 population in Madison has increased especially rapidly, and Green Bay's population was increased by its annexation of a neighboring community (see Table 4-1). They can all be classified as middle-sized cities with relatively high median family incomes and, compared to the national averages in urban areas, with fewer families with a median income under $3,000. All four communities are overwhelmingly white, ranging from Green Bay (.9 percent total non-white, less than .05 percent Negro), to Racine (5.4 percent total non-white, 5.3 percent Negro). The cities are also quite similar in their formal political structure. Each has a mayor-council form of government, and the aldermanic elections are non-partisan and by ward. Since they are all located in the same state, these cities are subject to somewhat similar political traditions and laws.[1]

These communities are different in some important ways, distinctions which will be further discussed in the case studies. At this point it is necessary only to present profiles comparing the communities according to the degree of police professionalization and the extent of group participation in the portion of the criminal justice process involving the police.

Professionalization

Police organizations were compared according to the stages of professionalization they had reached.[2] There is considerable agreement that specialization and expertise are important criteria for professionalization.[3] The extent of professionalization was thus established on the basis of criteria which measure the degree of expertise and specialization, and by criteria which indicate the nature of incentives that exist to sanction the development of expertise and specialization. The reports of the President's Commission on Law Enforcement best examplify the use of such criteria to measure police professionalization. From the recommendations made by this Commission the following characteristics of professionalized police forces can be listed: [4]

> 1. More general education ("enable them to administer the complex affairs of a police force"). An emphasis on education explicitly means more systematic and strict criteria for police recruitment.
> 2. Greater specialization ("specialist units, staffed by a variety of personnel trained in a variety of disciplines . . .")
> 3. Improved salaries. ("If the police services are to be an attractive career opportunity, it [*sic*] must offer compensation that is competitive with other occupations or professions that seek men of education or ability.")
> 4. Increased vocational training, both recruit and in-service.
> 5. Promotion on merit with much less emphasis on seniority.

Following these criteria, I used the following specific items to construct an index of professionalization (see Appendix B for more explicit reasons for the choice of these items):

> 1. Patrolmen's monthly salary.
> 2. Detective's monthly salary.
> 3. The percentage of full-time civilian employees in the department.
> 4. The percentage of criminal investigators in the department.
> 5. The percentage of officers with at least a highschool diploma.
> 6. The percentage of officers with at least some college.
> 7. Weeks of required recruit training.
> 8. Annual in-service training hours per officer.

In order to rank the departments on the basis of their professionalization, I computed the sum total of each of the eight variables and then established the fraction of the total that each department composed. For example, the Green Bay department required ten weeks of recruit training, Kenosha required eight and Racine and Madison required twelve and fourteen, respectively. The sum of the required hours equals 44. Thus for that item Green Bay received a score of .23, that is, 10/44, while Kenosha's score was .18, Racine's .27, and Madison's .31. For all of these items a higher score was equated with a greater degree of professionalization. Both Green Bay and Kenosha's mean score was .22. Racine's was .26, and the Madison department's was .30. According to this comparative index, the Green Bay and Kenosha departments are the least professionalized, followed in order by Racine and Madison.

The Alford and Scoble indices of local government bureaucratization are based on rank ordering without consideration of the *degree* of difference between the departments on each variable.[5] If such a method were used to compare the four police departments, Green Bay would be the least professionalized, followed in order by Kenosha, Racine, and Madison (see Appendix B). This finding is more consistent with Alford and Scoble's data. The combination of the two indices suggests that Green Bay is slightly less professionalized than Kenosha.

Participation

Advocates of police reform also relate the degree of participation to the ability to innovate. Generally the police are encouraged to consult other local governmental decision-makers as well as private groups, particularly bar associations. In the words of the President's Commission: [6]

> The creation of an institutional framework to encourage the development and implementation of law enforcement policies which are effective and also are consistent with democratic values is obviously difficult. To achieve this requires a basic rethinking of the relationship between the police, and legislatures, courts, prosecutors, local governmental officials, and the community as a whole.

Thus, according to the Commission, police organizations, in

order best to adjust to change, must look toward groups outside the police organization for guidelines to evaluate the extent and consequences of the perceived change. Presumably, the departments with the greatest facilities for communication with other groups can best adjust to new demands. The rating of the extent of group activity is based on data which were more difficult to measure rigorously than were professionalization data. Because of limited resources, this study only investigated the role of lawyers, bar association, local judges and prosecutors. Newspapers were also considered a form of potential group influence and were so analyzed. This limitation may not be too serious because through rudimentary investigation I am convinced that other groups or organizations had virtually no functions in police decision-making in regard to police interrogation procedures.

Disparities in bar association activities accounted for the greatest differences between the four communities. The Brown County (Green Bay) bar association had no committees concerned with the practice or problems of criminal law. None was formed after *Miranda*. Both Kenosha and Racine County bar associations have been somewhat active in this regard. Prior to *Miranda*, the Kenosha County bar association had furnished the local judges a list of attorneys willing to accept indigent cases. As a result of the *Miranda* decision, the association re-evaluated this policy and gave the police a list of attorneys who would be available at any hour. In 1963, the Racine bar association had seriously debated the adoption of a county public defender system. The proposal was voted down, but only after extensive debate. Although this association did establish an *ad hoc* committee to investigate the changes necessitated by *Miranda*, no meetings were held. In Madison some bar-initiated change in the system of furnishing counsel occurred after *Miranda*. Moreover, the Dane County (Madison) bar association was certainly the most active in the criminal law area. Since 1962, a very active "Subcommittee on Counsel for Indigents" has furnished the local judges with a list of attorneys eligible for appointment. It also encouraged increases in attorneys' fees for such cases. A special committee was appointed to investigate the *Miranda* decision. Though no changes in procedures were as yet adopted, this special committee met with the police chief and local judges in order to advise the chief.

The local judiciary is another potentially important group. Green Bay had no organized board of judges meeting regularly to discuss common judicial problems. Furthermore, one Green Bay judge heard virtually every criminal case in the county. The other judges were, for the most part, quite isolated from the criminal law process. Both the Racine and Kenosha judiciary also had no such organization. However, in each of these two communities at least two judges occasionally heard criminal law cases. In Kenosha, only one judge spent most of his time with criminal litigation. In Racine, both judges spent a considerable amount of their time hearing criminal cases. A board of judges did exist in Madison. It was not established primarily to discuss criminal justice administration, but the subject had been discussed periodically. A greater proportion of Madison judges handled criminal litigation. Though one county judge still bore the brunt of the load, another county judge was gradually assuming some of these duties. Circuit judges in Dane County (Madison) generally were also much more likely to dispose of criminal cases than were their associates in the other counties.

Newspaper activity is more difficult to compare. It was possible to review directly newspaper activities only during the first fourteen months after *Miranda*. Newspaper officials were interviewed in order to discover the local media's general activity in the crime area. Next to the Madison papers, the Green Bay paper published the most stories and editorials about *Miranda*. This activity, however, was exceptional for Green Bay. As a rule, the *Green Bay Press Gazette* displayed little interest in local crime and the administration of justice. The Kenosha newspaper displayed an interest in organized crime because of alleged organized crime activities in that city. Otherwise, it was not very concerned with criminal justice procedures. The Kenosha paper had minimal coverage of the *Miranda* decision, though it printed an editorial cartoon critical of the decision. While the Racine paper provided initial coverage of *Miranda*, the editors took no formal position on that case. A look at their clipping library and discussions with staff members convinced the writer that the Racine newpaper's interest in criminal justice administration seemed higher than that of the Kenosha paper. Activity in Madison was again highest. This city has two newspapers, and both papers manifested great interest in the criminal justice process. The papers took opposite positions on the *Miranda* issue, and one paper conducted a lively editorial campaign against it. Along with the Green Bay newspaper, the Madison newspapers were the only ones to follow closely the impact of *Miranda* over the fourteen-month period.

Green Bay undoubtedly had the lowest amount of group activ-

Table 4-1. Professionalization and Participation Four Wisconsin Cities

	Green Bay	Kenosha	Racine	Madison
Population	76,888[a]	62,899	89,144	160,000[b]
Alford-Scoble Bureaucratization rating	low	low-moderate	moderate	high
Police professionalization rating	low	low-moderate	moderate	high
Alford-Scoble Participation rating	low—much consensual, private decision making	moderate	moderate	high
Criminal Justice Participation rating	low	moderate	moderate-high	high
Summary	low level of both bureaucratization professionalization, and participation	lower bureaucratization than anticipated, low to moderate professionalization, generally moderate participation	moderation for all dimensions though criminal justice participation seemed relatively high	high at all levels

a. Includes 1963 annexation of about 14,000.   b. Special 1964 census.

ity, while Madison had the greatest amount. It is quite difficult to distinguish between Racine and Kenosha on this basis, but because more Racine attorneys attempted to broaden the scope of *Miranda*, Racine is rated slightly higher in group activity. One should remember that the differences in group activities were far more subtle than this brief sketch makes them appear.

Professionalization, Participation, and the Impact of Miranda

Table 4-1 summarizes the degree of professionalization and participation in the four cities.

Because there are few studies for guidance, no very specific hypotheses about the relationship between the two variables and policy consequences are offered. Yet there are some general considerations which should be kept in mind. In Chapter 1 we discussed the fact that under certain circumstances professionalization increased the amenability to innovation while in others it seemed to limit such change. Police reformers who emphasize professionalization often seem to assume that the Madison department should be most likely to make changes and to approve of the innovations. Racine, Kenosha, and Green Bay in that order should show less approval and there should be less likelihood of innovation. The remainder of this study spends much time investigating the validity of that assumption. Such reformers also suggest that a high level of participation, that is, group interaction with police, increases amenability to innovation. This, too, shall be considered.

The following four case studies each look at the consequences of *Miranda* in a single community. They are designed to facilitate comparison, the tables having the same number as those furnishing similar data in the other three chapters. The chapters all have the following format:

1. A brief discussion of the political culture of the community with special emphasis on the existence of professionalization and participation.
2. A look at the local groups which interacted with the police in regard to *Miranda*.
3. A discussion of the sources from which the police received information about *Miranda*.

NOTES

1. Except for the data on percentage non-white and median family income which came from the City-County Data Book, this preceding discussion was based on Robert R. Alford with the collaboration of Harry M. Scoble, *Bureaucracy and Participation* (Chicago: Rand McNally, 1969).

2. H. M. Vollmer and D. G. Mills, "Introduction," in H. M. Vollmer and D. G. Mills, *Professionalization* (Englewood Cliffs, N. J.: Prentice-Hall, 1966, vii-viii.

3. Richard H. Hall, "Professionalization and Bureaucratization." *American Sociological Review* 33 (1968), 92-104.

4. President's Commission on Law Enforcement and the Administration of Justice, *Task Force Report: The Police* (Washington: U.S. Government Printing Office, 1967), 43-61, 120-43. Also consult these pages for further references on police professionalization. Hereinafter this report will be cited *Task Force Report: The Police.*

5. Alford with Scoble, *op. cit.*, 122-23.

6. "Bar associations may make an important contribution by the maintenance of a standing committee which has as its mandate a continuing concern with important law enforcement policies. The police field would, in the long run, be aided by the critical, but at the same time, sympathetic, interest of the organized bar" (*Task Force Report: The Police*, 34).

Chapter 5

GREEN BAY

Although the four Wisconsin cities are similar in size and in formal governmental structure, they differ from each other in terms of their economic base. Green Bay is primarily a trading center. When compared to all 676 cities with 1960 populations over 25,000, Green Bay is near the top quartile in terms of trading, while it is in the lowest quartile in terms of persons engaged in finances, insurance, and real estate. Some other distinctions are critical for this analysis. First, Green Bay's population is considerably more immobile than any of the other four cities' population. Second, and more important, the city is lowest of the four in terms of the degree of governmental bureaucratization, an important indicator of professionalization. Finally, local poltitics in Green Bay have traditionally been passive and bland with much consensual decision-making and few active, potentially divisive interests.

These characteristics cannot be attributed merely to the fact that Green Bay is relatively small. In fact, if one considers the city's 1963 annexation of Preble (population approximately 14,000), then Green Bay (1960 population approximately 62,888) is larger than Kenosha and not much smaller than Racine. Moreover, the total size of the urbanized area of Green Bay (125,000) was larger than Kenosha's (101,000) and almost as large as Racine's (142,000). As we shall see, both of these cities have greater conflict in their local politics. Also, Green Bay, a Lake Michigan port city, has been affected considerably by the development of the St. Lawrence Seaway. It is not, then, an isolated small town.

Instead, the blandness and lack of conflict can be explained by various historical, economic, and political factors. At least since the nineteenth century there has been a tradition against active group participation in political decision-making. Labor unions, organizations which often changed traditional participation patterns in other communities, have not become vigorous participants in the local political process. Three factors help explain the reasons for their lack of participation. First, the Depression did relatively little harm in Green Bay. Thus, unions never developed the militance sparked by the Depression and fanned by New Deal legislation. Second, the individual unions are mostly small and craft-union oriented. Finally, two of the biggest corporations in the city have no outside unions (one of these has a company union). Other examples of this absence of conflict are the lack of group impingement on education policies and the lack of factions on the city council. Neighborhood aldermanic campaigns seldom include any intense organizational effort on behalf of a particular candidate.

Green Bay lacks many of Alford and Scoble's criteria of bureaucratization and professionalization, and the existing criteria are not as strong as they appear. For example, zoning laws exist, but zoning and planning commission recommendations are often voted down by the city council. When there is an issue where both the norms of professionalization and group activity are apparent and do conflict, the "localistic" interests advocated by groups are usually accepted over the interests advocated by a professionalized agency such as the city planning commission.[1]

The city of Green Bay faced no serious crime wave either before or after *Miranda*. It remained a city quite free of crimes against the person. There had been no homicides in the city since 1963. In 1966 there were two forcible rapes as compared to no reported rapes in 1965 and two in 1964. The number of robberies gradually declined from four in 1963 to one in 1966. The number of assaults varied from a high of eight in 1965, to five in 1964 and 1966, and a low of three in 1964. While in 1966 crimes against the person increased nationally among cities between 40,000 to 100,000, Green Bay's rate dropped.[2] If these figures are adjusted to population, to include Green Bay's annexation of Preble, the city's rates were even lower. Despite the 1963 Preble consolidation with Green Bay, there was no corresponding increase in the numbers of crimes against the person. Crimes against property, especially larceny, increased significantly, however, so that between 1965 and 1966 there was close to a 40 percent increase in the number of crimes reported to the police. In comparison, between 1965 and 1966 crime increased only 11 percent in cities of Green Bay's size (40,000–100,000).[3]

Police officers claimed that they were not too worried about the increase in these less serious crimes against property. The department's annual report stated that this rise "compared favorable [*sic*]" with the national 11 percent increase in cities of about the same size. The increase in crime was not great enough to increase specialization among detectives. In 1964 the rise in crime led to the adoption of a special squad of detectives. This squad was to work *only* on major cases such as murder, manslaughter, rape, robbery, and assault. According to the department's 1965 annual reports, this squad in fact did not devote all of its time to these major crimes.[4]

Neither the police chief nor the legal community perceived the crime problem as a serious one. The chief admitted that people in the community complained more about traffic than they did about crime. Indeed one view was pervasive among members of the legal community in Green Bay: no serious crime problem exists and none is anticipated. Attorneys in private practice, ex-district attorneys, judges, newspaper men, and police officials frequently expressed or supported the view that Green Bay is an "overgrown country town" with extremely stable social organizations. The variables associated with serious crime were not perceived to exist in Green Bay. There was indeed little concern with any need to mobilize the city's resources to fight crime. The *Miranda* decision had virtually no impact on the general pattern of consensus and informal negotiations. But some small though potentially important changes in the consensus did occur. By examining in more detail the groups involved in the administration of justice, we shall identify their relations with police departments and point out these changes.

Professionalization, Participation, and the Communications Process

THE BAR ASSOCIATION AND ATTORNEYS [5]

There is no specialized criminal law bar in Green Bay. The county bar association has displayed little more than passing concern with criminal law administration. If a Green Bay attorney is interested in criminal law, he usually seeks information from his own sources or from the criminal law section of the state bar association. The state bar also holds semi-annual meetings where such information is available. The state bar organization staff, however, made no attempt to disseminate information about *Miranda* in any systematic manner.

The local bar's most regular source of information on legal change are the monthly meetings of the local association. Here attorneys may give papers on important decisions. No paper, however, has been devoted to the *Miranda* decision, although in the past some papers on criminal law had been presented.

An increase in the amount of public money spent on attorneys' fees (Table 5-1) suggests that perhaps bar activities increased during the year of the *Miranda* decision. Table 5-1 shows the amount Brown County (Green Bay) spent for attorneys' fees for attorneys representing indigent defendants. The tremendous increase in attorneys'

Table 5-1.   Fees for Attorneys Representing Indigents in Brown County (Green Bay), 1961-1967

Year	Amount
1961	$ 835.00
1962	690.00
1963	795.00
1964	498.50
1965	842.00
1966	11,772.45
1967[a]	5,686.00

a. Through June 30, 1967.

SOURCE: Brown County Clerk's Office, Green Bay, Wisconsin.

fees in 1966 and the first part of 1967 did not reflect an organized effort on the part of the bar association to get increased compensation for local attorneys. This increase resulted from two other factors. First, the local attorneys themselves—without initial encouragement from the bar association—felt that the State Supreme Court had sanctioned the right to ask for greater fees. In addition, some attorneys believed that more people, aware of their rights, were seeking counsel. The county judge most involved in this appointment process accepted requests for increased fees because of these state court decisions, though he admitted that the local bar association had also encouraged this increase.

Unfortunately, the data in Table 5-1 shows only the costs per year, and not the number of cases. The latter was unavailable except for the year 1967. A closer look at these cases involved reveals that probably the greatest proportion of the 1967 increase can be explained by larger fees. Of 26 fees presented to the county by June 30, 1967, three attorneys charged over $500 each, and three others charged approximately $400 each. Over one-half of the $5,686 total was spent in less than one-fifth of the cases. The individual fees in *each* of these cases approached or exceeded the total charged in *any one year prior to 1966.*

The local bar association was inactive in another important area of criminal justice administration. Prior to *Miranda*, the local judges had no systematic means of appointing counsel. The judges followed no list of attorneys when they appointed a lawyer to represent an indigent. In two of the three other cities, local bar associations had either cooperated with local judges prior to *Miranda* or adopted them afterward. In the other local bar association this had been discussed extensively. Neither extensive discussion nor change occurred in Green Bay. According to the president of the local bar, the *Miranda* decision brought no large increase in the number of suspects demanding attorneys. The same few lawyers involved in most important criminal law litigation in Green Bay continued to be appointed to defend indigents accused of major crimes. Criminals accused of minor crimes usually continued to be defended by inexperienced attorneys.

The important point is that the appointing process remained unsystematic and unbureaucratized. The county judge who had appointed most attorneys continued to have sole discretion over appointments. This judge did not seem to encourage the bar association to offer a more systematic means of appointment. He attempted, however, to encourage a more active criminal bar in the city and insisted that the recent court decisions have increased the need for more criminal law specialists, even in Green Bay. It is interesting to note that the local bar association president defended Green Bay attorneys against the implication of the judge's suggestions. "We have," he claimed, "as fine a caliber of criminal attorneys here as there is in the state. Percentagewise, I'm sure more attorneys here take part in criminal practice than in your larger cities." [6]

This statement may indeed be true, but in Green Bay there was no impingement on police decision-making by lawyers representing the criminal bar. In the other investigated cities, there were always a few attorneys who formed a somewhat cohesive though informal subgroup that might be called a "criminal law bar." These men could be identified roughly by certain general characteristics. They were intensely interested in getting the police to adopt the new procedures and to expand these procedures. They were quite critical of upper-level police officials. They were also quite defensive about their practice in general. On the basis of these vague criteria, no such criminal bar exists in Green Bay. At least two Green Bay attorneys were well-known trial lawyers, but none felt called upon to exclaim that "we lawyers defend basic freedoms but are considered the dirt of the profession," a more common sentiment in the other cities. The interviewed attorneys had not used *Miranda* stipulations to challenge any confessions. Confessions had never been challenged successfully in the past. The police were perceived to be doing an adequate job in adopting the new warning procedures. Furthermore, other than occasional criticism of the police chief's attempt to pressure the district attorney into prosecuting a case, the attorneys were quite complimentary toward the police. Moreover, none of the criminal law practitioners' defensive esprit de corps existed among these attorneys.

There is some evidence to suggest that consensus and informal negotiation in the political culture here carried over to prosecutor-defense relations. According to one lawyer and ex-district attorney, who was well-known in the city as a practitioner with criminal law experience,

> There is a close cooperation between the district attorney and the defense. They cooperate with each other on furnishing information, though cautiously. Confessions are not too integral to this process.

Most criminal cases no doubt depend on a certain amount of such cooperation,[7] but in Green Bay this cooperation seemed to be particularly extensive. In the opinion of another attorney,

> There is not as much squabbling between the district attorney and the defense counsel as you find in other cities. Green Bay attorneys are not as determined to let their client go scot-free.

One must be cautious generalizing about this aspect of the legal culture. A more thorough study of bargaining or cooperation would be necessary before a generalization can be made. We can at least say that neither the bar association nor the best-known practitioners of criminal law became any more involved with the interrogation process after *Miranda*. The characteristic pattern of lack of involvement and unconcern with the need to correct police procedure remained.

JUDGES

In Green Bay there was no local judiciary organization which regularly and formally met to discuss common problems. Indeed, criminal law administration was handled almost completely by one county judge. From 1963 to 1966 all but four of the 2758 criminal cases in Brown County were disposed of in county court, and almost all of them were handled by the same judge. In 1966 all but one such case was tried in the county court. Thus there was a high degree of specialization, at least when criminal and non-criminal law are compared.[8] This type of specialization, however, limited the likelihood that an organization of judges would participate in the police decision-making process.

Miranda did not affect this specialization in any way. The same judge still continues to hear virtually all criminal cases. There has been no increase in circuit court jury trials. Generally, the other county court judges and, to a great extent, circuit court judges have professed only a cursory understanding of the *Miranda* decision. Their awareness of police department activities was also severely limited. The burden of interpreting and applying the *Miranda* decision fell upon one man with little guidance from his peers.

THE DISTRICT ATTORNEY

The prosecutor's office was undergoing a transition at the time of the *Miranda* decision. The position had become a full-time job only during the five years prior to *Miranda*, and the staff was not as yet established with any permanency. The district attorney's salary remained low ($10,700 a year), and the county had a difficult time hiring and keeping assistant district attorneys. The district attorney's office had not developed an entrenched lower level bureaucracy (assistant district attorneys) which normally develops expertise and informal channels of communication with police officials. Police officials, especially detectives, were limited in the opportunity to develop a dependable working relationship with an assistant prosecutor who had expertise in court-police problems. In fact, soon after the *Miranda* decision, two new men assumed the two assistants' positions. The district attorney lacked a buffer between himself and police officials. If police problems were channeled to the prosecutor's office at all, they were quite likely to be handled by the district attorney himself.

The district attorney's staff is the most important local organization imposing sanctions and rules on the local police. If the prosecutor's staff object to police procedures, they can refuse to prosecute. Prior to *Miranda*, the use of this power of refusal to prosecute was the primary source of friction in police-prosecutor relations. The present police chief had attempted, in the words of an ex-district attorney, to "interfere" with the discretion of the prosecutor. This conflict between the "police perspective's" emphasis on prosecuting all those arrested and the "legal perspective's" emphasis on the necessity for building a good case *before* a warrant is issued increased after *Miranda*. Police officers manifested the results of this friction by expressing great distrust and lack of confidence in the district attorney. Since the assistant prosecutors had limited experience in explaining the legal perspective, this conflict became almost a personal vendetta against the district attorney.

The district attorney was actually quite sympathetic toward the police view. Initially he perceived the *Miranda* decision as a sign that confessions were no longer usable in court. He felt that the Court was possibly eliminating the use of a legitimate tool and was forgetting about public protection.[9]

Rapid legal change required the district attorney to pay even closer attention to nuances in police procedure and increased the disparity between police perspective and legal perspective. The detectives, for example, often refused to accept the need for compromise between prosecutor and defense attorney. The prosecutor was considered "gutless" and "afraid of the defense attorneys." One detective's comment typified this view:

> The *Miranda* decision itself may not be so bad; we may not lose cases because of the decision. We lose cases not because of court decisions but because of the d. a.'s refusal to prosecute.

The district attorney viewed such friction as emanating from those who fail to "keep up with the law." From his perspective, these officers did not understand that a case which they thought similar to one previously presented might no longer be prosecuted because of changes in the law.

In a community where "lack of serious crime" seemed to be an accepted fact and where informal decision-making seemed to be the norm, police officers displayed little understanding and even less sympathy for the need to compromise. Perhaps the very lack of contact between police and other groups may have aggravated this difference in perspective. The lack of an established lower-level bureaucracy in the district attorney's office eliminated the possibilities of some informal, on-going, interpersonal relationships which might have helped to ease the difference between the police view and the legal view.

THE NEWSPAPER

Generally, police officials are supposed to be very sensitive about newspaper accounts of their job. One ex-police official has even suggested that police are probably more concerned with the type of newspaper coverage of their job than with any other aspect of police-community relations.[10] The Green Bay newspaper, while displaying an interest in police activity, has seldom acted as a watchdog over law enforcement procedures. The paper's police reporter emphasized that because of the scarcity of local crime, the paper's editors were not very concerned with the local crime problem.

The paper was in one way quite interested in the *Miranda* issue. Initially, it ran a short article which emphasized the new limits on interrogation procedures, but said nothing of the requirements for counsel. Four days later an editorial appeared which neither approved nor disapproved of the decision, but instead adopted a wait-and-see attitude. It accurately summarized the ruling as well as the tone of the dissent. The editorial also specifically noted that the use of confessions was not entirely prohibited. It cautiously stated that the "final test" of the decision will result from further elaboration of the decision, and it expressed some minor disapproval of the Chief Justice's views of the criminal law process.[11]

The editorial page, however, is not the most frequently read section of a newspaper. Therefore, perhaps the most important news information appeared two days after the editorial. Headlined " 'Mute' Ruling Hit by Police Officials," the story presented evidence of ringing criticism by local police officials. The objections of the police chief, district attorney, and county sheriff were all recorded in this first detailed coverage of local views of the *Miranda* decision.[12] The most interesting feature in this article was the absence of any attempt to present the opinions of local judges, attorneys, and anyone else who might be involved with criminal law administration. This article, at least by implication, accepted the view that in regard to interrogation the problems of police and prosecutor were isolated from the rest of the legal culture.

The editors did not engage in an active campaign for or against the decision, but nonetheless the media's function was somewhat unique. Other than the newspaper and the prosecutor's office, no other group displayed any significant interest in interrogation activities. The newspaper was thus the only source of opinion from outside the legal community. Yet, in some ways, the newspaper's involvement could have easily *reinforced* the view that police behavior was isolated from the rest of the community. The paper presented only police-prosecutor analysis of the decision's implications. The paper's police reporter, who wrote the article, admitted that in regard to *Miranda*, his "views are pretty much the same as the police." It is not surprising that, given his acceptance of the police perspective, he should look solely toward the police for comments about *Miranda*.

Police decision-making thus continued to take place in an isolated milieu. The newspaper, which seemed to increase its interest in local law enforcement, did not change this milieu by its activities. The *Miranda* communications process reflected this isolation, and the process was not basically changed by *Miranda*.

SOURCES OF *Miranda* INFORMATION

Table 5-2 shows that the police had different initial sources of information about *Miranda*. The newspaper was the most frequently mentioned first source although, among patrolmen, a superior was mentioned almost as often. Some rather interesting clues about the flow of communication emerge from these data. No detective mentioned a superior officer as the initial source of information. The detectives seemed more likely to look outside the police hierarchy for their initial information. Local officials played a miniscule part in initially furnishing information about the decision. Less than 2 percent of the officers listed a local judge or the district attorney as an initial source. Finally, the information from the attorney general's office initially seemed to permeate only the upper echelons.

The flow of *Miranda* information certainly continued after this contact between police and their initial sources of information. In Table 5-3 one can see a more complete composite of the sources of information.

Newspapers continued to be the most frequently mentioned source of information. Patrolmen listed the superior officer more often than did any of the other officers, but this source also ranked highly among both detectives and superiors. A superior officer usually spoke to the organization by means of short taped lectures presented fifteen minutes before each shift went on duty. These lectures could not present a detailed account of a subject as complex as the *Miranda* decision. They were usually perfunctory in nature and did not elicit much interaction between superior and the rank-and-file. The organization did hold special conferences on the interrogation issue. A majority of the force (61.4 percent) attended such sessions, but in one way this number may be surprisingly small. Close to 40 percent of the force did not remember attending such sessions, which were the department's most significant attempt to present an analysis of the *Miranda* decision. The local FBI agent spoke at these sessions. Detectives and superiors were more likely to attend such sessions than were patrolmen.

Of the information from sources who were not enforcement officials (the *Miranda* opinion itself, the district attorney, local judges, and the attorney general), only the Court opinion was ranked higher than were *any* of the other sources. (However, this source

Table 5-2. Rank and First Source of Information about *Miranda* (Green Bay), in Percentages

	Source	*All*	*Patrolman*	*Superior*	*Detective*
			R A N K		
(1)	TV, radio	8.6	7.3	11.1	10.0
(2)	Magazines not specializing in police activities	2.9	4.9	0.0	0.0
(3)	Newspaper	35.7	31.7	44.4	30.0
(4)	Police officer not a superior	1.4	0.0	0.0	10.0
(5)	Superior officer	18.6	27.9	11.1	0.0
(6)	Magazines specializing in police activities	2.9	2.4	0.0	10.0
(7)	Training sessions	10.0	12.2	11.1	0.0
(8)	Supreme Court opinion	12.9	12.2	16.7	10.0
(9)	Attorney General	4.3	0.0	5.5	20.0
(10)	Local judge	1.4	2.4	0.0	0.0
(11)	District Attorney	1.4	0.0	0.0	10.0
	TOTAL	100.1	101.0	99.9	100.0
	(N)	(70)[a]	(41)	(18)	(10)

a. Individual rank totals are less than 70 because there was one person of unknown rank.
Total may not equal 100 percent because of rounding.

was mentioned less in Green Bay than in the other cities studied.) The district attorney, attorney general, and local judge ranked lowest.

The infrequent mention of the local judge and the district attorney reflected the isolation of the Green Bay police. The district attorney had prepared a memorandum about *Miranda*, and gave it to one of the upper echelon officers. He admitted that he did not know if it was ever shown to the rank and file. Note that detectives, who have the most daily contact with the prosecutor's office, were no more likely to get advice about *Miranda* from him than were the other ranks. Regularized channels of communication did not exist. Moreover, *none* of the detectives mentioned the local judge as a source of information.

In comparison with the other men, the detectives were far more likely to receive information from the attorney general's office. (Again this source is listed less in Green Bay than in the other cities.) But the detectives were probably more isolated from the influence of the other important actors in the local judicial process—the prosecution and the local judges. These detectives on the average received their information from more sources (5.3) than did either the patrolmen (4.73) or the superiors (4.41), but on the whole they were cut off from these potentially important local sources.

These facts shed further light on the earlier analysis of police-prosecutor relations. The above data suggest that the prosecutor, as a local "outside" decision-maker, was not successful in becoming an important source of information in an area where the overlap between the legal process and the law enforcement process certainly increased. The judge may not have been mentioned as a source because there was virtually no local litigation involving challenged interrogation procedures. From the evidence we can nevertheless say that the judge did not seem to be perceived as a regular source of information. The 1966 annual report of the Green Bay department mentioned the district attorney as a participant in training programs, but no judge was mentioned.[14] Table 5-4 examines the police perceptions of the importance of the sources.

Both the superiors (44.4 percent) and the patrolmen (41.5 percent) most often ranked training sessions and conferences as the best source of information. Otherwise there was little agreement on the best source. Indeed the detectives showed no consensus about the

Table 5-3. Rank and All Sources of Information about *Miranda* (Green Bay), in Percentages

	RANK			
Sources	All	Patrolman	Superior	Detective
Superior officer	75.7	78.1	77.8	60.0
Newspaper	75.7	80.5	66.7	70.0
TV, radio	70.0	75.6	55.6	70.0
Conferences, training	61.4	58.5	66.7	70.0
Supreme Court opinion	40.0	39.0	38.9	50.0
Police officer not a superior	34.3	41.5	33.3	10.0
Magazines specializing in police activities	32.9	24.4	33.3	60.0
Magazines, nonspecialized	32.9	35.0	22.2	40.0
District Attorney	30.0	29.2	33.3	30.0
Attorney General	22.9	12.1	27.8	60.0
Local judge	11.4	14.6	16.7	0.0
(N)	(70)[a]	(41)	(18)	(10)

a. Individual rank totals are less than 70 because there was one person of unknown rank.

Totals exceed 100 percent because each individual could choose as many as eleven sources.

importance of any of these. Of course, in order to choose a source as "best," an officer would have to experience contact with the information. When we control for such contact, the training session became even more important as a "best" source of information. Over 60 percent of those who had listed the training session as an outlet of information chose it as "best." This ratio did not exceed 30 percent for any other source.

In order to illustrate more graphically the lack of agreement on the importance of sources, other than training sessions, Table 5-4 is presented without combining categories. Table 5-5 compares the importance of sources of information from within law enforcement with those from outside law enforcement.

Law enforcement sources (conferences and training sessions, superior officers, and law enforcement magazines) were by far the most important sources of information. Outside specialized sources (the Supreme Court opinion and the attorney general) accounted for only a small fraction of the total choices, and local officials (district attorney, local judge) for a more miniscule number. Outside non-specialized sources, such as newspapers, non-law enforcement magazines, and television were chosen as most important more often than were either the outside legal sources or local officials.

Thus the sources of information were either relatively informal or inbred within the law enforcement profession. In addition, the sources established a milieu which appeared hostile to *Miranda*. Seventy-one and four-tenths percent of the force, including 75.6 of the patrolmen, 72.2 of the superiors and 60.0 of the detectives perceived their sources of information to be critical of *Miranda*, while only 4.3 percent (two patrolmen and a superior) perceived the sources to be complimentary of the decision. Seventeen and one-tenth percent thought the sources were neutral. Perhaps predisposed negative attitudes led the officers to perceive that the sources were so disapproving. Yet these perceptions are significant whether or not they were accurate. At least they reinforced these attitudes. Thus the sources can be generally categorized as inbred and, at least from the officers' viewpoint, hostile to the decision.

Some changes did occur in these sources of information. Table 5-6 shows that over 47 percent of the force thought that some of these outlets of information were new. Unfortunately, the officers almost always failed to list what these new sources were. Nonethe-

Table 5-4.   Rank and Best Source of Information on *Miranda* (Green Bay), in Percentages

R A N K

Source	All	Patrolman	Superior	Detective
Conferences, training	37.1	41.5	44.4	10.0
Newspapers	15.7	17.1	11.1	10.0
Superior officer	10.0	9.8	11.1	10.0
TV, radio	8.6	7.3	5.5	20.0
District Attorney	7.1	9.8	0.0	10.0
Attorney General	5.7	0.0	11.1	20.0
Supreme Court opinion	5.7	7.3	5.5	0.0
Magazines specializing in police activities	5.7	2.4	5.5	20.00
Magazines, nonspecialized	4.3	4.9	5.5	0.0
Police officer not a superior	0.0	0.0	0.0	0.0
Local judge	0.0	0.0	0.0	0.0
TOTAL	99.9	100.1	99.9	100.0
(N)[a]				

a. Individual rank totals are less than 70 because there was one person of unknown rank. Totals may not equal 100 percent because of rounding.

less, this table gives further enlightenment about the flow of communications. The upper ranks, and especially the detectives, were much *less* likely to receive information through new sources. Detectives' sources changed only slightly, and little contact remained between detectives and "outside" sources associated with organizations having high levels of professionalization and participation.

Police Perceptions and Attitudes

It is impossible to establish a direct causal relationship between the content of the previously discussed information and the attitudes and perceptions of the police. Nonetheless we can at least investigate the attitudes and perceptions which are conceivably related to the information process. These include the officers' anticipation of the decision and the extent of their knowledge about the *Miranda* decision. In addition police perceptions of the effects of *Miranda* are investigated to some extent because they seem related to the police reactions to the sources of *Miranda* information. A most important possible effect—change in interrogation behavior—will be briefly mentioned here but will be more thoroughly considered in Chapter 10.

Because of its low professionalization and low amenability to participation, we would expect that the Green Bay department was least likely to anticipate a decision like *Miranda*. This percentage was lower (but, as we shall see, not much lower) than it was in any of the other cities. Furthermore, the superior officers in Green Bay showed less anticipation than did any of the other ranks in the department. Beside the chief, only one of the 17 superiors in the sample expressed such anticipation as compared to 2 of the 10 detectives, and 8 of the 41 patrolmen. These superiors, who in a formal organization supposedly are in the best position to disseminate information, were in fact least likely to anticipate change.

The action of the chief casts some insight on the limits or extent of application of Supreme Court decisions. He definitely anticipated a *Miranda*-like decision, but refused to take action to implement the anticipated requirements. In his words, "We waited for the Supreme Court to take specific action because we needed every advantage we could get." Because of the lack of any action based on anticipation, we would expect that perceived change would be especially high in

Table 5-5.   Rank and Categories of Best Sources of Information on *Miranda*
(Green Bay), in Percentages

		R A N K		
Source	*All*	*Patrolman*	*Superior*	*Detective*
Law enforcement	52.8	53.7	61.0	40.0
Outside specialized	11.4	7.3	16.7	20.0
Outside nonspecialized	28.6	29.3	22.2	30.0
Local officials	7.1	9.8	0.0	10.0
TOTAL	99.9	100.1	99.9	100.0
(N)	(70)	(41)	(18)	(10)

Totals may not equal 100.0 percent because of rounding.

Table 5-6.   Rank and New Sources of Information (Green Bay), in Percentages

		R A N K		
Sources	*All*	*Patrolman*	*Superior*	*Detective*
All new	1.4	0.0	5.5	0.0
Some new	45.7	53.7	38.9	20.0
None new	41.4	31.7	50.0	70.0
Don't know	11.4	14.6	5.5	10.0
TOTAL	99.9	100.0	99.9	100.0
(N)	(70)[a]	(41)	(18)	(10)

a. Individual rank totals are less than 70 because there was one individual of unknown
rank.

Green Bay. In fact, the opposite occurred. Of the four departments studied, the Green Bay department had *fewest* officers who perceived that *Miranda* led to a great or a very great change in their jobs. Less than one in four (24.3 percent) perceived such changes. The 45.7 percent of the Green Bay officers who did think that their department underwent considerable change was lower than that found in all but one of the other police forces. Again perceptions varied according to rank. Table 5-7 shows the breakdown by rank.

All detectives felt that the decision had changed their job to some extent. The superiors were more likely to perceive no change in their jobs. However, about the same percentage of each rank thought that the *department* had undergone considerable change (48.8 percent of the patrolmen, 41.1 of the supervisors and 40 of the detectives). Only one officer, a patrolman, said the decision did not change department activities.

Even though perceived change was somewhat limited, the Green Bay officers objected most strenuously to the decision. Only 11.4 percent approved of the decision. Only Kenosha showed less approval. The detectives, the group which unanimously perceived that *Miranda* would change their job, nevertheless were the most approv-

Table 5-7. Rank and Perceptions of Extent *Miranda* Changed One's Own Job (Green Bay), in Percentages

		R A N K		
Change	All	Patrolman	Superior	Detective
Great or very great	24.3	21.9	22.2	40.0
Some	62.9	65.9	55.5	60.0
None	10.0	7.3	22.2	0.0
Don't know	2.9	4.9	0.0	0.0
TOTAL	100.1	100.0	99.9	100.0
(N)	(70)[a]	(41)	(18)	(10)

a. Individual rank totals are less than 70 because there was one person of unknown rank.

Totals do not equal exactly 100 percent because of rounding.

Table 5-8.   Percentage Correct Perceptions of Stipulations in *Miranda* Decision
            (Green Bay), in Percentages

			R A N K	
Stipulation	*Total*	*Patrolman*	*Superior*	*Detective*
(1) Must tell of right to remain silent	98.6	100.0	100.0	90.0
(2) Anything suspect says may be held against him	95.7	95.1	100.0	90.0
(3) Right to attorney if he wants one	92.9	90.2	100.0	90.0
(4) If indigent, can have attorney appointed at court expense	91.4	87.9	100.0	90.0
(5) Can still ask person to come voluntarily to the station	40.0	34.1	44.4	60.0
(6) Suspect must have an attorney whether he wants one or not	95.1	96.3	94.4	100.0
(7) Confessions no longer evidence	87.1	82.9	88.9	100.0
(8) May no longer talk to anyone without informing him of rights	21.4	19.5	22.4	30.0
(9) No wire tapping	87.1	87.8	83.3	100.0
(10) Voluntary confessions no longer legal source of information	87.1	82.9	88.9	100.0
(N)	(70)[a]	(41)	(18)	(10)

a. Individual rank totals are less than 70 because there was one person of unknown rank.

ing of the decision. Three of 10 approved as compared to 1 of the 17 superiors and only 3 of the 41 patrolmen. Thus, there is some indication that the detectives, who were most central to the interrogation process, were relatively more approving, though the percentage of detective approvers was still only 30 percent.

Table 5-8 shows the amount of knowledge about the stipulations in the *Miranda* decision. The officers were asked to check which of those on the list were stipulations from the *Miranda* decision. The first five items in the table were those for which a check was required as a correct answer. For the next five a check was an incorrect answer. These items appeared in a different order in the questionnaire (for further comment see Appendix A).

As a whole, the officers showed a high level of knowledge about the basic elements of the decision. They did, however, *overestimate* the limitations of the *Miranda* decision. For example, only 40 percent of the officers correctly perceived that *Miranda* did not prohibit the police from asking a suspect to come voluntarily to the police station. FBI local police training procedures spend much time discussing the ways of keeping voluntary such personal "invitations." The attorney general's memorandum also mentioned this aspect. Such a response might be considered as an example of police anticipation of change or, in lawyer's terms, acceptance of the "spirit" of the law. In fact since *Miranda* the Green Bay police did ask a person to come voluntarily to the station, and the State Supreme Court has explicitly sanctioned this behavior in a case involving the Green Bay department.[15]

The State Supreme Court decision was handed down two months after the questionnaire was administered. Consequently, more officers might subsequently know that individuals may be invited to the station house. Nevertheless, prior to this state decision, over half (60.0 percent) of the detectives were aware that *Miranda* did not proscribe such interrogations. A greater number of detectives knew about this than did either patrolmen or superiors. This information evidently was not disseminated by the detectives.

There was similar confusion about a related item, concerned with the need to advise all persons of their rights (item 8). The chief himself admitted that he was most concerned about anticipated decisions which would require that all conversations be preceded by a *Miranda* warning. He felt that such stipulations would necessitate

Table 5-9. Rank and Effects of *Miranda* on Own Job (Green Bay), in Percentages

Effects	All	RANK Patrolman	Supervisor	Detective
(1) New methods of gathering evidence	47.1	43.9	55.5	50.0
(2) Better education and training	41.4	46.3	38.8	30.0
(3) Sympathy toward suspects	17.2	14.6	27.8	10.0
(4) Spending more time explaining activities to community	15.8	14.6	16.7	20.0
(5) More attention to others in the field of criminal justice	15.8	14.6	16.7	20.0
(6) New methods to obtain confessions	7.1	0.0	5.6	40.0
(7) More closely observed by people outside department	12.4	14.6	0.0	20.0
(N)	(70)[a]	(41)	(18)	(10)

a. Individual rank totals are less than 70 because there was one person of unknown rank.
Total may be greater than 100 percent because each officer could give two responses.

that all officers be trained in interrogation procedures. Yet it was apparent that most officers, including the detectives, believed that such stipulations were *already* required. In sum, on certain key procedures the overwhelming majority of the force perceived a change greater than the change adopted by the United States Supreme Court as well as by other decision-makers important in the administration of justice.

There is other evidence to suggest that a good number of the officers also felt that *Miranda* had affected the procedures related to the interrogation process. The need to adopt new means of gathering evidence was the most frequently mentioned effect on one's own job; 47.1 percent of the department listed this effect (see Table 5-9).[16] This table shows that 40 percent of the detectives thought that the *Miranda* decision caused them to seek new methods for obtaining a confession. Five and six-tenths percent of the supervisors and no patrolmen perceived this effect on their own job. This again emphasizes the continuing importance of the detectives in the interrogation process even in a relatively unspecialized department. The other officers did not perceive this change in their own jobs because they seldom interrogated. Only 15.7 percent of the department felt that the change in evidence-gathering procedure was the most important single effect on the department. (There was little difference by rank.)

Some of the other perceived effects in Table 5-9 are more relevant to the present analysis because they are more closely related to the process of communicating information about *Miranda*. Over two-fifths of the men listed changes in education and training programs as one of the two most important effects on their own jobs; these included 46.3 percent of the patrolmen, 38.8 of the superiors and 30 of the detectives. About the same percentage of patrolmen and superiors listed this as the most important effect on the department in general (34.1 percent of the patrolmen and 33.3 of the upper echelon). This response was chosen more frequently than all others except the "more responsibility to detectives" alternative. Only 20 percent of the detectives chose the education response, but again this was the second most frequent choice.

The emphasis on education and/or training did not mean that there was an immediate increase in professionalization or participation. There were no changes in the methods used to train officers although there was a special training session devoted to *Miranda*. Much of in-service training still depended on roll-call training programs, and these were not intensified. The department did not adopt an incentive pay plan which would encourage education. The chief discussed this possibility, but hinted that it would create friction on the force. Moreover, some of the upper echelon officers certainly expressed cynicism about the President's Commission on Law Enforcement and the Administration of Justice's recommendations concerning professionalization. The chief training officer, now deputy chief, responded in the following manner to the Commission suggestion that college-graduate police should not start as beat patrolmen: [17]

> Education alone is not enough. Police experience is necessary and the only way to get this experience is through proper police training over a period of years.

This officer did admit that recent changes in the law required better police training. He organized a police cadet program which allowed the department to recruit men who were not yet old enough to be policemen. These men were to serve a form of apprenticeship, and perhaps get a college education partially completed prior to becoming police officers.[18] As of the spring of 1967, there was one such cadet.[19]

Other, more subtle factors limited the emphasis on education. Compared to the other departments, Green Bay had the fewest respondents perceiving the education effect on their own jobs. For example, among the police in Kenosha (the next lowest force in professionalization) 71.4 percent said that perception of the need for more education was one of the two most important effects of *Miranda*. Moreover, this emphasis on education cannot be considered an indication that the Green Bay police have now become more cognizant of the need to make police behavior less isolated from the community. Public appearances by police officers decreased from 144 in 1965 to 121 in 1966.[20] Of the five least frequently mentioned effects of *Miranda*, four were related to greater participation (see Table 5-9).

Items 4, 5, and 7 can be considered indicators of increased participation on the part of local groups. Local participation might also have increased at the training sessions, but we saw this was not the case. Changes *within* the department's regular activities take precedence over changes in relations *between* department and community or between the department and other actors in the law enforcement process.

Conclusion

The traditional lack of emphasis on professionalization and participation continued in Green Bay after the *Miranda* decision. The isolation of police from their community on this matter was reinforced by the fact that the lack of crime prevented the use of interrogation and confessions from becoming a controversial, salient issue. Local police and FBI agents continued to be the most important sources of information. Thus, as one might expect in a department with low professionalization and participation, the *Miranda* decision did not result in pressure for great procedural change.

Yet, the Green Bay police indeed perceived relatively great changes and disapproved of the decision. It may seem paradoxical that in a department where pressure for change was relatively low, police perceptions of change were relatively great. Two interrelated factors may explain this paradox. First, the police generally overestimated the constraints resulting from *Miranda*. Second, those who had access to the police communications process did not emphasize the *limits* of the *Miranda* constraints. We shall see that in the more professionalized departments those with such access stressed the *Miranda* limitations rather than the strength of its constraints.

The low professionalization and participation were thus significant factors in maintaining police isolation. This isolation in turn seemed an important factor in explaining the continuation of low professionalization and participation. This cycle was also maintained because the lack of any great local interrogation issue limited the need for any changes either in police professionalization or their access to outside groups.

NOTES

1. Robert R. Alford with the collaboration of Harry M. Scoble, *Bureaucracy and Participation* (Chicago: Rand McNally, 1969), 13-16, 37-58, 118-54.

2. *Annual Report—1966* (Green Bay: Green Bay Police, 1967), 25. See also the annual reports of 1964 and 1965, hereinafter cited *Annual Report* followed by the appropriate date.

3. *Annual Report—1966*, 25. Of the 1411 crimes reported to the Green Bay police in 1965, 1025 or better than 70 percent involved some form of larceny.

4. Compare *Annual Report—1964*, 27, with *Annual Report—1965*, 27.

5. In each of the communities studied an attempt was made first to interview the local bar association president. After discussing the association's involvement in the *Miranda* question, he was asked to name some lawyers "who practiced more criminal law than the average." Seldom was this initial list greater than five. During the course of interviews with these "criminal" lawyers, they were asked to furnish more names. In almost all cases, these attorneys felt that the bar president's list was inclusive, perhaps too inclusive. Although no attempt was made to sample systematically the bar members in each community, the views of the interviewed attorneys did seem to support my original assumption that few attorneys are significantly involved with criminal law.

6. *Green Bay Press Gazette*, March 5, 1967.

7. See Donald J. Newman, *Conviction: The Determination of Guilt or Innocence Without Trial* (Boston: Little, Brown, 1966).

8. Letter from Janet M. Courtney, State of Wisconsin Judicial Council, to author, October 6, 1967.

9. *Green Bay Press Gazette*, June 19, 1966.

10. Arthur Niederhoffer, *Behind the Shield: The Police in Urban Society* (Garden City, N.Y.: Doubleday, 1967), 115-17.

11. *Green Bay Press Gazette*, June 17, 1966. However, after the second *Miranda* conviction an editorial appeared that gave more support for agreement with the Supreme Court that the "rights of the individual must receive first consideration." Undated editorial, article file, *Green Bay Press Gazette*, Green Bay, Wisconsin.

12. *Green Bay Press Gazette*, June 19, 1966.

13. The patrolman category also includes corporals. In fact, there is no distinction between the duties of these two ranks, and the department

is discontinuing the rank. Detectives includes supervisors in the detective bureau as well as juvenile investigators.

14. *Annual Report—1966*, 11.
15. *State v. Miller*, 35 Wis. 2d 454, 151 N.W. 2d 157 (1967).
16. Each respondent could check two effects on his own job.
17. *Green Bay Press Gazette*, March 5, 1967.
18. *Green Bay Press Gazette*, August 21, 1966.
19. *Annual Report—1966*, 4.
20. Compare *Annual Report—1966*, 6 with *Annual Report—1965*, 7.

Chapter 6

KENOSHA

Kenosha differs significantly from Green Bay in its economic base and in the degree of conflict that characterizes its political process. Kenosha is a manufacturing center which is basically a one-industry town; American Motors employs about 60 percent of the labor force. The difference in the degree of conflict is more important. More than any other city, Kenosha politics have been characterized by intense group conflict over substantive issues, the constitutional framework of local government, and minor procedural matters. Conflict over procedural matters has been especially intense. This traditional political turmoil, which extended to the activities of the mayor, city council, and the school board, was exacerbated by a heavily unionized working class and absentee ownership of many industries. Thus, unlike Green Bay, Kenosha has neither the cultural homogeneity nor the tradition of unsupervised decision-making.

The polarization of the city into one large union versus one large company, the absence of middle-level managers and businessmen from local politics, and the political activism of the local unions are all important factors making Kenosha a city of working class or lower middle-class homeowners who are longtime residents and whose views are extremely important in Kenosha politics. Because local councilmen are elected by the ward system, the views of these people have been forcefully represented. Such persons are typically concerned about taxation and they oppose bureaucratization and professionalization in many aspects of city government.

Consequently, despite many differences in group participation in governmental decision-making, there is not a great deal of difference in regard to professionalization between Green Bay and Kenosha. Kenosha,[1]

> lacking a sizable pool of leaders with a cosmopolitan orientation, and, having a city council dominated by a faction with strongly localistic and parochial orientations, has resisted such developments [of professionalization and bureaucratization]. . . . Government is not so professionalized as in other cities, where the public interest is assumed to be easily defined and non-political, in the sense that professionals can define the "best" way to organize.

The police reflect these characteristics. They, like Green Bay, are relatively unprofessionalized, but unlike Green Bay some groups have actively participated in the police decision-making process. Moerover, crime is a very salient issue in Kenosha. Kenosha has the dubious reputation of being one of the few places in Wisconsin which allegedly has elements of organized crime, although its existence is debated.[2] At least one killing attributed to the Cosa Nostra occurred in Kenosha within the past few years, and the existence of such crime here is often attributed to Kenosha's location, roughly mid-way between Milwaukee and Chicago. The President's Crime Commission has specifically stated that organized crime exists in those two larger cities.[3]

Crimes against the person are much more prevalent, relatively and absolutely, than they are in Green Bay. In each of the respective years, 1964 through 1966, there were two crimes classified as "murder or non-negligent manslaughter."[4] One, the alleged gangland killing, remains unsolved. In addition, in early 1967, Kenosha was the scene of a particularly brutal stabbing. There were four forcible rapes in 1964 and 1965, though none either during 1966 or during the first six months of 1967. The number of assaults varied from a high of 52 in 1966 to a low of 14 in 1965. At the same time, in Kenosha, robberies also increased from 14 in 1964, and 15 in 1965, to 19 in 1966. Between 1965 and 1966 crimes against the person (including robbery) more than doubled. This increase can primarily be attributed to the increase in the relatively minor assault cases. Disregarding assault cases, we find that the more "serious" reported crimes against the person increased 16 percent between 1965 and 1966. Kenosha's Class I offenses showed a little under a 10 percent increase between 1965 and 1966. This is close to the 11 percent national increase among cities in its category.[5]

Perhaps more important than these rather ambiguous crime statistics is the fact that unlike Green Bay no informants in Kenosha ever mentioned a lack of serious crime in the city. Both serious crime and the factors commonly (though, it must be emphasized, not necessarily accurately) related to crime were perceived to exist. In his 1966 report to the city, the Kenosha police chief expressed anxiety about the increase in crime. He directly related this problem to the interrogation decisions: [6]

> As you study this report, you will note that in Kenosha, as in many other parts of this country, the crime rate has increased over the past year, in spite of the fact that we have additional personnel patroling during the evening hours. The solutions of the crimes committed have been hampered to some degree by the decisions and decrees of the higher courts such as the *Miranda* and *Escobedo* rulings.

This attempt by the chief to demonstrate to people outside the department the problems raised by *Miranda* may be taken as a sign that there are groups taking part in police policy-making involving interrogation procedures. Our discussion of the existence of group conflict in Kenosha, coupled with the brief coverage in Chapter 4, suggests that some groups do impinge on this process, but not to the extent that they impinge upon other policy areas. On the one hand, the Kenosha chief emphasized the importance of other groups and specifically discussed the importance of the city attorney and the common council in police decision-making. Only in Kenosha did the chief require anyone outside the department (the city attorney) to approve this author's questionnaire before he agreed to allow its administration. On the other hand, certain groups which were important in other cities were substantially less important in Kenosha.

Professionalization, Participation, and the Communications Process

THE BAR ASSOCIATION AND ATTORNEYS

Few attorneys concentrate upon the practice of criminal law in Kenosha. There is, however, one lawyer who has a statewide reputation as a criminal law practitioner. His former partner, who now practices law in neighboring Racine but who still handles cases in Kenosha, also has a wide reputation.

The local bar association is by no means solely or even primarily interested in the problems of criminal law practice. A Kenosha attorney who is interested in criminal law has to rely on his own private resources rather than on the state or local bar association as the primary source of information. The Kenosha County Bar Association publishes a monthly newsletter which often gives a brief synopsis of important local decisions, but these synopses do not offer more than bare details.

Table 6-1 shows the amount of money spent by Kenosha County for attorneys representing indigents.

Table 6-1.   Fees for Attorneys Representing Indigents in Kenosha County, 1961-1967

Year	Amount
1961	$ 1,820.00
1962	2,356.24
1963	4,964.53
1964	7,518.70
1965	7,153.52
1966	6,101.07
1967[a]	10,521.92

a. Total 1967 expenditure.

Prior to the *Miranda* decision, the local bar association had already been involved in the process of furnishing counsel to indigents. It had given the local judges a list of attorneys who could be called to represent an indigent defendant.

The information in the table is of limited value because it does not tell the number of cases. Informants felt that the number of cases involving indigents has remained relatively stable, but we must still be careful with our conclusions.

These data suggest that the *Miranda* decision might have necessitated greater allocations in 1967. Unlike Green Bay, the greatest initial increases occurred in 1963 and 1964, the years when the State Supreme Court seemed to sanction higher attorney's fees for such cases. The local judge most involved in appointing attorneys agreed that the state court decisions led to the change. The bar association did not attempt any campaign to increase these fees. Although the reasons for the increase are not completely clear, one official who is closely involved with the finances of paying attorneys in such cases claimed that the earlier increases were indeed the results of requirements imposed by pressure from outside the city. In his words, the increase occurred because "there were to [*sic*] many damn fool laws passed." *Miranda* was such a new "outside" factor, but certainly not the first. There was no active conflict between the judiciary and the bar on the fees issue. In fact, the judges did not consider the increase in attorneys' fees to be a serious problem.

After *Miranda* the association and some individual lawyers took action which brought them into more direct involvement with law enforcement activities. A number of lawyers used the *Miranda* stipulations to challenge police interrogation procedures. Though the local judges were uncertain of the number of successful challenges, the district attorney claimed that he refused to issue a warrant in two cases because of the possibility of successful challenges. Perhaps more significant was the willingness of some attorneys, especially the two with statewide criminal law reputations, to expand the use of the *Miranda* rules and to try to make certain that the upper level police were aware of the broader implications of the decision. One of the attorneys had informally talked to some police officials about the adoption of new sophisticated evidence-gathering techniques. These police officials were aware of the attorneys' reputations, and were quite concerned over the willingness to expand upon the *Miranda* rule. Furthermore, one attorney refused to allow the police to speak to his client, whom the police considered to be a key suspect (as we shall see later, a more accurate term to the detectives involved was "guilty party") in a brutal stabbing. Again, because we have no systematic sampling of attorneys, we must be careful in our generalizations about police-lawyer relations. Nonetheless, it is safe to conclude that attorneys showed no reluctance to use *Miranda* and met with some success.

The bar association attempted to institutionalize greater lawyer impingement on police interrogation activities. Six months after *Miranda*, with the cooperation of the police, the president of the local bar furnished the police department with a list of attorneys who were willing to be called at all hours by indigent suspects. This list of 22 lawyers was given to the department "together with appropriate signs calling [the suspect's] attention to the availability of such lists.[7] The police were supposed to give the list of attorneys to the indigent who desires counsel at the interrogation stage and to allow him to choose any lawyer on the list.

JUDGES

The bulk of criminal justice litigation fell on two county court judges rather than on one judge as it did in Green Bay. The criminal caseload is divided by calendar months between two county judges. During a given month one judge acts as the preliminary police magistrate who decides whether warrants shall be issued. This judge also presides over the trials involving misdemeanors, and, if there is no objection, sits for the preliminary hearing in felony cases. After the preliminary hearing, felony cases are bound over to the other branch and to the other judge. At the end of the month the arrangement between the two judges is reversed.

Thus two judges not only have regular contact with criminal law cases, but also have regular contact with police officers, especially detectives, at the initial stage where decisions on warrants are made. Both of these judges must use the *Miranda* decision in their proceedings. Quite often the rather informal magistrate's hearings focus on the admissibility of a confession. At this stage the district attorney and the police must be prepared to discuss the means used in obtaining a confession. The detective thus works with either of the two judges at a very informal level. Despite the discussions, few confessions have been eliminated at this stage of the proceeding. One reason, as we shall see in the discussion of the district attorney, was the reluctance of the prosecutor even to ask for a warrant when he felt that the validity of a confession was dubious and there was no corroborating evidence.

THE DISTRICT ATTORNEY

Except for the district attorney himself, the Kenosha district attorney's staff was not an experienced organization when the decision was handed down. The district attorney, holding the position since 1955, hoped to make the office his career, but, at the time of the *Miranda* decision, the most experienced of the three-attorney staff of assistants had been an employee for only two years.

Compared to all other local organizations, the district attorney's office in Kenosha maintained the greatest day-to-day supervision and sanction control over police procedures. The district attorney was aggressive in the maintenance of this supervision. He quite thoroughly accepted the trend in Supreme Court decisions, and after *Miranda* quickly adopted the use of these new procedures as constraints on police behavior. His primary sanction was a refusal to issue a warrant. This led to conflict between the police and the prosecutor, a conflict which amplified an already existing mutual distrust. (As evidence of distrust, some detectives had campaigned actively for the candidate who opposed this district attorney in the last election.) Despite the fact that the police worked continuously with other members of the staff, the bulk of their criticism was levelled at the district attorney himself, probably because he took the initiative in forcing the police to adopt new procedures and because the rest of the staff was new.

Unlike the Green Bay prosecutor, the district attorney never objected publicly to the *Miranda* decision. Although he made no public statement about his opinion, his feelings favoring *Miranda* were well understood by the detective bureau. He believed that the effect of the decision was nominal, and that the perceptions in the *Miranda* majority opinion regarding police behavior were accurate.

Miranda increased the conflict between the police and the district attorney. The conflict centered around the requirements necessary for a warrant. The adoption of new police investigation and interrogation procedures unquestionably lagged behind procedures desired by the prosecutor. Consequently, he used his power to refuse to seek warrants as a means of forcing the police to be more thorough in following interrogation procedures which would be acceptable in the courts. The police view of this limit on obtaining warrants was best expressed by a detective who exclaimed, "He [the district attorney] expects the case to be tried before he charges a suspect." The detectives saw his procedures regarding *Miranda* as the actions of a lawyer and politician (both of which connote trickery) who had deserted the organization that must depend upon him to complete its job successfully. As a result, police and legal perspectives were further separated.

On the surface, this conflict, intensified by *Miranda*, seems similar to the police-prosecutor conflict in Green Bay. In fact there are some important differences in departmental reactions to prosecutor behavior; these differences are related to differences in professionalization and participation. The Kenosha department operated in a context of greater participation. Thus communications between the district attorney, his staff, and the police department were well established prior to *Miranda*. The department perceived that this prosecutor's office generally had a high level of expertise. The Kenosha officers also showed a greater amount of empathy with the district attorney's job.

The Kenosha police did not seem to consider the district attorney "chicken" or afraid to face other more competent attorneys. Neither his competence nor his experience was questioned. What was questioned was his unwillingness to see police perspectives and his refusal to compromise with police views. They understood to some extent his need to "bargain" with other attorneys, but found him uncompromising in his bargaining with the police. As one detective responded in a disapproving tone, he may not be an incompetent lawyer but, "He's [still] a lawyer."

Greater empathy with the prosecutor's job did not significantly limit the difference between the police and legal perspective which intensified after *Miranda*. This greater empathy was, however, an important factor in altering the reasons given for the conflict, but the nature of police-prosecutor conflicts was quite similar in both Green Bay and Kenosha.

THE NEWSPAPER

In the analysis of Green Bay it was suggested that the newspaper staff perceived the *Miranda* issue as important enough to consider it in detail seldom used in the reporting of that city's criminal justice activities. Though coverage was implicitly biased in favor of the police perspective, the decision itself was quite thoroughly reported. While avoiding such thorough coverage, the Kenosha newspaper certainly had this same bias.

The newspaper was exceptional in its avoidance of accurate consideration of the important issues. On the day of the *Miranda* decision, the *Kenosha News* included a very short synopsis of *Miranda* as part of the "Late Bulletins" on page one. The complete bulletin is printed below: [8]

> The Supreme Court ruled today that a confession by a suspect under police questioning may be introduced at his trial only if he was warned of his right to remain silent.

No mention was made of the requirement that counsel shall be furnished to the indigent suspect. Chief Justice Warren's statements that interrogation was still possible were not mentioned. No other story about the content of the decision appeared until one week later when a short article about the limits of retroactivity of the decision appeared on page one.[9] The *Kenosha News* presented no other discussion of *Miranda's* content.

The paper's editorial policy was quite a bit more explicit. Eight days after the decision a cartoon with the caption "New Uniform" appeared. It depicted a Supreme Court Justice pulling the strings to operate a puppet policeman.[10] Six days later the paper printed on its editorial page a fictional conversation between a police officer and a person who voluntarily wants to confess a crime. The officer insists that he cannot accept the confession unless the confessor has an attorney. Of course, this vignette is based on an inaccurate interpretation of the *Miranda* decision. *Miranda* specifically allows for such spontaneous voluntary confessions. The editorial concluded with the following: [11]

> Each and every American is entitled to his rights, of course, as the Supreme Court says.

> Presumably this includes the public law enforcers, and even the victims of crimes of violence.

Certainly the Kenosha officer could receive from the newspaper little guidance about the details of the decision. Unlike the Green Bay newspaper, the *Kenosha News* presented no stories about effects on local police. But the *Kenosha News* editors certainly tried to give the impression that the decision severely hampered local police work.

SOURCES OF *Miranda* INFORMATION

Table 6-2 shows that there was a wide variety of initial sources of information about *Miranda*. As one might expect from the analysis of the *Kenosha News*, relatively few officers received their initial information from the newspaper. In Green Bay, the newspaper was the most common first source among all ranks, while in Kenosha there was considerable difference among ranks. The most obvious rank differential relates to the activities of the district attorney. After *Miranda* was handed down, he made an immediate personal effort to disseminate information to detectives by means of a memorandum. Almost 54 percent of the detectives—but *no* uniformed officers—identified the district attorney as the initial source. The previously established channels of prosecutor influence on police decision-making facilitated this communication with detectives.

When all sources are considered, there is a little more consistency between the ranks (Table 6-3). Almost the same percentage of patrolmen and detectives received information from the generally most common sources—conferences and training sessions, television and radio, and newspapers. Superiors were less likely to receive information from television but more likely to receive it from newspapers. The local FBI conducted an 18-hour in-service training course dealing with the legal problems of arrests and searches and seizures. It was somewhat more extensive than Green Bay's and was Kenosha's only formal training program devoted to *Miranda*. Fifty-five officers, a little better than half the department, attended this course.[12]

The district attorney was a source of information for *all* detectives and for all but one superior. Thus the information from the prosecutor ultimately was channeled to the superior, but only 25 percent of the patrolmen received information from the district attorney. The district attorney admitted that, although he did have

Table 6-2. Rank and First Source of Information about *Miranda* (Kenosha), in Percentages

			RANK		
	Source	All	Patrolman	Superior	Detective
(1)	TV, radio	18.8	22.5	0.0	15.4
(2)	Magazines not specializing in Police activities	3.1	5.0	0.0	0.0
(3)	Newspaper	12.5	12.5	20.0	7.7
(4)	Police officer not a superior	3.1	2.5	10.0	0.0
(5)	Superior officer	15.6	22.5	0.0	7.7
(6)	Magazines specializing in police activities	6.3	7.5	10.0	0.0
(7)	Training sessions	10.9	15.0	0.0	7.7
(8)	Supreme Court opinion	4.7	5.0	10.0	0.0
(9)	Attorney General	9.4	2.5	40.0	7.7
(10)	Local judge	4.7	5.0	10.0	0.0
(11)	District Attorney	10.9	0.0	0.0	53.8
	TOTAL	100.0	100.0	100.0	100.0
	(N)	(64)[a]	(40)	(10)	(13)

a. Individual rank totals are less than 64 because there was one person of unknown rank.

a good channel of communication to these upper echelons, he was not able to communicate the rather complex legal points to the rank and file. He claimed that generally the supervisory police officials too quickly assumed that a written memorandum is sufficient to make the rank and file understand or comprehend legal change. There was thus a gap in communications between prosecutor and patrolman even before *Miranda,* and the *Miranda* information process showed that the gap remained. As a further example of the isolation· of the patrolman, the chief, who also considers the prosecutor to be one of his main sources of guidance, sent a memorandum about *Miranda* only to detectives and to other investigators.

The attorney general is frequently mentioned, but again there is a disparity between the ranks. The superiors were the most frequent recipients of his expertise. Dectives received information from this source somewhat less frequently, but both these ranks received such information far more frequently than did the patrolmen.

Each officer received, on the average, a little over five sources of information (5.20 as compared to Green Bay's 4.95) about *Miranda.* Like Green Bay, detectives had the most sources (5.92), but unlike the Green Bay department, the Kenosha superiors (5.60) received more information than the patrolmen (4.95).

The detectives and the upper echelon police officials, despite disagreements with the prosecutor, were not cut off from his influence. Indeed, he became an increasingly important participant in many aspects of the training program.[13] This suggests that for some ranks some sources outside the police department may often be perceived as the best for information about *Miranda.* Table 6-4 shows that this is indeed the case.

Such sources were not important for all ranks. The training session is by far the most frequent choice of patrolmen. The Supreme Court opinion itself, unimportant to detectives and patrolmen, is the most frequently selected source among superiors (though only 3 of 10 selected it). Almost twice as many detectives as patrolmen perceived the attorney general to be the best source. The district attorney was perceived as the best sources by 30.8 percent of the detectives while no member of any other rank chose the prosecutor.

But an officer can judge a source only if he were exposed to it. Table 6-4a controls for such contact with these sources.

Because of the particularly small numbers of cases we can only

Table 6-3.   Rank and All Sources of Information about *Miranda* (Kenosha), in
Percentages

	RANK			
Source	*All*	*Patrolman*	*Superior*	*Detective*
Conferences, training	67.2	67.5	70.0	69.2
TV, radio	62.5	65.0	50.0	61.5
Newspaper	54.7	52.5	70.0	53.8
District Attorney	51.4	25.0	90.0	100.0
Superior officer	50.0	50.0	30.0	69.2
Supreme Court opinion	46.9	42.5	60.0	53.8
Local judge	43.8	47.5	30.0	46.2
Attorney General	42.2	27.5	80.0	61.5
Police officer not a superior	35.4	40.0	20.0	38.5
Magazines specializing in police activities	31.3	30.0	40.0	23.1
Magazines, nonspecialized	25.0	27.5	30.0	15.4
(N)	(64)[a]	(40)	(10)	(13)

a. Individual rank totals are less than 64 because there was one person of unknown rank.

Totals exceed 100 percent because each individual could choose as many as eleven sources.

Table 6-4.   Rank and Best Source of Information on *Miranda* (Kenosha), in Percentages

RANK

Source	All	Patrolman	Superior	Detective
Conferences, training	34.4	42.5	20.0	23.1
Attorney General	17.2	12.5	20.0	30.8
Supreme Court opinion	9.4	7.5	30.0	0.0
District Attorney	6.3	0.0	0.0	30.8
Police officer, superior	6.3	10.0	0.0	0.0
Newspapers	6.3	5.0	10.0	7.7
Local judge	6.3	7.5	10.0	0.0
TV, radio	4.7	2.5	0.0	7.7
Magazines not specializing in police activities	4.7	7.5	0.0	0.0
Magazines specializing in police activities	3.1	5.0	0.0	0.0
Police officer not a superior	0.0	0.0	0.0	0.0
Other	1.6	0.0	10.0	0.0
TOTAL	100.3	100.0	100.0	100.0
(N)	(64)[a]	(40)	(10)	(13)

a. Individual rank totals are less than 64 because there was one person of unknown rank. Total may not exactly equal 100.0 percent because of rounding.

Table 6-4a.   Rank and Ratio of Best Source to Those Receiving Information
from Source (Kenosha), in Percentages

		RANK		
Source	*All*	*Patrolman*	*Superior*	*Detective*
Conferences, training	51.2	63.0	28.6	33.6
TV, radio	7.5	3.8	0.0	12.5
Newspapers	11.5	9.5	14.4	14.3
District Attorney	12.3	0.0	0.0	30.8
Superior officer	12.6	20.0	0.0	0.0
Local judge	14.4	15.8	33.3	0.0
Attorney General	40.8	36.4	25.0	50.1
Police officer not a superior	0.0	0.0	0.0	0.0
Magazines, nonspecialized	0.0	0.0	0.0	0.0
Magazines, specializing	9.9	16.7	0.0	0.0
Supreme Court opinion	10.0	11.1	16.7	0.0

be very general in our interpretations. This table does show, however, first, that among officers going through the *Miranda* training
session, only the patrolmen were generally likely to rate the session
most highly. The attorney general's memorandum was the most
frequently mentioned best source among detectives who were exposed to it. Indeed this memorandum, though received by relatively
few patrolmen, has a ratio second only to conferences in the force
in general and among patrolmen in particular.

By combining some categories in Table 6-4, Table 6-5 attempts
to compare important sources of information within the department with those from outside the department.

Only the patrolmen show a preponderance of law enforcement
sources. Fully one-half of the superiors chose the outside specialized

sources (Supreme Court opinion and the attorney general's office). Detectives were less inclined than superiors to choose outside specialized sources, but they were more likely to be impressed by local officials (district attorney and local judge).[14] Local officials were chosen quite infrequently by both superiors and their supervisors.

A large majority (62.5 percent) of the department perceived that their sources of information were hostile to the decision, but 40 percent of the superiors, over 23 percent of the detectives, and only 5 percent of the patrolmen felt that these sources approved of *Miranda*. Thus those ranks that were most likely to receive the "best" information from outside sources were more likely to perceive their sources of information as approving of *Miranda*.

But was there a trend toward the reception of information from new sources? Table 6-6 shows that better than 80 percent of the detectives received information on *Miranda* from sources that were new to the officers. Other ranks are considerably *lower* in this respect. In Green Bay the detectives were *least* likely to receive new sources. As in Green Bay, few Kenosha officers listed the nature of these new sources. We can only suggest that in response to *Miranda* more groups and agencies did at least indirectly impinge upon the detectives.

Police Perceptions and Attitudes

Like the policemen on the Green Bay force, few Kenosha policemen anticipated or approved of the *Miranda* decision. Only 10.9 percent of the Kenosha department approved, and there was no important inter-rank difference. Only 15 percent of the patrolmen, 30 percent of the superiors, and *no detectives* anticipated such a decision. It is interesting to note that the detectives, who do most of the interrogation, did not anticipate this change. The superiors, who at least formally sit at the hub of the information network, were more likely to expect such a ruling, but they evidently did not convey their expectations to the detectives. (This may be indicative of the isolation between these superiors and the detective bureau, a characteristic often mentioned by the Kenosha detectives.) The Kenosha chief definitely did not anticipate a *Miranda*-like decision.

Because of this lack of anticipation we might expect that officers would perceive a great change resulting from the *Miranda* decision.

Table 6-5. Rank and Categories of Best Sources of Information on *Miranda* (Kenosha), in Percentages

		R A N K		
Source	*All*	*Patrolman*	*Superior*	*Detective*
Law enforcement	43.8	57.5	20.0	23.1
Outside specialized	26.6	20.0	50.0	30.8
Outside nonspecialized	15.7	15.0	10.0	15.4
Local officials	12.6	7.5	10.0	30.8
Other	1.6	0.0	10.0	0.0
TOTAL	100.3	100.0	100.0	100.1
(N)	(64)	(40)	(10)	(13)

Total may not exactly equal 100.0 percent because of rounding.

Table 6-6. Rank and New Sources of Information, in Percentages

		R A N K		
Source	*All*	*Patrolman*	*Superior*	*Detective*
All new	6.3	5.0	20.0	23.1
Some new	45.3	57.5	30.0	61.5
None new	43.8	35.0	50.0	7.7
Other; don't know	4.7	2.5	0.0	7.7
TOTAL	100.1	100.0	100.0	100.0
(N)	(64)	(40)	(10)	(13)

Totals may not equal 100.0 percent because of rounding.

Generally, this hypothesis is supported. (It is not supported in Green Bay.) Table 6-7 shows that over 62 percent of the department felt that the decision led to a great or very great change in their own jobs. An even greater number, 76.5 percent, perceived department activities changing extensively. *Every* officer saw some change at both his own and the departmental level. Almost 77 percent of the detectives, 70 percent of the superiors, and 57.5 percent of the patrolmen perceived a great or a very great change in their own jobs.

As the Green Bay study showed, lack of anticipation does not necessarily create perceptions of such great change. This overwhelming agreement on the extensiveness of change in Kenosha can best be explained by considering certain events which have made the impact of *Miranda* especially visible to the Kenosha police force. Possibly one factor was the introduction of the printed list of attorneys, which was clearly visible to many of the officers. More important was the aftermath of a brutal, unsolved stabbing which received much publicity because of its proximity to the scene of the unsolved murder of United States Senator Charles Percy's daughter. The Kenosha detectives had a suspect who they felt certain was guilty of the Kenosha crime. His lawyer would not allow them to question the suspect. This case and the obstacles to its investigation were well known among the officers. Thus the proscriptions against the use of some pre-*Miranda* procedures were clearly salient.

Table 6-8 tells us more about knowledge of the *Miranda* deci-

Table 6-7. Rank and Perceptions of Extent *Miranda* Changed One's Own Job (Kenosha), in Percentages

	RANK			
Change	*All*	*Patrolman*	*Superior*	*Detective*
Great or very great	62.5	57.5	70.0	76.9
Some	37.5	42.5	30.0	23.1
None	0.0	0.0	0.0	0.0
TOTAL	100.0	100.0	100.0	100.0
(N)	(64)[a]	(40)	(10)	(13)

a. Individual rank totals are less than 64 because there was one person of unknown rank.

Table 6-8.   Correct Perceptions of Stipulations of *Miranda* Decision (Kenosha),
            in Percentages

			RANK		
	Stipulation	Total	Patrolman	Superior	Detective
(1)	Must tell of right to remain silent	100.0	100.0	100.0	100.0
(2)	Anything suspect says may be held against him	98.4	97.5	100.0	100.0
(3)	Right to attorney if he wants one	95.3	97.5	90.0	92.3
(4)	If indigent, can have attorney appointed at court expense	93.8	90.0	100.0	100.0
(5)	Can still ask person to come voluntarily to the station	37.5	27.5	50.0	53.6
(6)	Suspect must have an attorney whether he wants one or not	93.8	92.5	90.0	100.0
(7)	Confessions no longer evidence	92.2	92.5	90.0	100.0
(8)	May no longer talk to anyone without informing him of his rights	34.4	30.0	50.0	38.5
(9)	No wire tapping	89.1	90.0	80.0	92.3
(10)	Voluntary confessions no longer legal source of information	96.9	95.0	100.0	100.0
	(N)	(64)[a]	(40)	(10)	(13)

a. Individual rank totals are less than 64 because there was one person of unknown rank.

sion. Generally, the officers; especially the detectives, were quite familiar with the basic rudiments of the decision, but again we find that the officers overestimated the constraints that the *Miranda* decision puts on their behavior (items 5 and 9). A considerably lower percentage of patrolmen (27.5 percent) than detectives (53.6 percent) or superiors (50.0 percent) correctly understood that a person may still be asked to come voluntarily to the police station. More superiors (50.0 percent) understood this possibility of talking to a person without advising him of his rights than did patrolmen (30.0) or detectives (38.5). Again this information has not been disseminated from the organization leaders to those quite likely to use such procedures in their work.

All ranks agreed that the two most important changes that *Miranda* made in their own jobs related to the need to find new ways of gathering evidence and the need for better education (Table 6-9).

There is some difference according to the type of tasks the officers perform. For example, the number of patrolmen perceiving the education effect is about the same as the number choosing the evidence-gathering effect. Superiors, who are not often directly involved in interrogation, were much more likely to feel the impact on education. The detectives, who were well established as the main interrogators, were most likely to perceive the change in the evidence-gathering process. These men did not perceive increased education to be as important as changes in gathering evidence. The uniformed officer-detective difference is also apparent in regard to changes in the department. Better than 46 percent of the detectives saw the greatest departmental effect as more responsibility for detectives, while only 15 percent of the patrolmen and 20 percent of the superiors felt this way. Though this is the second most frequent response among the uniformed officers, they were much more likely to see the education effect as the most important for the department. Sixty-five percent of the patrolmen, 80 percent of the superiors, and only 46.2 percent of the detectives perceived increased education as the most important effect.

The rhetoric of the training officer certainly reflects what seems to be an increasing emphasis on education. Calling training one of the "cornerstones of modern police science," this officer offered the following ringing phrases in support of professionalization as a tool to cope with social change: [15]

We must have the assurance, in order to meet this new challenge, that the police officer of today can function in a role that
lies outside the area of his personal sentiments. Therefore, it is
necessary that we develop in that officer, a real sense of professionalism. Just as in other professions, his is a 'high' calling. It is
not merely another occupation, distinguished only by the uniform and the size of the wage or salary. Policing is increasingly
recognized as requiring a high degree of technical knowledge
and skill. This, however, is only one mark of a profession. There
is the distinguishing emphasis upon public duty and service to
the community.

In fact, there was little immediate formal educational change. In-service training was not revised. The annual report of the training officer showed no new emphasis on college education. Though there is
definitely greater discussion about the recently developed two-year
police-science course at the Kenosha Technical Institute, no incentive
pay plan was adopted to facilitate taking this course, which counts
for college credits, though the department officials certainly are now
more concerned with making these facilities available.

Table 6-9 also furnishes evidence that shows further limits in
Miranda's effect on professionalization. Items 4, 5, and 7 can be considered *Miranda* effects that would bring police decision-making more
outside the control of the police themselves. Again one should remember that every officer could list only two effects. With this
caveat in mind we nevertheless can conclude that the changes within
the department are generally far more important than changes in
relationship between department and groups in the community. One
interesting exception should be noted. Thirty percent of the superiors
and almost 31 percent of the detectives perceived that, because of
Miranda, they must pay more attention to others in the field of criminal justice. This may reflect activity on the part of the bar association
and, to some extent, that of the local judges and prosecutors. Obviously, much of the department failed to be so affected, since only
one patrolman perceived this change. This is lower than the number
of the Green Bay patrolmen (10) who perceived such change despite the fact that groups in Green Bay have less contact with police.

Conclusion

The existing levels of participation and professionalization were related to some of the patterns of change resulting from the *Miranda* decision.

Crime and the administration of justice was a visible issue in Kenosha, and, as with other such visible local issues, there were groups actively attempting to deal with it. This milieu facilitated an increase in group interaction with police departments after *Miranda*. For example, the previously existing important network of communication between prosecutor and upper echelon police (particularly detectives) was an important factor in facilitating prosecutor impingement in regard to the adoption of the new *Miranda* rules. The bar association, which prior to *Miranda* was already involved with the use of procedures related to interrogation, increased its involvement after the decision. Its new involvement on the surface increased interaction between attorneys and the police.

Some of these suggested changes required greater bureaucratization and regularization of police procedures. In Chapter 10 we shall take a closer look at the ways police limited the effect of these procedures on interrogation behavior. Here it is only necessary to point out that the Kenosha department manifested attitudes and perceptions associated with a less professionalized department in moderate levels of participation. Few officers approved, and few anticipated the decision. Officers generally overestimated the limits of *Miranda* and, perhaps as a result, perceived great change in their jobs. Detectives and superiors depended fairly frequently upon outside sources for information about *Miranda*, but for the most part these outside sources did not penetrate the lower ranks.

Furthermore, innovations related to increased professionalization were also limited. Changes in education and training programs were discussed more thoroughly in Kenosha than in Green Bay, but the proposed Kenosha changes did not effectively pass the discussion stage during the first fourteen months after the decision. The police did indeed perceive that *Miranda* resulted in great change, but the reason for this perceived change more likely stemmed from the relationship between *Miranda* procedures and the important investigation of the local stabbing.

Like Green Bay, the relatively low level of Kenosha police professionalization seemed to limit certain actual innovations which could
have resulted from the *Miranda* decision. The higher pre-*Miranda*
level of participation increased the likelihood that at least the upper
echelon police officers would be exposed to outside sources of information. This was not the case in Green Bay where both low professionalization and the low participation reinforced the isolation of that
community's police department.

Table 6-9.   Rank and Effects of *Miranda* on Own Job (Kenosha), in Percentages

	Effects	All	Patrolman	Supervisor	Detective
			RANK		
(1)	New methods of gathering evidence	70.3	72.5	40.0	84.6
(2)	Better education and training	71.9	77.5	80.0	38.5
(3)	Sympathy toward suspects	18.8	20.0	0.0	23.1
(4)	Spending more time explaining activities to community	9.4	12.5	0.0	7.7
(5)	More attention to others in the field of criminal justice	12.5	2.5	30.0	30.8
(6)	New methods to obtain confessions	7.8	10.0	10.0	0.0
(7)	More closely observed by people outside department	1.6	2.5	0.0	0.0
	(N)	(64)[a]	(49)	(10)	(13)

a. Individual rank totals are less than 64 because there was one person of unknown rank.
Total may be greater than 100 percent because each officer could give two responses.

NOTES

1. Quotation from Robert R. Alford with the collaboration of Harry M. Scoble, *Bureaucracy and Participation* (Chicago: Rand McNally, 1969), 78. See also *Ibid.*, 13-16, 59-79, 118-54.

2. "Organized Crime in Wisconsin" (Madison: Office of the Attorney General, 1966).

3. President's Commission on Law Enforcement and the Administration of Justice. *Task Force Report: Organized Crime* (Washington: U.S. Government Printing Office, 1967), 5-10.

4. Unless otherwise stated all the data on Kenosha's crime are found in the 54th, 55th, and 56th Annual Reports (Kenosha, Wisconsin: Kenosha Police Department, 1964, 1965, and 1966, respectively), hereinafter cited *54th Annual Report*, etc.

5. *Uniform Crime Reports*, 1966, 92.

6. Introductory letter to *56th Annual Report*.

7. *Kenosha County Bar Association October Newsletter*, October 14, 1966.

8. *Kenosha News*, June 13, 1966.

9. *Kenosha News*, June 20, 1966.

10. *Kenosha News*, June 21, 1966.

11. *Kenosha News*, June 27, 1966.

12. *Annual Report—1966*, 28. The Kenosha sample may have been somewhat biased in favor of those who attended the conferences since 67.2 percent said they attended. Some of this increase, however, can be accounted for by those who may have considered, as training, various comments from their superiors.

13. Compare *Annual Report—1966*, 27-29, with *Annual Report—1964*, 26-30. In the latter report the district attorney is not mentioned as a participant in training. In the 1966 report he is mentioned twice. One of the programs, a shoplifting institute, was given in 1964 but without the prosecutor's help. In 1966, presumably because of the greater legal complexities now involved with arresting a shoplifter, the district attorney participated in this institute.

14. The main reason for the difference between detectives and superiors regarding outside specialized sources results from the superiors' much more frequent choice of the Supreme Court opinion. See Table 6-4.

15. *Annual Report—1966*, 27.

Chapter 7

RACINE

Like Kenosha, Racine is basically a manufacturing center. It also resembles Kenosha in the relative mobility of its population. They can both be classified as satellite cities of Milwaukee and Chicago. There are, however, important differences which help to explain Racine's higher level of professionalization and participation. Racine's industries are, for the most part, locally owned. No firm predominates in that city the way American Motors does in Kenosha. Because of local ownership business firms have been more likely to encourage political participation on the part of their executives.

While labor unions are active in Racine, labor-management conflict has abated, and there is no pervading class conflict. Because no single company predominates, there is not the pitting of a single labor union against a large company. In fact the third largest company in Racine—and one of the most community-oriented—has never been organized.

Thus Racine lacks most of the important characteristics which explain the existence of group conflict and anti-professionalization in neighboring Kenosha. According to Alford, Racine conforms to the stereotype of a progressive twentieth-century city. Its politics are controlled by a coalition of labor and business leaders. Participation is encouraged as long as it does not raise intense conflict or threaten the basic professionalization norms. The kind of localism that was common in Kenosha occasionally raises its head but seldom with any success. Middle-class and working-class citizens have actually withdrawn from civic affairs, but others, who are not nearly as likely to participate in Kenosha, are encouraged to and do participate in Racine.

The city has a very high crime rate. According to the FBI statistics, Racine generally has the highest crime rate of any reporting city in Wisconsin. In 1966, it had the highest rate among these Wisconsin cities for robbery, rape, assault, and burglary.[1] Its crime rate was relatively low only for the less serious grand-larceny and auto-theft offenses. With the exception of burglary, these offenses are most likely to be juvenile crimes.[2] From 1962 through 1964, the city's Class I crime index increased between two and three times faster than the national average, and over twice as fast as the average of other cities with populations of 50,000 to 100,000. In 1965, the disproportionate increase ended temporarily; from 1964 to 1965 the Racine rate increased only .4 percent, compared to an increase of 6 percent in cities of similar size and 9 percent nationally. In 1966 the increase was again slightly greater than either the national or similar cities' average.[3]

As is typical of such cities, professionalization of government is considered to be a legitimate goal. The ethos of administrative efficiency and rationality—an ethos encouraging professionalization—is accepted by the political leadership in Racine. Although the city does not have a city manager, Racine's elected leaders are quite willing to give deference to local administrative expertise. For example, 25 school districts in 1961 voted to consolidate with the city of Racine into a unified school district. The newly elected school board for this unified district is completely independent of the Racine City Council on budgetary matters. There are no provisions for aldermanic challenge to the budget. According to the proponents of this system, the primary advantage of the unified district is this very lack of control by a city council, whose veto, it is believed, would be "irresponsible." This action is typical of the local trend toward accepting administrative efficiency, even in the case of the city council, at the expense of some divestment of power.

This emphasis on expertise and efficiency establishes an environment seemingly amenable to the acceptance of the rationale of police professionalization. After all, such professionalization also emphasizes the need for specialization and the idea that social change creates a greater need for expertise. Analysis of Racine must also consider the tension between professionalization and group activity because political decision-making in that city seems to emphasize professionalization at the possible expense of participation.[4] The nature and extent of group activity does not necessarily typify the nature of group activity in the legal community. Kenosha is a case in point; legal conflict and legal group impingement, though strong, were certainly not as intense as the general group conflict in the community. In Racine, the opposite pattern exists. The legal process conflict is probably greater than are the relatively placid group politics in general.

Professionalization, Participation, and the Communications Process

THE BAR ASSOCIATION AND ATTORNEYS

The bar association organization, as a rule, exhibits the typical lack of emphasis on criminal justice matters. In recent years the association seriously considered the adoption of a public defender for Racine County, but the idea was dropped.[5] Soon after the *Miranda* decision, with the encouragement of the district attorney, the local association appointed a committee to develop a systematic plan for furnishing counsel at the interrogation stage. The local prosecutor, as well as other attorneys who practiced some criminal law, were appointed to this committee, but the committee never met. The chairman of the committee expressed little concern about this failure to meet because he felt that the district attorney could continue to handle the problem without procedural change. In appointing counsel for an indigent, the judge merely continues to follow the alphabetical list of all Racine County attorneys. There were still no institutionalized provisions for furnishing an indigent with counsel when the judge is not around, *i.e.*, during a late evening interrogation.

As in Kenosha and Green Bay, attorneys' fees have increased since 1965 (no data are available before 1965 because the item was not kept as a separate part of the budget). In Table 7-1 note that, as of June, 1967, the county spent almost as much money on this item as it did throughout 1966. In fact, the county board appropriated an extra $10,000 for the remainder of 1967. In 1965 the amount was not much different from the fees paid to Green Bay attorneys in 1966 (almost $12,000). Racine, of course, has much more crime and more criminal litigation than does Green Bay; thus the relative amount

Table 7-1. Fees for Attorneys Representing Indigents in Racine County, 1965-1967[a]

Year	Amount
1965	$11,503.00
1966	12,700.00
1967[a]	11,659.00

a. Through June, 1967.
SOURCE: Racine County Clerk's Office, Racine, Wisconsin.

paid in Racine was probably smaller than the amount paid in Green Bay. Again we are limited by the fact that we do not have the number of cases for which attorneys were appointed. Because of the great 1967 increase in Racine, this conclusion based upon a comparison between Racine and Green Bay may no longer be a valid one.

As in the other two previously discussed cities, the bar association is given little credit for this increase. According to various informants, most of the increase can be attributed to two factors: (1) greater sensitivity by the judges toward the problem—a sensitivity reinforced by the visibility of court decisions dealing with attorneys' fees; and (2) more significantly, the appointment of counsel to represent certain misdemeanants. Both of these factors led to change prior to *Miranda,* and both involved a response to events occurring outside the domain of the local bar association. The great 1967 increase, which was also apparent in Kenosha, suggests, however, that *Miranda* may have increased the trend.

Since crime and ethnic problems in Racine are somewhat similar to those of other contemporary industrial cities, it should not be surprising that the structure of the legal profession is also similar. Characteristically, such cities have a legal profession divided into the relatively well-off "WASP" corporate or firm lawyers, who go to the better law schools and more or less ignore the practice of criminal law, and the struggling non-"WASP" or Negro solo practitioner with inferior education, who must depend upon the financially ill-rewarding criminal law practice in order to make a living. Bar associations are usually more concerned with the former type of attorney.[6] Racine does show some signs of following this pattern. There is some evidence that local attorneys who have a reputation for practicing some criminal law are of non-"WASP" or Negro descent. For example, of the five attorneys who, in the view of the local bar association president, practiced the most criminal law in Kenosha, two are Negro while one each had a Jewish surname and an Italian surname, respectively. The one exception is a former district attorney whose contacts would obviously be in the criminal law field. As one attorney (not one of the five) who does handle some criminal law claimed, "The [legal] elite in Racine doesn't like to get its hands dirty with criminal law cases."

Also, those who do have a reputation for practicing some criminal law are aggressive, distrustful of the police, and quite willing to challenge the police on the basis of recent court decisions. These local attorneys have used *Miranda* to challenge law enforcement procedures. This aggressiveness is recognized by the upper-echelon police officers. In the words of the police chief,

> There is a defense counsel atmosphere which makes the impact of a decision greater in Racine. There are a few well known defense attorneys who learn the [new Supreme Court] decisions so well that the pressure to close our loopholes is greater.

This "defense counsel atmosphere" is made particularly visible by the activities of one of the criminal law specialists who, as the police are the first to admit, has a statewide reputation for his work in criminal law. The Racine bar, especially the criminal bar, is small enough to allow this man to exert significant influence on the activities of criminal lawyers. Other attorneys used his briefs for their criminal cases and considered him an expert on criminal law. This process of disseminating information takes place completely independently of the organized bar association. He is, of course, not the only attorney interested in criminal law, but he certainly is the hub of an informal communications network.[7]

The nature of the criminal law practice as well as the influence of the most famous local criminal law attorney are clearly seen in the activities involving a particular litigation with *Miranda* implications. Unlike the one "big" murder case in Kenosha, this case merely involved a relatively minor traffic violation. Also unlike the Kenosha case, charges were actually filed in Racine: a man was charged with failure to stop at an arterial stop sign. The situation in Racine was different in another way. The Kenosha police department's methods of solving the murder case were directly constrained by the *Miranda* procedures. In Racine, the *Miranda* decision and police behavior were involved in a much more indirect manner.

In the traffic case, the defendant's attorney challenged the validity of the charge on the grounds that no traffic citation can be granted without a magistrate's determination that there was probable cause for issuance of the citation. He cited a recent Wisconsin Supreme Court decision requiring that no warrant can be issued without a magistrate's determination of probable cause.[8] According to the assistant city attorney who was prosecuting the case, a ruling consistent with this argument would require all police officers to present their evidence to a magistrate for determination of probable cause, prior to any voluntary court appearance by the individual violator. This issue, on the surface only peripheral to the *Miranda* case, in fact masked a deeper, more subtle, yet intense conflict over both the nature of police procedures in Racine and the defense attorney's responses to them.

In his reply brief regarding the traffic case, the assistant city attorney in charge of the case took the opportunity to castigate the activities of Racine's criminal lawyers. He left little doubt that he was referring to their use of the *Miranda* stipulations. He criticized the "present day fashionable issue of putting the police on trial." To him the lack of confidence in the police, and defense attorneys' extremely broad interpretation of decisions affecting police procedure, are slowly destroying the possibility of any cooperation between an individual and a law enforcement agency. He warned that "the new philosophy if carried too far may result in a [new] defense manual for lawyers defending traffic violations." Following this statement was a list of procedures which would be part of this hypothetical manual. These procedures strongly implied that the Supreme Court decisions and the local lawyers' use of the decisions will encourage a lack of faith in law enforcement and an obstruction of the administration of local justice.[9]

This addendum to the otherwise ordinary brief created an uproar among those who practice in Racine courts. Indeed, the well-known criminal attorney, previously described, who was not directly involved in this case was, nevertheless, moved to reply by letter to the assistant city attorney. His letter offered a "defense manual for prosecutors prosecuting traffic violators." He somewhat sarcastically claimed that such a manual could result because "recent Supreme Court cases have engendered such passionate resentment on the part of law enforcement." The lawyer specifically mentioned *Miranda* and insisted that the prosecution and police in traffic cases tried to "pretend *Miranda v. Arizona* was never decided and hope[d] that it will go away." [10]

The traffic case was significant for several reasons. It focused much of the *Miranda* controversy on the issue of traffic violations, a subject far different from the brutal murder in Kenosha but still one which possibly involved a change in some very common police procedures. It increased awareness of the broader implications of *Miranda* and associated these implications with the existence of a "defense counsel atmosphere." Interrogation procedures *per se* were not questioned, but, because of the conflict, attention was focused upon the relationship between the specific *Miranda* procedures and the broader implications of general police behavior. Technically *Miranda* did not affect this case because it was not the primary precedent under consideration by the local judge. But both the upper-echelon police and the city attorney associated this case with the implications of the *Miranda* decision. Thus, the decision increased the conflict between other key participants in the criminal justice process. Certainly the tone of the city's brief and the reply by a well-known attorney suggest that the law enforcement and defense attorney views were becoming more polarized. In fact, in his letter the local attorney himself suggested to the assistant city attorney that the conflict was serious enough to require a meeting between the defense attorneys and the city. Unlike Green Bay and Kenosha, the Racine district attorney was not the center of this police-lawyer conflict.

JUDGES

Almost all criminal litigation is handled by two county court judges. One of those judges predominately hears misdemeanors and traffic cases while the other judge initially hears all the felony cases. Circuit judges hear appeals for felony cases and act as a court with trial *de novo* jurisdiction for appealed misdemeanor cases.

As in Kenosha these two county court judges have continuous contact with the criminal law process. They do not, however, have the degree of informal contact with detectives that the two Kenosha judges had. This lesser contact results from rather unique use of court commissioners in Racine. These commissioners, private attorneys who perform this job in addition to their regular practice, act as magistrates who make the final decision about granting warrants. The detectives thus have further contacts with the legal profession, but in a sense this occurs at the expense of contact with the judiciary. The upper-echelon police seek legal advice from the local judiciary, but, as we shall see later, the judges' role in the training and education process is peripheral at best. This pattern of local police-court inter-action did not change after *Miranda*. The court commissioner system was not modified. Perhaps the greatest consequences on the local judiciary resulted from the intense pressure from the criminal lawyers who wanted the judges to consider the broad implications of *Miranda*, but by mid-1967 the pressure had produced no substantial policy change.

THE DISTRICT ATTORNEY

The Racine district attorneyship is definitely a full-time job. At the time of this study the present prosecutor had been in office for only three years, but he had served previously as assistant district attorney. Both of his assistants had held the job for over two years, a considerably longer period than that of their counterparts in Green Bay and Kenosha.

There is an absence of the intense police-prosecutor conflict apparent in both Green Bay and Kenosha. The more experienced assistants form a buffer between the chief prosecutor and the detectives. The detectives depend upon the assistants for much of their everyday assistance. There seems to be little friction over the attempt to obtain warrants. Some detectives, especially those specializing in cases involving worthless checks and forgery, spend much of their time working in the district attorney's office.

The district attorney has usually been a dependable source of expertise for at least some members of the police department. Unlike the majority of the police force, the district attorney approved of the *Miranda* decision. In his view the decision offered some greatly needed guidance about what he considered to be the Supreme Court's earlier highly ambiguous police interrogation decisions. He attempted to convince the police of these advantages. But the problems inherent in trying to convince the police were similar to those found in the

Kenosha and, to some extent, the Green Bay district attorney's office. The prosecutor faced a serious handicap, accentuated by *Miranda*, explaining difficult legal points to men with little understanding of the legal process. In the words of the Racine district attorney, "As in all of these cases [involving court sanctions on police behavior] the problem is getting the policeman of limited intellect to comprehend." This difficulty increased as a result of *Miranda*.

Moreover, the lack of conflict cannot be attributed to complete prosecutor identification with the police perspective because the district attorney identified his position more as a part of the legal community than as a part of the law enforcement community. As he puts it,

> My code of ethics and my oath of office make me a quasi-judicial official, and one of my jobs is to prevent the innocent from being convicted.

A hard-bitten defense attorney might blanch at the statement, but it is at least significant that the prosecutor defined his role in terms of the norm established by the legal community with an implicit emphasis on the Rule of Law.

Miranda necessitated few changes in prosecutor procedures. The greatest immediate problem resulted from the twenty to thirty cases already prepared for trial when *Miranda* was handed down. These cases were re-worked before the trial, but there is no record about how many were dropped as a result of the new requirements. As in the other cities, the district attorney prevented some cases from getting to court, but the police in Racine did not seem to consider this change significant. Despite the chief prosecutor's approval of the decision, there appeared to be no strong sentiment in the police department that the district attorney feared or sold his soul to the defense.

THE NEWSPAPERS

The *Racine Journal Times* reported the decision quickly and thoroughly. In front-page articles both on June 13, and June 14, 1966, the newspaper printed Associated Press dispatches which listed quite carefully the main stipulations of the decision, the relationship of the case to *Escobedo*, the facts of the companion cases, and a brief discussion of the dissenting opinion. In addition, these articles discussed the nation-wide response of police officials. The article of June

14 claimed that most of these responses were critical, but that many police agencies felt it was too early to comment. On that same day there appeared another Associated Press dispatch suggesting that convictions may become more difficult to obtain.[11]

This emphasis on broader, nation-wide implications of the decision continued during the week following the decision. More than the newspapers in Green Bay or Kenosha, the *Journal Times* focused outside the community for *Miranda* news. Except for a story mentioning the challenge of a local confession obtained prior to *Miranda* without advisement of the right to counsel,[12] the paper printed nothing about local implications during the first week following the decision. The paper also presented an article about a change in New York City arrest procedures, a story about Danny Escobedo, and an article explaining the limits of *Miranda's* retroactivity.[13]

The *Journal Times* took no direct editorial position on *Miranda*. But on the basis of other editorials both preceding and following the decision, it is clear that the editorial policy emphasized both a need for innovation in the criminal justice field and a need to develop expertise to cope with such innovation. In an August 11, 1965, editorial entitled "Confusion, Dispute Born of Change," the newspaper emphasized the need to adapt the Constitution to changing socioeconomic conditions. The editorial sympathized with police anxiety but approved of the legal changes giving equal rights to the indigent accused.[14] The *Miranda* decision seems to have accentuated this position. In an editorial appearing about six months after the decision, the newspaper put it this way: [15]

> If the courts are going to expect policemen to meet their new and higher requirements in law enforcement and criminal law, it stands to reason that we must provide law enforcement officers capable of meeting those standards.

> No longer can we take a strong young fellow with little education, put him on the street as a foot patrolman and hope that a few years of on-the-job training under the watchful eye of the patrol sergeant can make a 'good cop' out of him. Unless he understands an amazing number of things from the technical to the theoretical . . . he will do more harm than good. He may even be obliged to know a fair amount of sociology, criminology and law to be an effective policeman.

Table 7-2.   Rank and First Source of Information about *Miranda* (Racine), in Percentages

	Source	All	Patrolman	Superior	Detective
			RANK		
(1)	TV, radio	3.4	6.5	0.0	0.0
(2)	Magazines not specializing in police activities	5.2	9.7	0.0	0.0
(3)	Newspaper	24.1	35.8	0.0	18.8
(4)	Police officer not a superior	0.0	0.0	0.0	0.0
(5)	Superior officer	39.7	38.5	55.6	37.5
(6)	Magazines specializing in police activities	3.4	0.0	11.1	6.3
(7)	Conferences, training	3.4	3.2	11.1	0.0
(8)	Supreme Court opinion	8.6	6.5	11.1	12.5
(9)	Attorney General	5.2	0.0	11.1	12.5
(10)	Local judge	0.0	0.0	0.0	0.0
(11)	District Attorney	5.2	0.0	0.0	12.5
(12)	Other	1.7	0.0	0.0	0.0
	TOTAL	99.9	100.2	100.0	100.1
	(N)	(58)[a]	(31)	(9)	(16)

a. Individual rank totals are less than 58 because there were two persons of unknown rank.

Total may not equal 100 percent because of rounding.

The editorial went on to support the establishment of state-wide minimum police education standards.

More than any other group involved in the administration of justice in Racine, the newspaper editors emphasized these basic tenets of professionalization, tenets whose acceptance was generally characteristic of the political culture. Social and legal change was both accepted and desired, according to the newspaper, but the complexities inherent in these changes could only be overcome by developing greater specialization along with the education and salary requirements that facilitate this specialization.

Thus in Racine, more than in Kenosha or Green Bay, the groups impinging on criminal justice administration certainly emphasized the broader implications of the decision. The active criminal law practitioners created a milieu in which these broad implications were highly visible to the police. The relatively great amount of crime in the community reinforced this visibility, since the confession issue can be—and was—frequently raised. Group impingement, already greater and more concerned with professionalization than Kenosha or Green Bay, increased. Conflict between the police and some groups was exacerbated. The newspaper's view about the implications, however, was that all participants in the process could adjust to such change. It emphasized socially desirable and legally acceptable means, *i.e.*, adoption of norms of professionalization, which the police should use to adjust to *Miranda*. Thus in a community whose police department ranked relatively high in professionalization and whose groups were quite actively involved in impinging on police decision-making, both the desire for professionalization and group activity increased as a result of *Miranda*. We must keep in mind this milieu of conflict, accompanied by emphasis on long-range implications and the need for professionalization, when we investigate the effect of *Miranda* on the police department itself.

SOURCES OF *Miranda* INFORMATION

Table 7-2 reflects some evidence of greater specialization in the Racine department. A relatively high percentage of officers in all ranks, *including superiors*, received their first source of information from superior officers.

The Racine department primarily depended on its captain of de-

Table 7-3. Rank and All Sources of Information about *Miranda* (Racine), in Percentages

R A N K

Sources	All	Patrolman	Superior	Detective
Superior officer	84.5	80.6	88.9	93.8
Conferences, training	69.0	58.1	88.9	81.3
Newspaper	63.8	71.0	22.2	75.0
District Attorney	60.3	38.7	77.8	87.5
Supreme Court opinion	48.3	38.7	33.3	81.3
TV, radio	48.3	51.6	11.1	62.5
Magazines specializing in police activities	44.8	38.7	44.4	56.3
Attorney General	34.5	25.8	22.2	50.0
Magazines, nonspecialized	29.3	35.5	0.0	37.5
Police officer not a superior	27.6	32.3	11.1	32.3
Local judge	25.9	22.6	33.3	31.2
(N)	(58)[a]	(31)	(9)	(16)

a. Individual rank totals are less than 58 because there were two persons of unknown rank.

Totals may exceed 100 percent because each individual could choose as many as eleven sources.

tectives for its main source of legal expertise. Consulting with the local judges and district attorney, this officer prepared a memorandum about *Miranda* which became the primary instructional literature as far as the chief was concerned. The superior officer is the source of information most frequently chosen by all ranks in Table 7-2. Indeed, no superiors received their first source from the newspapers, the other channel of information quickly attuned to the decision. The detective.captain's specialization and his activities relating to this specialty are reflected in the responses. The upper echelons, including the detectives, seemed most likely to depend upon the superior.

This dependence seems even more apparent when we look at all the sources of information which the officers received (Table 7-3). All but one detective (93.8 percent) and all but one superior (88.9 percent) received information from a superior. In comparison, only 30 percent of the Kenosha superiors and 69.2 percent of the Kenosha detectives received information from this source. Conferences and training sessions were frequently mentioned, but considerably more among the upper echelons than among patrolmen. On the average, detectives list the greatest number of sources (6.81). This is higher than any rank in any of the previously discussed departments. Patrolmen, on the average, list slightly more sources (4.74) than do superiors (4.33).

According to the information in Table 7-3, the district attorney and the attorney general quite frequently contributed information about the decision, but only to superiors and detectives. Thus, there is some evidence of the importance of specialization and the importance of outside sources of the kind encouraged by advocates of police professionalization. But, as in Kenosha, these outside sources furnish information predominantly to the upper ranks.

The perceived importance of these sources, including the outside sources, varied according to rank (Table 7-4). No single source was important enough to be chosen as "best" by more than about one-quarter of the men (the most frequently mentioned, conferences, was chosen by only 24.1 percent). Though superiors and detectives were more likely to receive information from superior officers (see Table 7-3), patrolmen were far more likely to consider the superior as the best source of information. Detectives seemed more influenced by the conferences. The patrolman's most frequent choice of superiors probably reflected the emphasis on roll-call training while the detec-

Table 7-4. Rank and Best Source of Information on *Miranda* (Racine), in
            Percentages

		R A N K		
Source	*All*	*Patrolman*	*Superior*	*Detective*
Conferences, training	24.1	19.4	11.1	43.8
Superior officer	20.7	32.3	0.0	6.3
Supreme Court opinion	19.0	12.9	22.2	25.0
District Attorney	12.1	9.7	33.3	6.3
Attorney General	6.9	3.2	11.1	12.5
Magazines specializing in police activities	6.9	9.7	11.1	0.0
Local judge	5.2	3.2	11.1	6.3
Magazines, nonspecialized	3.4	6.5	0.0	0.0
TV, radio	1.7	3.2	0.0	0.0
Police officer not a superior	0.0	0.0	0.0	0.0
Newspaper	0.0	0.0	0.0	0.0
TOTAL	100.0	100.1	99.9	100.2
(N)	(58)[a]	(31)	(9)	(16)

a. Individual rank totals are less than 58 because there were two persons of unknown
rank.

tive's choice of conferences no doubt reflected the development in the detective bureau of a subsequently discussed in-depth study of Court decisions.

If we control for access to the sources by finding the ratio of the number of persons who choose the source as best to the number who receive information from the source, we find that the highest ratio, for the Supreme Court opinion, is only 39.3 percent. In other words, 39.3 percent of the officers who were exposed to the Court opinion feel that it was the best source. Among superiors the ratio is highest for this opinion; two-thirds of the superiors (2 of 3, admittedly a small number) were most impressed by the opinion itself. The highest ratio among patrolmen, only 40.1 percent, is for the source of superior officers. Detectives showed a fairly high degree of cohesion since 53.9 percent (7 of 13) who received information in conferences chose it as best.

Thus, the information process remained quite decentralized, particularly if one considers the supposed emphasis on specialization and the relatively high ranking professionalization of the department. Moreover, the sources of information remained predominantly inbred. Only superiors chose an outside local source (the district attorney) more frequently than any other source; two-thirds of the superiors chose this source (see Table 7-4).

Table 7-5 shows that for the majority of the department and for all ranks with the exception of superiors, inbred law enforcement sources were indeed the most significant. Local officials (district attorney, local judges) were quite insignificant except for the superiors. Few detectives received their most important information about the decision directly from the local officials. Even though the majority of all officers received information from these local officials, communications from the law enforcement sources themselves are generally considered better sources of information.

Local officials were slightly more important sources in Racine than in Kenosha, primarily because a much higher percentage of Racine superiors (44 percent) than Kenosha superiors (10 percent) chose that source.

The sources were primarily perceived as being critical of the decision by a majority (53.4 percent) of the department. However, fewer officers in Racine than in Kenosha (62.5) or Green Bay (71.4) felt that these sources were critical. Still, only 8.6 percent of Racine

Table 7-5. Rank and Categories of Best Sources of Information on *Miranda*
(Racine), in Percentages

		R A N K		
Source	*All*	*Patrolman*	*Superior*	*Detective*
Law enforcement	51.7	61.4	22.2	50.0
Outside specialized	25.9	16.1	33.3	37.5
Outside nonspecialized	5.1	9.7	0.0	0.0
Local officials	17.3	12.9	44.4	12.5
TOTAL	100.0	100.1	99.9	100.0
(N)	(58)	(31)	(9)	(16)

Total may not equal 100.0 percent because of rounding.

Table 7-6. Rank and New Sources of Information (Racine), in Percentages

		R A N K		
Source	*All*	*Patrolman*	*Superior*	*Detective*
All new	3.4	0.0	11.1	6.3
Some new	39.7	48.4	33.3	31.3
None new	46.6	35.5	55.6	56.3
Don't know	10.3	16.1	0.0	6.3
TOTAL	100.0	100.0	100.0	100.2
(N)	(58)[a]	(31)	(9)	(16)

a. Individual rank totals are less than 58 because there were two individuals of unknown rank.

Totals may not equal 100.0 percent because of rounding.

officers felt that their sources generally think the decision a good idea (32.8 percent think that these sources were neutral). Despite the greater importance of local officials or superiors, only one of nine superiors perceived that his sources approved of the decision. Only one of sixteen detectives—the rank most likely to approve of the decision—received information from such sources.

Table 7-6 shows that almost half of the force did not receive information about *Miranda* from any new sources. Some of this lack of new sources might be explained by the fact that these officers were in contact with a great many sources of information *prior* to the *Miranda* decision. More Kenosha officers received information from new sources. This is particularly true among detectives. In the Kenosha department, one with less professionalization but still great activity regarding crime, only 7.7 percent received no information from new sources. In Racine 56.3 percent of the detectives had no new sources of information. In Green Bay, a city with the lowest level of professionalization, the lowest number of sources of information, and the lowest amount of crime, 70 percent of the detectives received no information from new sources.

Police Perceptions and Attitudes

In his letter of introduction to the department's 1965 *Annual Report*, the Racine police chief left little doubt about the anticipation of change in the area of police interrogation: [16]

> Your police officers have been confronted with unfavorable court decisions based on standards set by Supreme Courts [*sic*] in their zealousness to protect the accused. Police officers must face the drastic and sometimes radical changes in the format of law enforcement. In the offing are changes in procedures that will completely erase the methods used for nearly a century by recognized police departments. Our officers will face new laws that will outlaw bail and bond, [and outlaw] confessions unless made in the presence of attorneys. Strict regulations are being developed that will prohibit law enforcement officers from revealing circumstances surrounding arrests.

The chief felt that many of the upper echelon of the department, in fact, did not accept his predictions about legal change. The majority of these men, he claimed, were aware that the interrogation issue was again before the Supreme Court but felt that the Court would rule contrary to its ultimate ruling. The data from the questionnaire support the chief's views of his department. Only 22.4 percent of the department anticipated a decision similar to *Miranda*. This is almost twice as large as the percentage of Green Bay and Kenosha officers who anticipated *Miranda*. Nonetheless, this certainly shows no pervasive feeling of anticipation. Surprisingly, more patrolmen (29.0 percent) than superiors (22.2) or detectives (12.5) expected such a decision. Thus, among superiors, the men in the best position to relate information, and among detectives, who are most likely to use such information, there was little expectation that a *Miranda* decision would occur.

This lack of anticipation did not lead to unanimous perceptions of great change as a result of *Miranda*. Table 7-7 shows that less than one-half the sample perceived a great change in their jobs as a result of *Miranda*. The vast majority of the force did perceive at least some change even though the Racine department encountered no crime similar to the Kenosha murder and its ramifications. The Racine detectives did not face the problem, as did the Kenosha force, of being constrained by new rules while trying to solve a particularly brutal crime.

Table 7-7. Rank and Perceptions of Extent *Miranda* Changed One's Own Job (Racine), in Percentages

| | | *R A N K* | | |
Change	All	Patrolman	Superior	Detective
Great or very great	44.9	45.2	33.3	50.0
Some	48.3	45.2	55.6	50.0
None	5.2	,6.5	11.1	0.0
Don't know	1.7	,3.2	0.0	0.0
TOTAL	100.0	100.0	100.0	100.0
(N)	(58)[a]	(31)	(9)	(16)

a. Individual rank totals are less than 58 because there were two persons of unknown rank.

Though only 17.2 percent of the department approved of the decision, the Racine department had more approvers than did the other previously discussed, less professionalized departments. The detectives were more likely to approve of the decision. Twenty-five percent of the detectives (4 of 16), compared to 22.2 percent of the superiors (2 of 9) and only 12.9 percent of the patrolmen (5 of 31) approved of the decision. The detectives, who as a group are more experienced in the interrogation process, are more likely to approve.

Table 7-8 gives some further clues about both the detectives' perceptions of change and the reason for great concern about the *Miranda* decision. Overestimating the *Miranda* constraints was again the rule (see items 5 and 8). Most detectives were aware of the leeway still possible while discussing a crime with an individual (item 8), but only a limited number of patrolmen realized the existence of this latitude. Surprisingly, of the three ranks, patrolmen were most likely to understand that a suspect can still be asked to come voluntarily to the police station. The detectives generally thought that they can still talk to a person without advising him of his rights, yet were less likely to see the legal feasibility of being able to convince a person to come to the station without his becoming a suspect.

The superiors fall between the detectives and patrolmen on these two items. In addition, their response to item 6 is interesting. One-third of the superiors in the sample thought that *Miranda* completely eliminated the use of confessions. The officers' other views on changes resulting from *Miranda* reflect further rank differences. These responses of the Racine department were generally quite similar to those of the less professionalized departments.

Table 7-9 shows that detectives were more likely than other officers to perceive the effects of *Miranda* on the relationship between their job and the jobs of others. Detectives were most likely to claim that because of *Miranda* they now spend more time explaining their work to others in the community (item 3). Though the percentages are much smaller, the detectives also claimed that they were now more closely observed by people outside the department. Supervisors are notably unaffected by these "outsiders."

These effects involving increased local impingement and participation by other outsiders are somewhat more frequently mentioned by Racine officers than by their Green Bay and Kenosha colleagues. But changes within the department's organization again are far more

Table 7-8.   Percentage Correct Perceptions of Stipulations of *Miranda* Decision
(Racine), in Percentages

			RANK		
Stipulation		Total	Patrolman	Superior	Detective
(1)	Must tell of right to remain silent	98.3	96.8	100.0	100.0
(2)	Anything suspect says may be held against him	98.3	100.0	100.0	93.8
(3)	Right to attorney if he wants one	98.3	100.0	88.9	100.0
(4)	If indigent, can have attorney appointed at court expense	94.2	90.3	100.0	100.0
(5)	Can still ask person to come voluntarily to the station	34.5	41.9	22.2	25.0
(6)	Suspect must have an attorney whether he wants one or not	98.3	100.0	89	100.0
(7)	Confessions no longer evidence	89.7	90.3	66.7	100.0
(8)	May no longer talk to anyone without informing him of rights	32.8	19.4	33.3	56.3
(9)	No wire tapping	86.2	93.5	77.8	81.3
(10)	Voluntary confessions no longer legal source of information	89.7	87.1	88.9	93.8
	(N)	(58)[a]	(31)	(9)	(16)

a. Individual rank totals are less than 70 because there were two persons of unknown rank.

important than these changes involving the impingement of others outside the department. Table 7-9 also shows that once again changes in evidence-gathering methods and changes in education are the most frequently mentioned modifications on an individual officer's job. What is most interesting about these responses was the fact that, unlike Kenosha, the detectives were *less* likely than other officers to perceive changes in their methods of gathering evidence. Furthermore, the detectives were far less likely to see any increase in their education as a result of *Miranda*. In fact, in choosing the greatest effect *Miranda* had on the department, almost one-half the patrolmen, two-thirds of the superiors, but only one-quarter of the detectives felt that the change in education has been most important.

There is a certain amount of irony present in this lack of perceived change in detective education. Racine ranks rather highly on our index of professionalization. Education is both an indicator on our scale and, in the eyes of advocates of police reform, an integral part of the process of increasing professionalization and improving responses to innovation. In none of the other departments have the goals of professionalization been so thoroughly and publicly emphasized as they have in Racine. The Racine chief, a great admirer of Orlando Wilson, prior to *Miranda* had adopted many of Wilson's suggestions for more efficient use of police personnel. In his presentation of the department's annual reports to the mayor and city council, he increased his advocacy of the need for education to meet the problems of social change. In 1965, while discussing problems raised by legal changes, the chief asserted, "How do we plan to meet these problems? Education is the only answer." [17]

After the *Miranda* decision the emphasis on problems of, and responses to, legal changes became greater. Said the chief,[18]

> The year 1966 will undoubtedly be recalled many times in the future as the year of the beginning of drastic changes in law enforcement.

1966 was the year of research by the President's Commission on Law Enforcement, the adoption of the Law Enforcement Assistance Act, as well as the year of the establishment of the Wisconsin Governor's Commission on Law Enforcement. The research by these organizations, along with change in the law and society, the chief claimed, radically altered the concept of law enforcement. How must law en-

Table 7-9. Rank and Effects of *Miranda* on Own Job (Racine), in Percentages

RANK

Effects	All	Patrolman	Superior	Detective
(1) New methods of gathering evidence	63.8	64.9	66.7	56.3
(2) Better education and training	53.4	61.3	66.7	31.3
(3) Spending more time explaining activities to community	22.4	12.9	22.2	39.6
(4) Sympathy toward suspects	17.2	13.0	33.3	18.8
(5) New methods to obtain confessions	13.8	6.5	11.1	18.8
(6) More closely observed by people outside department	6.8	6.4	0.0	12.6
(7) More attention to others in the field of criminal justice	5.2	3.2	0.0	6.3
(N)	(58)[a]	(31)	(9)	(16)

a. Individual rank totals are less than 58 because there were two persons of unknown rank.

Totals may be greater than 100 percent because each officer could give two responses.

forcement respond? "Better education and training must be provided, more personnel must be employed, and entirely new police procedures must be adopted." [19] This statement was certainly a succinct plea not only for education but also for the need to adopt new procedures (for example, evidence-gathering methods) in order to cope with change.

Prior to *Miranda*, because of his admiration for Wilson's ideas, the chief took action which increased the specialization in his department. Detectives were assigned to investigate the specific types of crimes. In 1964 a robbery squad was added to the existing burglary, check, "violent," and confidential squads.[20] The head of the detective bureau reported that in 1967 "there will be a definite trend toward specialized assignments as opposed to general shift assignments" in the detective bureau.[21]

Indeed, much of the educational changes also concentrated upon the detectives. According to the head of the detective bureau, in 1966 the detectives undertook an innovation in local training. These officers were supposed to study "in depth, a particular phase of law enforcement, draw up teaching procedures and then under the command of the bureau head, teach all other plain clothes personnel the subject." [22] One of the earliest topics considered was Supreme Court decisions, and plans for 1967 included—actually for the first time—a study of the effects of these decisions.[23] Training hours were also increased for the entire department.

There are, however, important limits to the extent of these changes. The "in depth" study of Court decisions was still concentrated in the detective bureau and perhaps also upon superior officers. As the analysis of sources of *Miranda* information showed, much of this information was concentrated at the upper levels. The detectives, as Table 7-9 shows, simply did not see this as an important innovation. The general increase in training occurred mainly through a stepping-up of the rather cursory roll-call training programs.

Thus in some ways this advocacy of professionalization had not yet reached beyond the pleading stage. Achievement of the goals of professionalization was further hampered by other activities within the department. As the chief himself admitted, there was a difference in his own perspectives of police work and the perspectives of many of the lower echelon officers. He was not completely successful in convincing these officers that such innovations were both necessary and helpful. According to some detectives, the advocacy of increased education has created some dissension between some of the younger detectives who desire the increase and a number of older detectives who fear it as a threat to their jobs.

No clear pattern emerges. There was neither unilateral acceptance of these changes, as a consequence of *Miranda*, in professionalization nor an agreement that such changes had occurred. Yet there are certainly signs that prior to *Miranda* the department was led by a man quite concerned with specialization and education. His concern increased after *Miranda*. The *Miranda* communications process reflected these contradictions. It showed characteristics of the professionalization and participation, but it also showed some of the characteristics of less professionalized departments.

Conclusion

In some ways both the communication process and the consequences of the *Miranda* decision differed from those in Green Bay or Kenosha. Though there was a resulting conflict between the police perspective and the legal perspective in all three cities, the Racine conflict was different because it involved a broader group struggle. Furthermore, the Racine conflict centered on an issue which was related to a much broader interpretation of the *Miranda* decision. As we suggested about more professionalized departments, the Racine department was more approving of the decision and was more likely to anticipate it.

Local groups tried to set standards for compliance that were different than those established in Kenosha or Green Bay. In neither of those two cities did the criminal bar make such an extensive attempt to use *Miranda* as a weapon to modify police interrogation behavior. Perhaps even more important was the fact that upper-echelon police officials perceived that the Racine attorneys were especially aggressive. Thus, like the other cities, Racine had a conflict between police and legal perspectives, but in Racine the conflict did not focus directly upon the district attorney. He was able to impinge upon police decision-making without incurring the wrath of the police officers. Instead, the conflict was more explicitly manifested between the police, the city attorney's office, and the criminal bar.

Our discussion of the three cities has suggested that a low number of new sources of information may reflect a lack of pressure to establish new channels (Green Bay), or it may reflect the previous existence of a relatively high number of groups interacting with the police. Racine is closer to the latter model. The goals of professionalization were strongly advocated in Racine prior to *Miranda*, and after that decision their espousal increased both through outside groups and through some members of the police department. Nonetheless, this ethos of professionalization, whether advocated by police officers or other groups (both of which were more likely in Racine than in the other two cities) may not have pervaded the rank and file. The chief's interest in change led to little immediate modification in the methods used to convey information about Court decisions affecting police behavior. The changes that have occurred apply primarily to the detectives, but the detectives themselves perceived *Miranda* as leading to a relatively insignificant change in their educational process, an important factor in police professionalization.

The extent of these changes should not be overemphasized. The communications process still emphasized inbred sources of information, sources which are not closely attuned to empathy with the legal community and the related emphasis on anticipating change. According to some local criminal lawyers, this lack in police-"outsider" communications is the greatest problem facing the Racine police. Though perhaps for different reasons, the chief would agree. In addition the rate of approval and anticipation of the decision was still quite low.

Conflict over the implications of *Miranda* will probably increase in Racine, not necessarily because the police are "unprofessionalized" since, in fact, they rank relatively high in professionalization. Rather, conflict will increase because group participation frequently leads to the calling of police behavior into question without having channels of communication which facilitate the understanding of these demands.

NOTES

1. *Uniform Crime Reports*, 1966, 78-90. The cities included in this report are actually the center city plus the surrounding county. Only Milwaukee, Green Bay, Kenosha, and Racine are specifically listed.

2. In 1966, 86 percent of the persons arrested in Racine for auto theft, 81 percent for burglary, and 69 percent for larceny, were under 18 years old. For crimes against the person, no murders, half the forcible rapes, and 36 percent of the aggravated assaults resulted in arrests of persons under 18. See *Annual Report—1966* (Racine: Racine Police, 1967), 39. Hereinafter all these reports will be cited as *Annual Report* followed by the appropriate year.

3. *Ibid.*, 3.

4. Robert R. Alford with the collaboration of Harry M. Scoble, *Bureaucracy and Participation* (Chicago: Rand McNally, 1969), 13-16, 80-95, 118-54.

5. Martin Showers, "Public Defender . . . Racine County Rejects It." *Wisconsin Bar Bulletin* 37 (August, 1964), 17.

6. Jerome Carlin, *Lawyers on Their Own* (New Brunswick: Rutgers University, 1962).

7. Informal face-to-face communication is a characteristic of the criminal law community even in a much larger city. See Jerome H. Skolnick, *Justice Without Trial* (New York: Wiley, 1966), 30.

8. *White v. Simpson*, 28 Wis. 2d 590, 137 N.W. 2d 590 (1965).

9. From the city's reply brief in *City of Racine v. Cotton*, Racine County Court, Branch II, undated.

10. Letter from this attorney, who shall remain nameless, to an assistant city attorney, April 25, 1967. Copy in author's possession.

11. *Racine Journal Times*, June 13 and 14, 1966.

12. *Racine Journal Times*, June 18, 19, and 20, 1966.

13. *Racine Journal Times*, June 16 and 18, 1966.

14. *Racine Journal Times*, August 11, 1965.

15. *Racine Journal Times*, January 27, 1967.

16. *Annual Report—1965*, 1.

17. *Annual Report—1965*, 1.

18. *Annual Report—1966*, 1.

19. *Ibid.*

20. *Annual Report—1964*, 11; *Annual Report—1965*, 14.

21. *Annual Report—1966*, 18.

22. *Ibid.*

23. *Ibid.*

Chapter 8

MADISON

Madison is best classified as a modern professional center. Education, finance, real estate and public administration form Madison's economic base. It ranks in the top quartile of American cities over 25,000 in all of these industries. The other three Wisconsin cities ranked much lower. Unlike the two manufacturing centers, Racine and Kenosha, Madison industries are service oriented. Almost from Madison's inception its political leaders deemphasized and even discouraged the need for heavy industry in that community. In 1955 the city had the highest proportion of people in professional service occupations of any city in the country.

Madison differs from the other cities in some other important ways. Its population is far more mobile and cosmopolitan than the other cities'. Madison began as a center for state government and for the university, and today it remains such a center. Since Madison's type of industry requires a high level of education, it should not be too surprising that in 1962 nearly 40 percent of all Madisonians had some college training. This is an extremely high percentage, especially when compared to Green Bay's and Kenosha's 14 percent and Racine's 20 percent.

Since Madison does not have a large working class base, the more "bread-and-butter" economic issues are less important than they are in Racine and Kenosha and even to some extent in Green Bay. Political controversy is more likely to center around such aesthetic issues as the use and location of recreational facilities. By no means does this emphasis automatically lead to genteel, non-controversial politics. Struggles involving the politics of beauty have been bitter and hard fought; group activity is ever present. Instead of class conflict or cosmopolitanism versus localism, this strong conflict is characterized by an intense middle-class activism. The two Madison newspapers quite obviously reflect both the nature and intensity of this conflict.

Interest in aesthetics makes the community more amenable to the professionalization of local governmental services. At a very early stage in Madison history a park commission was established and a landscape architect was hired. In fact, contrary to Kenosha, the participation of local groups reinforces rather than limits the acceptance of professionalization. Many active pressure groups participate primarily to get measures adopted which tend to professionalize local government. This is typical of a predominantly middle-class, professional center. Because political controversy centers around relatively abstract issues, and because of the relatively homogenous nature of the population, Madisonians seem surprised that conflict occurs over local issues. Compared to economic issues, it is more difficult clearly to perceive that differences over aesthetics ought to exist. Who can be against beautification? Yet the norms of participation in government and "stating your views" are also characteristic of the very middle class which is so prevalent in Madison. Conflict, while perhaps surprising to the community, is nonetheless endemic.

The degree of group impingement on decision-making is also increased by the presence of state and federal governmental bureaucracies. Their presence increases the general interest in the relationship between local events and political activities at the state or even national level. The existence of these "outside" bureaucracies in Madison probably adds to the cosmopolitan political culture of the city. Furthermore, there are many informal contacts between local political officials and the readily accessible state and federal officials.[1]

The police department thus operates in a milieu emphasizing professionalization and encouraging group activity. The university-government milieu encourages impingement on police activity by outside experts. The law school, with a number of professors extremely interested in criminal law, serves as a potential source of information. This source is not so readily available in the other three communities. The chambers of the State Supreme Court, federal dis-

trict court, the attorney general's office, and the office of the state
public defender, are all located within a distance of one block from
the Madison police station. The headquarters of the State Bar Association of Wisconsin is located only a few blocks away. Furthermore, the Madison police department shares its building with almost
the entire city and county-level bureaucracy, including the district
attorney and the local judiciary. Of course, physical propinquity
does not guarantee that lines of communication will exist. But many
of these potential sources of information in fact have often impinged
upon police activities.

Before dealing with that analysis, however, a word must be said
about crime. If the crime problem were great enough in Madison, it
is conceivable that the police themselves would not be very attuned
to the advice or views of "progressives," such as law school professors, public defenders, and the attorney general. The upper-echelon
police bureaucracy might take the position that concentration on
stopping crime takes all their resources, and they do not have time
for the more long-range but less pressing problems. But in fact, next
to Green Bay, Madison had the lowest 1966 crime rate of the studied
cities. It had 100 less reported Class I crimes per 100,000 population
than did Kenosha, and over 200 less per 100,000 population than did
Racine. It had the second lowest rate for murder, assault, robbery,
burglary, and auto theft. Except for rape, where it ranked second,
the city had a relatively low rate for crimes of violence. Only for the
less serious crime of theft over $50 did Madison rank highest of the
four. Madison, however, did experience a sharp increase between
1965 and 1966 in the *number* of reported crimes. There was a 64
percent increase in the number of reported crimes, as compared to
an average of only 8 percent for 96 cities with a population between
100,000 and 250,000. There was only one murder in 1965; in 1966
there were three. In 1966 there were 15 forcible rapes, as compared
to only one in 1965, but assaults rose only about 10 percent, and another potentially violent crime, robbery, decreased from 28 in 1965
to 24 in 1966. The greatest rise can be attributed mostly to increased
burglaries, thefts over $50, and auto theft. These crimes accounted
for about 90 percent of the reported crimes in 1965 and 1966. In
1966, their total number increased by better than 67 percent.[2]

The significance of these increases is limited by four factors.
First, the greatest increase occurred in less serious crimes. Second,

although rape and murders increased, none of the included crimes could be considered cases which struck enough terror in the community to put intense pressure on the police. Third, as in Green Bay, there seemed to be a feeling among informants (including some detectives) that Madison does not have a serious crime problem. Finally, as previously discussed, the Madison Class I crime rate was still lower than that of all the studied cities except Green Bay. Crime may potentially be more serious, but the problem did not seem overwhelming.

Professionalization, Participation, and the Communications Process

THE BAR ASSOCIATION AND ATTORNEYS

Like Racine, Madison does have some semblance of a criminal law bar. There are approximately six to eight attorneys who are usually identified as regular practitioners of criminal law. None of these attorneys exerts the informal influence comparable to the Racine attorneys whose actions regarding *Miranda* were so important, though at least two attorneys regularly handle criminal cases in cities outside of Madison. These Madison criminal attorneys do not seem to share the ethnic characteristics often associated with criminal law practitioners, but they do share a common defensive ethos about the practice of criminal law as well as a common distrust of police officials. Furthermore, the professional interests of these attorneys generally differ from the professional interests of the local bar-association leaders.

Instead of further separating the criminal law practitioner from the local bar association (the result in Racine), this difference in fact forced the bar association to pay *more* attention to the criminal law process well before the *Miranda* decision. In 1962 a large increase in the number of indigents' criminal cases led to requests for fees of unprecedented size. As a result, the local judges requested that the local bar association establish some fee guidelines. The bar association's executive committee decided that two-thirds to three-fourths of the recommended minimum bar fees would be adequate. A vocal minority of criminal lawyers, however, demanded at least the minimum bar schedule. There was evidence of both bar association impingement on the process of furnishing counsel to indigents and conflict between the association and criminal lawyers.[3] This association's involvement and the conflict over fees increased after *Miranda*.

The conflict manifested itself in a rather peculiar way. Since 1962 the local bar association continuously encouraged all attorneys to agree to represent indigent defendants. Anticipating a greater demand for such attorneys, the local bar association's Sub-committee on Counsel for Indigents in 1963 adopted a statement which explicitly encouraged a "maximum number of members of the Bar engaged in private practice" to represent indigents. A panel of all Dane County (Madison) attorneys was made available to the local judges with the suggestion that the judges use some means of systematic rotation in choosing attorneys.[4] With the encouragement of the local judges, the bar became an active and effective pressure group to increase the number of available lawyers. The association attempted to spread the "wealth" of indigent attorney representation by encouraging more attorneys to take such cases. The more attorneys involved the less likely an accusation that an individual attorney was getting rich from fees received for representing many poor defendants.

As in the other cities, a great increase in fees occurred prior to *Miranda* (see Table 8-1).

Table 8-1. Fees for Attorneys Representing Indigents in Dane County (Madison), 1963-1967

Year	Amount[a]
1963	$ 7,488.00
1964	28,615.00
1965	26,537.00
1966	31,123.00
1967	30,000.00[b]

a. Includes fees for representation of juveniles.
b. The amount appropriated.

The increase occurred for several reasons. The judges began to be more liberal in their criteria for determining defendants' eligibility for free attorneys. Since 1964, judges furnished counsel to indigent defendants accused of serious misdemeanors—those with potential prison terms of at least six months. In addition, State Supreme Court decisions encouraged greater fees. Because of the greater number of attorneys now involved, the local judges became less fearful of granting large fee requests. Since the same few attorneys no longer received all such cases, the judges felt that they could no longer be accused of favoritism. The local bar association's actions were important only in regard to this latter reason. The first two reasons are quite similar to the reasons for fee increases in the other cities, especially Racine. The third factor is perhaps more significant because it shows that the local association was definitely more involved in the increase in fees than were the associations in any of the other three cities.

Despite the 1963 change, the local judges continued to complain about the methods of assigning counsel. The two local judges most involved with appointing counsel often had difficulties in finding an attorney willing to accept a case. Furthermore, because of *Miranda* the police chief asked the judges for further guidance about furnishing counsel. Once again the bar association was called to take action in response to the judiciary. A few months after the *Miranda* decision the association decided to review the methods of counsel assignment. The problem was investigated by a committee which included two attorneys not in private practice—the state public defender and a professor of criminal law at the University of Wisconsin. These two men, along with two criminal law practitioners (again using this term in the broad sense), recommended that a local court administrator be appointed whose job would be the procurement of an attorney for an indigent. Presumably this administrator would use his discretion to appoint the best attorney for the job, not necessarily the next man on the list.[5]

Instead of increasing the number of attorneys participating in the criminal law process, this attempt at professionalization of the process of counsel assignment was suggested explicitly to *decrease* the number. The procedure implied that the trend toward greater, but more indiscriminate, lawyer participation should be modified. Prior to this report, the association had encouraged greater breadth of lawyer participation in order to meet the increasing demands of indigents in need of legal counsel. There was again a conflict between the majority of the association leaders and those who practice a significant amount of criminal law. The leaders were concerned about the possibilities that the newly suggested method would again allow a few criminal law specialists to get what they, at least, felt were lucrative fees. After all, the bar association had originally become formally involved with this problem in order to prevent such concentration of fees. Criminal law practitioners insisted that, as specialists, they were entitled to such fees. The nature of this rekindled conflict was best expressed by a noted local criminal law practitioner in his discussion of the organized bar's objections to this new plan:

> The bar thinks anyone can practice criminal law. They expect us to represent indigents as a duty to society. Hell, I don't see any lawyers practicing non-criminal law or do any widows and orphans work for nothing. Criminal law is my specialty. I should get properly paid for it.

In fact, a compromise plan was finally adopted, though not immediately implemented. Stipulations for a full-time administrator and a small staff were adopted.[6] This administrator will assign counsel at the request of the judge. He will not, however, have complete discretion because the association decided to keep in operation the entire list of attorneys. Only in serious cases will the administrator definitely appoint a criminal law specialist. Even prior to the adoption of this method, however, local judges departed from the list in serious felonies in order to appoint such specialists.

This administrator will have other duties which perhaps are more significant than his discretion over counsel selection. He will investigate guilty pleas to see if they were intelligently made. Thus a new outside source will investigate the competence of the defendant. Thse investigations could quite readily touch upon police interrogation behavior. This new plan, however, says nothing about establishing a procedure to furnish counsel to an indigent suspect at any hour. The plan does allow an administrator to appoint counsel, but only at request of the court. Therefore, the police still have no clear procedure to follow in arranging for an indigent's counsel. (This will be discussed more fully later in Chapter 10.)

Certainly all attorney activities in regard to *Miranda* problems did not center on this conflict. The criminal lawyers were quite willing to use the *Miranda* decision. Most of these attorneys complained about the local judges' unwillingness to accept broad interpretations of *Miranda*. On the basis of *Miranda*, two attorneys had unsuccessfully challenged police procedures in a city drunk-driving case. One of these attorneys planned again to challenge a similar procedure. Another successfully challenged two confessions, and has appealed an unsuccessful challenge of a third. Although these attorneys as a rule admitted that the police were now more careful in their interrogation procedures, they also continued to distrust them, especially upper echelon police officials whom they castigated for failure to accept the decision.

From the viewpoint of the bar, the *Miranda* decision reinforced existing conflicts both between criminal law practitioners and the bar association organization, and between such practitioners and the police. There were both increased participation by non-law enforcement groups and possibilities of an entirely new group (the administrator's staff) impinging on police decision-making. These changes in group participation were effected by organizations that had previously made policy regarding the indigent accused.

It is also significant that the decision-making related to these procedures was also related to the issue of professionalization. In no other city did the criminal lawyers so strongly push for procedures which would have professionalized the process of furnishing an attorney to an indigent. Professionalization was emphasized not only because (according to the recommendations) an expert would use his discretion in appointing attorneys but also because an important proposed function of the procedure was the granting of a greater number of appointments to experts in the criminal field.

JUDGES

Changes in judicial procedures in Madison are usually considered by the County Board of Judges. This board is composed of all judges presiding over courts of record in Dane County. The organization is designed to "provide for orderly, efficient, and expeditious handling" of court matters.[7] None of the other three communities has such an organization. Prior to *Miranda* this board had considered the problem of furnishing counsel to the indigent. After the *Miranda* decision, both top police officials and the local bar association perceived that this board was a source of information about *Miranda*. The police chief turned to the board of judges for advice about furnishing counsel to an indigent suspect. It was at the initiative of the board (rather than at the initiative of the district attorney, as in Racine, or the bar association, as in Kenosha) that the local bar association took action.

Compared to the other cities, the local judiciary as a whole is less isolated from the criminal law process. Two of five county judges regularly hear criminal cases. Although in the 1966-67 term only 2.8 percent of the criminal cases were disposed of in circuit courts (a small increase from 1.9 percent in 1965-66), each circuit judge did hear some criminal cases.[8] The circuit court judges have jursidiction over jury trials in criminal cases, and cases are assigned to them by lot. Thus the Madison judiciary has not only a formal organization involved· at least partially with criminal law, but also a group of judges who in their decision-making functions are likely to handle some criminal law matters. Indeed, on the surface, it appears that police-judiciary relations are typical of the actions we would expect in Madison. A number of the local judges, including one most regularly involved in the early stages of criminal law cases, emphasized the amount of interaction between police officers and judges. Such interaction, according to these judges, is commonly of the informal type. "We are easily available to answer police questions" is a typical comment.

The effectiveness of this source of information, however, can easily be overemphasized, because after *Miranda* the local judiciary as a formal organization failed to live up to police expectations as a solver of problems created by *Miranda*. The board did not really answer the police chief's question about the methods to be used for furnishing counsel to the indigent suspect. When the chief asked for clarification, the judge presiding at the meeting said, "Now, Chief, that's our [the judges'] problem, not yours. You let us worry about it." One judge made a further comment of a type not likely to reconcile the police and legal perspective. He exclaimed, "Give them [the police] a little law, and they think they are experts." [9]

Few confessions were invalidated on *Miranda* grounds. Again the exact number is not available, but an educated estimate based on discussions with the judges would be anywhere from two to six. None of these involved any highly salient issue which caused much conflict among participants in the legal process.

Although the Madison judiciary, through the Board of Judges, became the focal point for some important *Miranda* problems, it was not the focal point for much police guidance on questions of particular concern to law enforcement.

THE DISTRICT ATTORNEY

Perhaps the most significant characteristic of the district attorney's office was its stability in light of change both in *Miranda* policy and upper-level personnel. Within the first year after the *Miranda* decision, there were three different district attorneys in Madison. The early 1967 death of the prosecutor who outpolled the incumbent district attorney in the 1966 election led to these peculiar circumstances. Yet the relationship between the police and the prosecutor's office generally remained the same throughout this period.

This relationship reflects characteristics of police-prosecutor relationships in cities on both extremes of the scale of professionalization and group activity. For example, there was a great deal of friction between the police chief and the prosecutor. Both former district attorneys and former assistant district attorneys accused the chief of attempting to put pressure on the district attorney to prosecute certain cases. Often this conflict centered around the issue of plea bargaining. It was an open secret that in 1966 the chief favored the defeat of the incumbent district attorney.

In Madison, however, this conflict did not affect the rather stable and friendly relationship between the prosecutor's staff and the detective bureau. Neither the prosecutor nor the detectives were concerned about an increase in the number of cases which the district attorney would not prosecute because of the new *Miranda* procedure. Although some such cases were evident, the detectives did not accuse the district attorney of selling out to the supposedly smarter, more aggressive defense attorneys.

Again the primary reason for this can be attributed to the relationship between the detectives and assistant district attorneys. The district attorney had five assistants; their experience in the office ranged from five months to seven years. A total of twelve men were employed as assistants since *Miranda* (not including an attorney who lasted only four weeks). These attorneys worked for the prosecutor for an average of two years. Because of the size of this staff and the number of warrants to be sought, neither the district attorney nor the chief was directly involved with all police-prosecutor questions. As one former deputy district attorney put it, "each detective can pick out an assistant d.a. with whom he works especially well." Every legal problem thus did not force a confrontation between the police and the prosecution. .These informal relations were important because they furnished an outlet of information to the detectives, and they also created within the detective bureau some empathy with the legal perspective. In this way, the two most professionalized departments were similar.

The Dane County district attorney, however, played only a minor role in law enforcement response to *Miranda*. Though he regularly sent department memos about important court decisions to the police chief, the chief did not consider the district attorney to be an important source of information about *Miranda*. The reason for this relates to the difference in perspectives of the chief and the district attorney. According to the chief, "he [the district attorney] is not a law enforcement official; he's an attorney." An ex-assistant district attorney stated this difference in another way. "The upper level police administrators do not seek the prosecutor's advice because he [the prosecutor] is too objective." The most ardent defense attorneys generally agree with this latter statement. As a *formal* source of information the prosecutor remained quite isolated from the police even after *Miranda* although the informal channels of communication between the prosecutor's staff and the detectives limited this isolation. In our later discussion of the communication process we shall take a closer look at the reasons for and the effect of this isolation on the district attorney's role in police training.

THE NEWSPAPERS

Both Madison newspapers frequently commented about local law enforcement activities. The *Capital Times* editorially was more critical of the police than was its competitor in Madison, the *Wisconsin State Journal*. Both interest in police activities and difference in newspaper views of police behavior manifested themselves in the newspapers' responses to the *Miranda* decision.

The *Capital Times*, the newspaper which favored the decision, gave it immediate coverage. On June 14, 1966, the paper carried a headline story featuring the Associated Press dispatch about the case. The article listed the specific rules listed by the Chief Justice, but little other discussion was offered.[10] This newspaper took no immediate editorial position, and in fact, during the remainder of the month, no mention was made of any of the ramifications of the decision.

The *State Journal* reported the decision in a completely different manner. Initially little was printed about the *Miranda* decision; however, a week after the decision that newspaper carried a front page story about the *Johnson* decision which held that *Miranda* did not apply retroactively. On this same day the *State Journal* printed a cartoon showing a police officer holding a gun on a suspect while simultaneously reading from a pamphlet entitled "What to Do Until the Lawyer Comes." On the same editorial page the editors reprinted a *U.S. News and World Report* article discussing the Warren Court "revolution." [11] In the next edition there was more of this reprint, plus an editorial warning of the dangers of the Supreme Court's attacks on accepted standards of law enforcement.[12]

With this editorial began the strongest attack against the decision by any newspaper in the four cities. Its theme was that the American people had become too complacent. Now was the time for the public to stand up and show the Court that the pendulum had swung too far in favor of the criminal. The editors encouraged letters from the public stating their views about the decision (note the typical encouragement of participation as a desired norm), and for about a week the *Journal* printed letters, virtually all of which condemned the Court. These letters were accompanied by additional anti-Court cartoons and another editorial with the same theme.[13]

Neither newspaper immediately ran any stories about Madison law enforcement response although some comments by local officers are found in a June 14, 1966, *Capital Times* article. What is most interesting is the continuing visibility of the *Miranda* decision as a source of conflict. Almost one year after *Miranda* the *Capital Times* featured an editorial supporting the decision. It also criticized the Madison police chief and the local sheriff for their testimony, before a Senate Subcommittee, that *Miranda* hampered their jobs. The editorial was a classic defense of the legitimacy of the Rule of Law as a constraint on police behavior: [14]

> We wonder if Sheriff Haas and Chief Emery have really found their jobs more difficult since the *Miranda* decision or whether they are merely joining with the popular outcry that constitutional rights constitute "pampering of criminals. . . ." We can understand that men charged with the responsibility of law enforcement are anxious to have their jobs made as easy as possible. But they should understand, too, that free men have rights that have been born through centuries of struggle. . . .

Moreover, the editorial was also critical of the police chief's comments that "lawyers and newspapers have been stressing non-police cooperation [*sic*] and fictitiously pointing [to] the police as the bad guys for the past three or four years."

The *State Journal* continued its editorial theme that "there can be little doubt that citizens generally" have been disturbed by *Miranda*. The editors in fact attributed the electoral defeat of the chief justice of the Wisconsin Supreme Court partially to this anti-*Miranda* feeling.[15]

SOURCES OF *Miranda* INFORMATION

Table 8-2 shows that like their counterparts the Madison officers received information about *Miranda* from many diverse sources; however, because of the activity of Madison newspapers the press was by far the most common initial source. The superior officer was the second most common source, but this superior did not quickly transmit information to the detectives. As a comparison, in Racine the superior was the more frequently mentioned first source of information for the detectives than it was for the department generally, but even among detectives the prosecutor was listed by only 13 percent. Thus, to a great extent the Madison department's initial sources were more like the sources in Green Bay and Kenosha than in Racine, where a response by the department itself was more quickly organized.

When we look at all the sources of information, however, we can see evidence that the communications process was quite systematic and pervasive. The Madison department was exposed to many sources of information. Madison officers received information from more sources than did the officers in any other community. Every officer received, on the average, close to six (5.82) sources. Patrolmen received slightly over five (5.15) sources, superiors were exposed to 5.92 sources, while the detectives received information from an average of 6.30 sources.

Table 8-3 shows that there is relatively little difference between the ranks in their access to sources of information on *Miranda*. Compared to those of the other cities, the channels of communications in Madison were not only more numerous, but also were likely to penetrate all ranks with equal success. The response to the training session

Table 8-2. Rank and First Source of Information about *Miranda* (Madison),
in Percentages

	Source	*All*	*Patrolman*	*Superior*	*Detective*
			R A N K		
(1)	TV, radio	11.5	12.2	23.1	4.3
(2)	Police officer not a superior	1.3	2.4	0.0	0.0
(3)	Superior officer	15.4	19.5	23.1	4.3
(4)	Newspaper	39.7	36.6	46.2	43.5
(5)	Magazines not specializing in police activities	2.6	0.0	7.7	0.0
(6)	District Attorney	6.4	4.9	0.0	13.0
(7)	Magazines specializing in police activities	1.3	0.0	0.0	4.3
(8)	Supreme Court opinion	11.5	9.8	0.0	21.7
(9)	Attorney General	7.7	9.8	0.0	8.7
(10)	Local judge	1.3	2.4	0.0	0.0
(11)	Training sessions	1.3	2.4	0.0	0.0
	TOTAL	100.0	100.0	100.1	98.8
	(N)	(78)[a]	(41)	(13)	(23)

a. Individual rank totals are less than 78 because there was one person of unknown rank.

Table 8-3. Rank and All Sources of Information about *Miranda* (Madison), in Percentages

	RANK			
Source	*All*	*Patrolman*	*Superior*	*Detective*
Conferences, training	92.3	87.8	100.0	95.7
Newspaper	74.4	78.0	61.5	78.3
Superior officer	70.5	70.7	69.2	69.6
Attorney General	67.9	61.0	69.2	78.3
TV, radio	61.5	61.0	69.2	56.5
Supreme Court opinion	59.0	48.3	53.8	78.3
District Attorney	57.7	58.9	46.2	60.9
Magazines not specializing in police activities	37.2	31.3	53.8	34.8
Magazines specializing in police activities	30.8	17.1	46.2	43.5
Police officer not a superior	21.8	24.4	15.4	21.7
Local judge	10.3	7.3	7.7	17.4
(N)	(78)[a]	(41)	(13)	(23)

a. Individual rank totals are less than 78 because there was one person of unknown rank.

Totals exceed 100 percent because each individual could choose as many as eleven sources.

exemplifies such pervasive lines of communications. Over 90 percent of the department, including seven-eighths of the patrolmen, *all* the superior officers and well over nine-tenths of the detectives, received information from such sessions. In fact, of all departments, the Madison department prior to *Miranda* had the most systematic and complete in-service training process. Every officer was required to complete forty hours of training courses (in addition to short roll-call training sessions) each year. FBI officials were often used as advisors and lecturers for these sessions. The other three departments also made use of FBI agents both generally and as sources of information about *Miranda*. But none of the other departments so thoroughly depended upon the FBI sessions. In Madison one of the local FBI agents, along with a special agent from the main office in Washington, D.C., spent three days lecturing on *Miranda* to the Madison officers. According to the chief, the agents were asked to remain for three days so that *every* officer could hear their discussion. The *Miranda* decision seemed to increase the department's dependence on this source. In strongly advocating the advantages of such FBI training, the chief claimed:

> FBI agents are the best teachers of the police because they know the law and know how to speak to the police. Most attorneys don't know how to talk to the police. This includes the district attorney. He is not a law enforcement official; he's an attorney and his perspective differs.

Some outsiders served as fairly frequent sources of information. The attorney general's memorandum was a source for a far greater percentage of Madison police than it was for any of the other departments. Within a month after *Miranda* the Madison police chief circulated to all personnel copies of the attorney general's *Miranda* memorandum. Accompanying the memorandum were the following instructions: [16]

> The impact of the United States Supreme Court decisions in the *Escobedo v. Illinois* and *Miranda v. Arizona* cases has affected all law enforcement. . . .

> You are expected to understand and comply with the opinions of the high court particularly as it applies to the "Fifth Amendment" privileges of the United States Constitution.

This method of disseminating information from the staff of the attorney general was also used prior to *Miranda*.

Nevertheless, these outside officials, especially outside local officials, definitely played a subordinate role. The activities of the district attorney best exemplify this minor role. About half of the department (57.7 percent) received some information from the prosecutor's office. In comparison, the district attorney was a slightly more frequent source of information for the Racine department, where over 60 percent of the department received information from the prosecutor or his staff. Much of this information was probably elicited by the Madison prosecutor through lectures at police in-service training programs, but the district attorney himself admitted that these lectures played only a subordinate role in the training process. According to him, the chief relied on the FBI for information about all important *Miranda* questions. For once the chief agreed with the district attorney's evaluation of his role. When this author asked the chief to describe the district attorney's contribution to the training process, he replied, "He and his staff contributed very little. In fact, I invited his staff to sit in on the FBI lectures. I felt they could learn something." [17]

Table 8-4 gives a clearer picture of the lack of importance of men who are not police officials. Almost no officer considered the judges the best sources, while only 3.8 percent of the force felt that the district attorney was the best source; no superior officer and only 8.7 percent of the detectives so rated the prosecutor. (In Racine, over 22 percent of the superiors and 25 percent of the detectives picked the district attorney as the best source despite the effort of that department to act as its own source of expertise.) Only the attorney general fared relatively well. The second most frequently mentioned best source, he was chosen by 20.5 percent of the force. Few superiors (7.7 percent) picked the attorney general, probably because his memorandum was basically a brief of the *Miranda* decision, and the superiors more frequently found the *Miranda* opinion itself to be the best source of information.

The training session is the most frequently mentioned best source for all ranks. (The detectives did cite the Supreme Court opinion just as frequently.) Within no other department did all ranks choose the same "best" source. The FBI session certainly not only successfully pervaded all departmental levels, but also the men at each of these levels generally perceived the value of the program. Close to half of the department who had access to the training session, including 58.3 percent of the patrolmen, 38.5 percent of the superiors and 40.9 percent of the detectives, claimed that the training sessions were the best sources. Even when we control for access to sources, the training session is the most frequently cited source for all ranks except the superiors. Among the superiors who received information from the Supreme Court opinion, 71.6 percent felt that the opinion was the best source. Note that there was more agreement about the importance of one source even though the Madison officers received information from more sources than did any of the other departments.

By combining the categories in Table 8-4, Table 8-5 presents a clear indication of a communications process with characteristics similar to those on both ends of a professionalization and group activity scale. Of all departments, the Madison police most frequently received information from outside specialized sources, particularly the attorney general and the Supreme Court opinion. Indeed, members of *each* of the individual Madison ranks mentioned such sources more frequently than do their respective rank members in the other cities. Certainly this shows the apparent access to non-police sources of expertise, sources to which professionalized departments are supposed to be amenable. However, in regard to other such sources, that is, local officials, the Madison department ranks *lowest*. Thus the highly professionalized Madison department has established particularly systematic and pervasive contacts with other law enforcement sources of information and with other specialized sources not directly involved with the administration of criminal justice in the city of Madison. Despite the high group activity and the department's amenability to sources of information, these local officials were not able to establish important lines of communication in regard to *Miranda*.

The district attorney's staff readily participated in everyday police decision-making, and the Madison detectives showed an empathy for the prosecutor's job. This empathy, it should be remembered, was characteristic of the professionalized Racine department but not as apparent in Kenosha and especially Green Bay. The effects of professionalization seemed to work another way in regard to

Table 8-4.   Rank and Best Source of Information about *Miranda* (Madison), in Percentages

	RANK			
Source	*All*	*Patrolman*	*Superior*	*Detective*
Conferences, training	44.9	51.2	38.5	39.1
Attorney General	20.5	22.0	7.7	26.1
Supreme Court opinion	15.4	7.3	38.5	13.0
Newspapers	6.4	7.3	0.0	8.6
District Attorney	3.8	2.4	0.0	8.7
TV, radio	1.3	2.4	0.0	0.0
Magazines specializing in police activities	1.3	0.0	7.7	0.0
Magazines not specializing in police activities	1.3	2.4	0.0	0.0
Superior officer	1.3	0.0	0.0	4.3
Local judge	0.0	0.0	0.0	0.0
Other	3.8	4.9	7.7	0.0
TOTAL	100.0	99.9	100.1	99.9
(N)	(78)[a]	(41)	(13)	(23)

a. Individual rank totals are less than 78 because there was one person of unknown rank.

Table 8-5. Rank and Categories of Best Sources of Information on *Miranda* (Madison), in Percentages

	RANK		
Source	*All*	*Patrolman*	*Superior*	*Detective*
Law enforcement	47.5	51.2	46.2	43.4
Outside specialized	35.9	29.3	46.2	39.1
Outside nonspecialized	9.0	12.1	0.0	8.7
Local officials	3.8	2.4	0.0	8.7
Other	3.8	4.9	7.7	0.0
TOTAL	100.0	99.9	100.1	99.9
(N)	(78)	(41)	(13)	(23)

Table 8-6. Rank and New Sources of Information (Madison), in Percentages

	RANK		
Source	*All*	*Patrolman*	*Superior*	*Detective*
All new	2.6	2.4	7.7	0.0
Some new	38.5	43.9	38.5	30.4
None new	47.4	39.0	53.8	60.9
Don't know	11.6	14.6	0.0	8.6
TOTAL	100.0	99.9	100.0	99.9
(N)	(78)[a]	(41)	(13)	(23)

a. Individual rank totals are less than 78 because there was one individual of unknown rank.

prosecutor influence on long range departmental interrogation policy. The upper-echelon Madison administrators distrusted the district attorney's ability to develop and communicate this type of policy. The police chief stressed instead the law enforcement profession's own expertise. The chief did initiate attempts to consult with other outside groups, such as the local board of judges, but *only* on relatively specific interrogation matters.

Perhaps because of their dependence on these law enforcement sources, Madison officers perceived that their sources of information were quite hostile. Only 12.8 percent of the force claimed that the sources had a favorable opinion about *Miranda*, and 76.9 percent of the superior officers perceived that their sources usually were critical of the decision. No other rank in any department was so unanimous in its perceptions of its sources' hostility toward *Miranda*.

Some changes in the communications process did occur in Madison. Generally these changes followed a pattern similar to that found in the other cities (see Table 8-6). Approximately the same, very low, percentage of officers in all four cities received information from entirely new sources as a result of *Miranda*. In the Madison departments, like the others, slightly less than half the men receive information from *some* new sources. In regard to rank differences, the Madison department generally follows the pattern of Green Bay and Racine, where detectives were least likely to receive information from new sources, or rather than the pattern of Kenosha where detectives were more likely to receive such information. Like Racine, the lack of increase in new sources, especially on the part of detectives, may be attributed to the fact that such sources were used prior to *Miranda*.

Police Perceptions and Attitudes

In spite of its relatively high degree of department professionalization and the high degree of impinging group activity, few Madison police officers anticipated the changes made by the Court in *Miranda*. The chief had not expected the Court to make such a decision. He did not know that the Court had been considering a case involving the issue ultimately decided in *Miranda*. Only 12.8 percent of the force expected the Court to make a *Miranda*-type of decision. Surprisingly, this is *lower* than any of the other three departments. Only one of 23 detectives (4.3 percent), 2 of 13 supervisors (15.4) and 6 of 41 patrolmen (14.6) said that they expected this decision. Certainly the degree of group activity did not seem to increase significantly the officers' amenability to anticipation of legal change.

Even though the decision was seldom anticipated, the officers saw a relatively small degree of change elicited by *Miranda* (see Table 8-7). Thirty-two percent of the department perceived a resulting great or very great change in their jobs; only among the Green Bay officers is there a smaller percentage. Racine and Madison detectives are virtually the same in this regard.

In their attitudes about the decision, however, all ranks of Madison officers differed from their counterparts in other cities. A whopping 35.9 percent of the department approved of the decision. This number is twice as large as Racine's, the next highest. Furthermore, there is not a very great difference between ranks; 31.7 percent of the patrolmen, 46.2 of the superiors and 39.1 of the detectives registered approval. The percentage of approving detectives is not too much larger than the percentage of such detectives in the other departments; but the other Madison ranks are far more approving than

Table 8-7. Rank and Perceptions of Extent *Miranda* Changed One's Own Job
(Madison), in Percentages

| | | | RANK | |
Change	All	Patrolman	Superior	Detective
Great or very great	32.0	26.9	15.4	52.2
Some	59.0	65.9	61.5	43.5
None	6.4	4.9	23.1	0.0
Don't know	2.6	2.4	0.0	4.3
TOTAL	100.0	100.0	100.0	100.0
(N)	(78)[a]	(41)	(13)	(23)

a. Individual rank totals are less than 78 because there was one person of unknown rank.
Total may not equal 100.0 percent because of rounding.

are their counterparts.[18] As police reformers would expect, the most professionalized department gives the greatest amount of approval to the *Miranda* decision. Unlike our expectations, however, this approval attitude did not develop as a result of greater anticipation that such a decision would be made. The combination of a highly professionalized department and a milieu of highly active interest groups did not foster such anticipation.

One important reason for the greater approval is that the department had a relatively greater amount of knowledge about the procedures *Miranda* does *not* proscribe. The knowledge of the basic rudiments of the decision was again quite great (see Table 8-8), but in addition over 60 percent of the officers were aware that they can still ask a person to come voluntarily to the police station (item 5). Almost the same percentage of each rank was aware of this possibility. A comparatively high percentage of Madison officers (53.8) understood that a policeman may still talk to some people without giving them the *Miranda* warning. Compared to item 5, there is greater inter-rank difference in regard to the understanding of the acceptance of this latter procedure. Patrolmen were less likely to recognize its legality. Nevertheless, there was not only greater knowledge, but also greater inter-rank consensus, within the Madison department than there is within any of the other departments. This information had more effectively pervaded all ranks of Madison police officers.

Despite the difference in attitudes and knowledge the Madison department generally perceived effects of *Miranda* similar to those perceived by the less professionalized departments (see Table 8-9). As usual, increased education and new techniques of gathering evidence were the most common effects seen by all ranks. Of all the cities, Madison officers were most likely to declare that the *Miranda* decision made them more sympathetic toward suspects. The state attorney general and other advocates of police professionalization would have expected such a finding. On the other hand, next to the Green Bay detectives, the Madison investigators were most likely to declare that the decision results not in a deemphasis upon obtaining confessions but rather in an attempt to continue their use.

Unlike the case in other departments, some important educational changes actually did occur relatively quickly. The Madison department instituted a merit pay plan, a rather radical change regard-

Table 8-8.   Correct Perceptions of Stipulations in *Miranda* Decision (Madison), in Percentages

Stipulation	All	RANK Patrolman	Superior	Detective
(1) Must tell of right to remain silent	96.2	100.0	84.6	100.0
(2) Anything suspect says may be held against him	98.7	100.0	100.0	100.0
(3) Right to attorney if he wants one	97.4	97.6	100.0	100.0
(4) If indigent, can have attorney appointed at court expense	96.2	97.6	100.0	95.7
(5) Can still ask person to come voluntarily to the station	62.8	61.0	69.2	65.2
(6) Suspect must have an attorney whether he wants one or not	97.4	100.0	92.3	95.7
(7) Confessions no longer evidence	94.9	92.7	92.3	100.0
(8) May no longer talk to anyone without informing him of rights	53.8	96.3	69.2	60.0
(9) No wire tapping	92.3	90.2	92.3	95.7
(10) Voluntary confessions no longer legal source of information	93.6	90.2	100.0	95.7
(N)	(78)[a]	(41)	(13)	(23)

a. Individual rank totals are less than 78 because there was one person of unknown rank.

Table 8-9. Rank and Effects of *Miranda* on Own Job (Madison), in Percentages

			RANK		
	Effect	All	Patrolman	Superior	Detective
(1)	Better education and training	50.0	56.1	38.5	47.8
(2)	New methods of gathering evidence	48.7	53.7	38.5	47.8
(3)	Sympathy toward suspects	28.2	31.7	23.1	30.4
(4)	Spending more time explaining activities to community	19.3	12.2	23.1	30.4
(5)	New methods to obtain confessions	15.3	12.2	0.0	30.4
(6)	More closely observed by people outside department	7.7	4.9	15.4	8.7
(7)	More attention to others in the field of criminal justice	2.6	4.9	0.0	0.0
	(N)	(78)[a]	(41)	(13)	(23)

a. Individual rank totals are less than 70 because there was one person of unknown rank.
Total may be greater than 100 percent because each officer could give two responses.

ing the formal (as opposed to in-service) education of their officers. As a result of this plan the pay scales of officers no longer depend purely on rank and seniority. Under the new plan, officers may receive extra pay commensurate with their attendance at a college or with credits earned from another similar institution. Specialized training is also rewarded. Seniority continues to serve as a criterion for salary, but its importance is diminished. This plan was not adopted until four months after the questionnaire in this study was administered. Nevertheless, the merit pay plan had been under consideration for some time, and we can assume that prior to its formal inception many officers were aware of it. Certainly, in Madison more than in any other department, the officers' perceptions of educational change is supported by observable and significant change. This change emphasizes specialization and higher education, while it decreased emphasis on seniority. Unquestionably such emphasis reflects the acceptance of values of professionalization.

But there is further evidence which might be disconcerting to advocates of police professionalization. Only 7.7 percent of the department claimed that because of *Miranda* they were now more closely observed from the outside. Superiors seemed a little more likely to experience this change, but none of the detectives or superiors claimed that he now pays more attention to others. This lack of change might be attributed to the relatively great amount of police-group interaction already existing in Madison prior to *Miranda*. The three departments with the highest levels of participation were all less likely to perceive this effect than was the Green Bay department. On the other hand, it has been shown that much of these groups' activities in response to *Miranda* did not answer some important questions raised by the police. In fact the Madison process of disseminating information about *Miranda* is a curious combination of characteristics. Some of these characteristics were associated with well-established lines of communication between the police and other groups, while other segments of the process reflected an *increase* in the very inbreeding supposedly characteristic of the less professionalized, more isolated police agencies.

Conclusion

In several ways, the Madison department's response to *Miranda* was unique. Moreover, this uniqueness reflected characteristics expected of a professionalized department with a high level of participation. Approval of the decision was relatively frequent. Greater information about *Miranda* was disseminated to *all* ranks. Outside specialized sources (though not local officials) were more accessible. Madison officers generally knew more about the decision than did their counterparts. The adoption of a merit pay plan quite explicitly reflects the values of professionalization. Other groups had previously attempted to professionalize and formalize some parts of the criminal justice process related to *Miranda*, and after *Miranda* their new attempts were more complete than those in any other city.

A "professionalized" response did not guarantee great amenability to the advice of non-police groups, even in a community with generally intense group activity in the criminal justice area. Local officials like the district attorney and municipal judges played an exceedingly minor role in the advisement of the police even, as in the case of the local judges, when certain police officials desired such help. None of these groups successfully aided the Madison department in anticipating the decision. Madison is a community where the ethos of professionalization and some types of group participation seem extremely, if not uniquely, strong and interrelated. Yet local groups do not impinge upon possibly the most important process of communicating information. Outside law enforcement agencies, that is, the FBI, have a virtual monopoly on discussions of this aspect of police behavior.

The evidence strongly suggests that a highly professionalized department is not necessarily amenable to effective participation by outside groups. In fact professionalization may discourage such participation. The next chapter, the first of two which more explicitly compare the consequences of *Miranda*, looks more closely at this possibility.

NOTES

1. Robert R. Alford with the collaboration of Harry M. Scoble, *Bureaucracy and Participation* (Chicago: Rand McNally, 1969), 13-16, 96-154.

2. The crime data came from the following sources: *Uniform Crime Reports—1966*, 78-90, and *Annual Statistical Report—Madison Police Department—1966* (Madison: Madison Police, 1966), 28. Again it should be remembered that the comparative *Uniform Crime Report* data cited in this study are computed according to crimes reported both in the city and the surrounding county, *i.e.*, the data measure crime in "standard metropolitan statistical areas."

3. Neal Milner, "The Impact of *Gideon*—A Study of the State and Local Judicial Process." Unpublished M.A. thesis, University of Wisconsin, 1965, 129-31.

4. "Indigents in Criminal Cases," Resolution by subcommittee on Counsel, Dane County Bar Association, November 13, 1963, quoted in Milner, *op. cit.*, 140.

5. *Wisconsin State Journal* (Madison), December 1, 1966.

6. The Ford Foundation through the National Defenders Project will pay part of the expenses, and the County will pay the remainder.

7. "Rules of County Board of Judges of Dane County," January 11, 1963.

8. Letter from Janet B. Courtney, State of Wisconsin Judicial Council to author, October 6, 1967.

9. Two participants at that meeting directly quoted the judges saying this, and others talked about the incident in a similar manner.

10. *Capital Times*, June 14, 1966.

11. *Wisconsin State Journal*, June 21, 1966.

12. *Wisconsin State Journal*, June 22, 1966.

13. *Wisconsin State Journal*, June 29, 1966.

14. *Capital Times*, February 18, 1967.

15. *Wisconsin State Journal*, April 10, 1967.

16. Madison Police Department, "Inter-Departmental Correspondence," August 22, 1966.

17. Another incident, told to me by a district attorney during the first few months after *Miranda*, gives a clearer picture of the chief's lack of confidence in the prosecutor. The department had trouble with searches, and, as a result, the chief wrote the FBI for legal advice. When the district attorney offered the services of his staff to help solve these

search and seizure problems, the chief replied, evidently in all sincerity, "Do you know anything about it?"

18. Because of the relatively smaller sample of Madison officers (see Appendix), some of this disparity between Madison and other cities may be explained by sampling error. The sample may be biased because those who approved of *Miranda* were possibly more willing to complete the questionnaire. But *even if every man who did not complete the questionnaire did so, and disapproved of the decision, the percentage of approvers would still be higher than any other department.*

Chapter 9

ATTITUDES, PERCEPTIONS, PROFESSIONALIZATION, AND PARTICIPATION
A Comparative Analysis

Advocates of police professionalization, as we saw in Chapter 3, were certainly interested in having the police develop a positive attitude toward the *Miranda* decision. Presumably increased professionalization, along with greater interaction by local groups, increases the likelihood that police approve of *Miranda*. We have already introduced some evidence to support this view. The degree of approval of *Miranda* varies directly with the degree of professionalization and participation.

Initially, a brief summary of the supposed, and partially demonstrated, effects of professionalization and participation is appropriate. According to police reformers the process of professionalization creates an organizational environment amenable to innovation, particularly when the innovation involves adoption of the Rule of Law as a job constraint. Greater participation on the part of outside groups facilitates the acceptance of such innovation. The previous case studies illustrate that a high degree of professionalization and a high level of participation do not necessarily develop simultaneously. Indeed, in the most professionalized Madison department, that characteristic was an important factor in limiting participation levels. From this we can develop—and to some extent investigate—a hypothesis which, if valid, modifies the rather sanguine view many police reformers have about the congruity of the two key variables: professionalization increases the amenability to outside groups primarily if these groups furnish information which is consistent with the professionalization norms.

In order to look more closely at this hypothesis we must take a closer look at the officers' attitudes and perceptions regarding *Miranda*. First, we investigate the extent to which an ideology consistent with professionalization is apparent in the officers' more general perceptions about the *Miranda* decision. Next, we take a closer look at the difference between those who approve and those who disapprove of *Miranda*. Finally, we attempt to hypothesize further about the relationship between the two variables and response to *Miranda*.

In this study professionalization has been used not as a measure of individual officers but rather as a measure of whole departments. Thus, for the most part, we cannot really compare *individual* officers on the basis of the extent of their *own* professionalization. Instead we must compare them only on the basis of the degree of professionalization of the milieu in which the police officers work. We can also investigate the frequencies of certain responses which seem characteristic of professionalized officers. These should be most prevalent in Madison, next most prevalent in Racine, less in Kenosha, and least in Green Bay.

A milieu which stresses higher professionalization should include an ideology which reinforces this dominant ethos, particularly if groups impinging on the organization also accept this ideology or ethos. The opposite effect might be expected in Green Bay and Kenosha where the organizational context deemphasizes and even discourages professionalization. A highly professionalized department, then, would be expected to have more officers who have an ideology consistent with the norms of professionalization. This ideology is called professionalism.[1] (The criteria for professionalism are further refined later in the chapter.) In order to illuminate the relationship between professionalization and *Miranda's* impact, we shall see whether the frequency of a professionalized view of *Miranda* varied according to the degree of departmental professionalization. Advocates of police professionalization would expect to find positive relationship between the two.

At the outset one must remember that no attempt was made to observe systematically the difference in *behavior* between those who approved and those who disapproved of *Miranda*. Here we deal almost completely with the relationship between professionalization and attitudes.

Perceptions about Miranda

The following data are taken from the last question on the questionnaire presented to all police officers in the four communities (see Appendix A). Unlike the others, this question was purposely kept open-ended so that the officer would have at least one opportunity to discuss in some detail his perceptions and attitudes about *Miranda*. The question reads as follows:

> If you so desire, please make any other comments about the *Miranda* rule. Why, for example, do you think the Supreme Court decided the *Miranda* case the way it did?

Of the 270 coded responses to the questionnaire, 161 chose to answer this question.[2] Most of these respondents discussed both their attitudes toward the decision and why they thought the Court made the *Miranda* decision.

Professionalism is defined in a way that would seem consistent with the themes commonly emphasized by those who advocate it among police departments. A police officer with professionalism should fulfill one or both of the following criteria:

> 1. His perceived reasons for the Court's decision should be roughly consistent with the reasons usually given by advocates of police professionalization. In other words, he should mention the Court's desire for stricter, more formal police guidelines or its desire to protect citizen's rights, but should not attribute this desire to a lack of realism. (This does not necessarily mean that he specifically approves of the decision.)

> 2. He should specifically approve of the decision on the grounds that it will improve the police profession.

The following are the most important themes appearing in these responses. They generally show a low level of legal sophistication and an almost complete emphasis on efficiency as opposed to Rule of Law aspects of criminal-justice administration.

LACK OF UNDERSTANDING OF POLICE WORK

The most frequently mentioned conceptualization of the Court's *Miranda* decision very clearly demonstrates that many policemen see a difference between police and legal perspective. The Justices are given little credit for understanding the job of the police officer.

Approximately 45 percent of the responses could be classified under this category. This theme has two levels of abstraction. First, about half of these officers generally criticize the Court for its failure to appreciate the consequences of the decision on society. As one officer stated, "The honest, the good, the meek of society will suffer losses untold at the hands of the criminal because of this decision." The *Miranda* rule obstructs justice and encourages criminals because of the protection it provides. Among advocates of this viewpoint there is little doubt that the decision "pushes the pendulum too far" in favor of the "criminal" at the expense of the innocent, law-abiding citizen. One patrolman succinctly summarizes the viewpoint in the following way:

> They [the Justices] thought innocent persons were being unduly harassed, forgetting the general public has the right to protest if they felt they were being harassed. Also they are protecting the criminal's rights. There is nothing in the rule about the rights of the innocent public.

The law-abiding majority, especially the injured party, is flaunted, and only law breakers benefit. The Court, however, is seldom accused of willfully aiding the criminal. Instead the Justices are perceived as misguided idealists who have inadvertently harmed society. Or, in the words of an experienced detective, "This ruling must have been decided without properly realizing the rights of victims of crimes." The end result, whether desired by the Court or not, is increasing crime in the streets.

The second level of this theme emphasizes in more specific terms the Court's lack of understanding of the police officer's perspective and problems. In the words of a young patrolman,

> It is obvious that some of our Supreme Court Justices are not familiar with the complexities of everyday police work. They can make decisions, by a very small margin, that can completely undo what police officers have to spend many days to accomplish. We should put our nine Supreme Court Justices in a few police departments to show them a few problems of common everyday police work.

The Justices have not merely lost sight of the problems of police departments. They have made at best only a feeble attempt to discover the nature of these problems.

There are many variations on this theme. The Court is accused of operating with a presumption of guilt against the police officer. The officers insist that the Justices overemphasize the extent of police brutality and underestimate the obstacles found by the police officer in performing his public duty. Those critics feel that society has, unfortunately, a group of Justices too intent on protecting the rights of the criminal. Because of this emphasis and corresponding lack of "realism," the police cannot do their job effectively. These officers have no doubt that greater exposure to police departments would change the Court's perspective.

The decision raises particular resentment among those who claim that it punishes many innocent police departments because of the misdeeds of one or two:

> As a professional, well trained police officer, I strongly resent being handcuffed by the Supreme Court for the misdeeds of my fellow officers. I feel that the pendulum of justice which seems to swing so far left in favor of the criminal, may some day swing far right in favor of the police. This is something no honest policemen desires either.

In sum: I do not use duress to obtain a confession, nor do other members of my department. Therefore we should continue to operate with the pre-*Miranda* procedures. These men deny the validity of the argument that all interrogations are coercive enough to require formal rules.

Others are more explicit in their critique of the decision. Good, efficient police work suffers at the hands of this misguided decision because of its proscription of the use of indispensable tools. An experienced detective put it this way:

> I believe a man's right should be protected, however, I believe the police should be able to question a person without advising him of rights. Police work has been mostly bluff in the past and now you have nothing. The very good aspect of being a detective was to match wits with the criminal. Now that can't be done.

The officer is unfairly and unnecessarily forced to change his behavior in regard to police interrogation. Both the police and the rest of society suffer at the hands of the Justices who in effect unrealistically interfere with the policeman who, after all, can best judge his own job. This common viewpoint is particularly interesting because it closely parallels what Skolnick found to be typical police reactions to legal sanctions on police behavior. According to Skolnick the police consider themselves craftsmen with enough expertise and ability to determine innocence or guilt. He further found that this police conception of the law enforcement role leads the officer to view criminal law, with its presumption of innocence, as unrealistic. The officer believes he would not take action against an innocent person, and has great faith in his presumption of guilt.[3] Significantly, this presumption of guilt is almost unanimously acknowledged by the officers who accuse the Court of a lack of understanding about the problems of crime or law enforcement. *Never* is the word "suspect" used in the officers' comments. Only two of the hostile responses even used the somewhat generous phrase "the accused" to describe the suspect. "Criminal" and "guilty party" are the overwhelmingly predominant words. The *Miranda* decision "lets the criminals go free." It "makes it easier for the criminals." "The guilty party" has too many rights. The "rights of the guilty" predominate over the "rights of the innocent."

A police officer thus assumes that the suspect is guilty not because of malice but because of qualifications which, he feels, entitle him to make this assumption. In the opinion of such officers, one which seems most prevalent, the Justices do not consider either the "realities" of police work or the competence of police to deal with these "realities." Again the words of an officer (an inspector with 25 years of experience) best express the perceived differences between the Court's view and the officers' view. After agreeing quite explicitly that all officers must obey the decision, the inspector goes on to say:

> Naturally, the police officer feels that he is operating under a disadvantage. They feel that most of the protection is being afforded to the criminal without any regard for the rights of the innocent. *Certainly only the criminal would take advantage of the Miranda decision, the innocent need not worry* [emphasis added].

OBJECTION TO LEGAL
PROCEDURES AND PRACTITIONERS

About 16 percent of the responses reflect more explicit objection to the legal *procedures* used by the Court. These objections do not show a very high level of sophistication about the legal process. They again reflect quite obviously the difference between legal and police perspective.

This police perspective toward the legal process is manifested in several ways. The Justices are, first of all, criticized because, in making the decision, they *made* rather than interpreted law. As one detective said critically, "I feel that the Supreme Court is trying to make legislation by judicial decree." The Justices are castigated because they have acted in a manner which, in the eyes of the officers, reflects an improper *judicial* role. As a corollary, the Court is accused of destroying the certainty of the law so clearly established by our founding fathers. In example are the words of a young patrolman:

> For as long as our land has been, we have lived by the constitution and the bill of rights of man. Now we must live by what someone thinks it means. This is done by adding words and ideas that our Supreme Court inserted.

The Court, then, is wrong for "toying with the law," and changing the presumably immutable meaning of the original Constitution. None of these officers presents an argument explicitly based on precedents. No other decisions are cited. These officers simply feel that the Court's function was to discover the unchanging law. This perspective characterizes an acceptance of what Jerome Frank called the "basic myth" about the legal process.[4] Furthermore, the rhetoric is similar to that used many times by other critics of the Court.[5]

Six officers questioned the legitimacy of the decision because the Justices themselves were in such disagreement. Each of these men mentions that the outcome of the decision was only by the barest of margins and that a single vote should not be decisive in legal matters. If the Justices cannot agree on interpretation, surely the interpretation must be suspect.[6] For example,

> I feel any Supreme Court decision which is based on a 5 to 4 decision leaves much to be desired! When 9 learned men can't agree, the rule is open to debate.

The activities of the lawyers are criticized almost as often as are the activities of the Justices. To those officers (12 in all) who criticize lawyers, the *Miranda* decision increased the opportunity of the legal profession to take advantage of "loopholes" and/or to make money at the expense of the public. The *Miranda* decision gives the wily attorney further opportunity to find what the police disapprovingly call "technicalities" in order to free their guilty clients. These attorneys distort the actual characteristics of police behavior. They are not, as attorneys would probably argue, using newly granted constitutional procedures, but rather "getting around the law." Some officers go so far as to say that the decision could conceivably protect the citizen, but attorneys have destroyed this benefit by using the decision for their own selfish ends. What are these selfish goals? As the two following comments show, these ends usually involve money:

> It [the *Miranda* decision] appears to be a selfish effort by the legal community to make their profession as indispensable as medicine without the responsibility to a statute.

> Politics—it's just another way for the lawyers to gouge the public out of more money!

Like the officers who stress the Court's lack of understanding of the problem of crime, these officers perceive a great difference between what they consider and what other participants in the criminal-justice process consider to be legitimate legal procedures. In sum, there is indeed a great and recognized difference among Court, lawyer, and police perspectives in regard to *Miranda*. These responses suggest that the disparity between the two viewpoints may have increased after *Miranda*. Police recognition of legal uncertainty may well create or increase a negative attitude toward criminal law and its administration.

LACK OF RELATED ISSUE CONTENT

Fourteen percent of the officers responded in a manner devoid of any information about the interrogation process itself. Slightly less than half (9) of these officers see the decision as part of a rather insidious civil rights revolution. Some specifically blame civil rights organizations. Others merely mention that the Court seems to be so concerned with protection of these rights that they have developed a tendency to go too far in favor of minority groups. The decision is part of the trend exemplified by emphasis on civil rights, minority group activities, and civilian review boards. This trend, in the officers' opinion, will destroy law and order.

Of the remaining fourteen officers whose responses were classified under this theme, seven criticized the morals and general competence of the Justices. These comments have little specific issue content. A typical example is a patrolman who says that the Justices "should have their head(s) examined." Four others, including a superior officer and two detectives, feel that the decision was made as part of an increasingly active Communist plot to destroy law and order. Three others suggest that the Court made the decision because it was involved in some kind of conspiracy, probably with organized crime.

PROFESSIONALISM

There is a significant number of officers who do seem to view the reasons for change in terms of a professionalism ideology. Twenty-five percent of the officers might be so classified. Such officers do not necessarily agree with the decision. The greatest number of these officers, 21 in all, believe that the Court so acted because of the need for stricter guidelines for police behavior. These men usually commented about police abuses without criticizing the Court for taking general action to protect individuals from them. In the words of a patrolman, the Court so acted because "too many police departments in the country were operating in a manner that deprived a citizen of a right to counsel."

Nineteen others are more explicit in their emphasis on the Court's desire to protect the rights of all individuals, whether guilty or not. The Court is not condemned for this desire. Moreover, the distinction is made between a guilty party and a suspect. The following comments serve as good examples:

> The Court made the decision to protect the average citizen who is usually unaware of his full rights, when arrested.

> . . . so a person's rights would not be violated. As a rule some people are not aware of their rights and also the rich and poor would have equal rights as well as the educated and uneducated.

Six others fit into our second sub-category relating the decision to the need for a more highly professionalized police department. Not all six completely approved of the immediate results of the decision. A young patrolman claims:

> I think they [the Justices] did it to protect the right of everyone and not to make it hard for us. But it has hurt some but in

the long run I think it just makes for better and more complete police work.

Professionalism is directly related to professionalization; 14 percent of the Green Bay officers, 23 percent of the Kenosha officers, 28 percent of the Racine department and 33 percent of the Madison officers had professionalized responses.

Approval of the Miranda Decision

Since professionalization is a rather vague concept, it would seem valuable to test the relationship between certain more specific professionalization criteria and response to *Miranda*. Again one should remember that this study's stress on the organization rather than the individual officer precluded much of this type of analysis. We can nevertheless test the relationship between one important criterion, formal education, and attitudes toward *Miranda*. Advocates of police reform usually assume that the more educated officer will have greater understanding of and thus a more positive attitude toward this innovation.

Approval of the decision was measured by questionnaire responses to the following question: "What is your personal opinion of the *Miranda* rule?" The officers could choose from four responses, varying from strong approval to strong disapproval. In the following analysis these categories are combined to include only approval versus disapproval. The approvers constitute a small minority; 19.6 percent (53) approve of *Miranda*, 78.9 percent (213) disapprove, and 1.5 percent (4) are undecided.

EDUCATION

Most advocates of police reform would expect a positive relationship between education and the degree of approval of a decision like *Miranda*. Table 9-1 suggests that this view is partially correct.

Those with some college are most likely to approve, but there is only a small difference between the response of the highest and the lowest educational levels. The high school graduates, who compose by far the larger group, were considerably less likely to approve. Other data suggest that college graduates are not too sympathetic about the rule. There were only six college graduates in the sample, so they were

Table 9-1. Degree of Education and Attitude toward *Miranda,* in Percentages

EDUCATION

Attitude	Some Highschool	Highschool Graduate	Some College or College Graduate
Approve	24.1	14.6	28.0
Disapprove	75.9	82.7	72.0
Don't know	0.0	2.7	0.0
Total	100.0	100.0	100.0
(N)	(29)	(151)	(75)

combined with those who had completed some college work. Of the six, only one approved of the decision.[7]

Table 9-2 gives an indication of the combined effects of education and length of service.

Only among the oldest and newest officers does education seem to be strongly related to attitudes. The responses of the newest officers are the most interesting. College men are almost five times more likely to approve of the decision than are those who at most were highschool graduates. Furthermore, there is a real polarization of attitudes in the group. Of all groups, non-college officers with less than five years' experience were least likely to approve, while their college-attending counterparts were the most approving.[8] Nevertheless, there is no consistent positive relationship between education and approval among those in the middle levels of tenure.

The importance of education is further minimized because in another way job experiences seems to have an effect on attitudes. The detectives, who have the most experience in interrogation procedures and still handle the bulk of such work, are almost twice as likely to approve of the decision as are the patrolmen. Twenty-nine percent of the detectives approve, compared to 16.1 percent of the patrolmen and 22.4 percent of the superiors. This greater approval among detectives is not related to increased formal education. There is not a great difference between the percentage of patrolmen with some college (26.3 percent) and the percentage of detectives with such education (30.6). Moreover, in regard to approval, there is only less than 1 percent difference between college-educated detectives and less-educated detectives.

KNOWLEDGE AND SOURCES OF INFORMATION

Formal education itself does not seem to be an important factor, but we still might hypothesize that those who approve of the decision know more about the decision than those who disapprove. The data bear out this hypothesis. The approvers are more likely to identify correctly the procedures *not* proscribed by *Miranda*. Over 45 percent of the approvers understand that an officer can still talk to some people without advising them of *Miranda* stipulations. Only 33.8 percent of the disapprovers show this understanding. Slightly over 60 percent of the approvers, as compared to 40.8 percent of the disapprovers, correctly perceive that an officer may still ask a person to come voluntarily to the police station. Although the great majority of both groups continue to recognize the possible validity of some confessions, 10.2 percent of the disapprovers and only 3.8 percent of the approvers feel that *Miranda* invalidated all confessions. Because of the smallness of the cells, we cannot really look at the inter-city difference between the approvers. If we compare Madison with the combined non-Madison approvers (and the data suggest this comparison is not misleading), about one-third of the non-Madison approvers as opposed to 55 percent of the Madison approvers correctly understand that an officer can still talk to an individual without advising him of his rights. About half the non-Madison approvers as compared to 62 percent of the Madison approvers correctly perceive that an officer may still ask a person to come voluntarily to a police station. Thus, in this regard the non-Madison approvers are more like the disapprovers than they are like the Madison approvers.

The approvers are also more likely to think that the *Miranda* decision is quite clear in its pronouncements. Over 92 percent of the approvers think the decision is a clear one; 73.3 percent of the disapprovers think so. Better than 23 percent of those who find the decision lucid approve of it, while only 5.9 percent of those finding *Miranda* unclear approve of the Court's ruling.

The relationship between approval and knowledge may be further strengthened by the fact that approvers are considerably more likely to anticipate the Court's decision. Almost one-quarter

Table 9-2. Length of Service, Education, and Attitude Toward *Miranda*, in Percentages

LENGTH OF SERVICE	5 years or less		6-9 years		10-19 years		20 years or more	
Amount of Education	*Highschool graduate or less*	*At least some College*	*Highschool graduate or less*	*At least some College*	*Highschool graduate or less*	*Some College*	*Highschool graduate or less*	*Some College*
Approve	9.6	45.5	22.2	23.8	20.4	13.6	17.5	37.5
Disapprove	90.4	54.5	77.8	76.2	79.6	86.4	82.5	62.5
Total	100.0	100.0	100.0	100.0	100.0	100.0	100.0	100.0
	(N=32)	(N=22)	(N=27)	(N=23)	(N=54)	(N=22)	(N=40)	(N=8)

Total N less than 266 because some men did not indicate their length of service, education, or attitude.

of the approvers had expected the Court to make such a decision. This was twice the number of disapprovers who anticipated the decision. Almost 32 percent of those who had anticipated *Miranda* approve, but only 16.2 percent of those who had not expected such a decision approve.

There is, however, no difference in the average number of sources of information received by each group. Both approvers and disapprovers received information from an average of 5.6 sources. Both groups rank the best sources of information in a similar manner (see Table 9-3). The training session conference is most frequently chosen by each group.

When all of the sources, rather than just the best sources, are considered, there are some differences between approvers and disapprovers. Those differences involve information from two sources, the attorney general and the training sessions. Differences in access to both the attorney general and the Supreme Court opinion can be explained by conditions peculiar to Madison. In regard to the attorney general, more approvers (56.6 percent) received information from this source than did disapprovers (40.4); the disproportionate number of Madison approvers explains the difference. Over 71 percent of the Madison approvers compared to only 41 percent of the disapprovers used this source.

Conferences and training sessions are, on the surface, the only source of information which cannot be explained by conditions peculiar to Madison. Over 90 percent (90.6) of the approvers and only 69.5 percent of the disapprovers received *Miranda* information from these sessions. Looking at it another way, we find that 24.2 percent of those who received information from this source approve of the decision, while only 6.9 percent of those not attending approve of *Miranda*. There is no difference between Madison approvers and those of other cities in regard to frequency of attendance at these sessions, but there was an important difference in the types of training sessions that were held.

The Madison department's *Miranda* training sessions were not only more pervasive but also relied more completely on the FBI. As pointed out in Chapter 2, the FBI's emphasis was on interrogation behavior *not* proscribed by the *Miranda* decision. Madison officers, most likely to identify the limits of the constraints, were more likely to approve because their training sessions minimized the impact.

Table 9-3.   Attitude Toward *Miranda* and Best Sources of Information, in
             Percentages

	ATTITUDE	
Best Sources	*Approvers*	*Disapprovers*
TV, radio	1.9	4.2
District Attorney	9.4	6.1
Police officer not a superior	0.0	0.0
Superior officer	9.4	8.9
Newspapers	7.5	7.5
Magazines not specializing in police activities	1.9	3.8
Magazines specializing in police activities	3.8	3.8
Conferences, training sessions	39.6	35.2
Supreme Court opinion	13.2	12.2
Attorney General	13.2	13.1
Local judge	0.0	1.9
Other	0.0	3.1
TOTAL	100.0	100.0
(N)	(53)	(213)

Total may not equal 100.0 percent because of rounding.

On the surface, it appears that professionalism generally was related to approval. Thirty-five percent of the men who discussed *Miranda* with an ideology of professionalism approved of the decision, as compared to only about 17 percent of the other men. But when we control for the city, we again find that these Madison officers were quite different even from the non-Madison officers who displayed professionalism. Only one officer with professionalism approved of *Miranda* in each of the cities except Madison. In Madison, however, *eleven of fifteen or 73 percent* of officers with professionalism approved of the decision.

These distinctions between Madison and non-Madison officers might lead one to emphasize local factors rather than professionalization and participation. There is, however, a plausible explanation which again shows the importance of these two variables.

The findings followed the expected patterns with regard to the relationship among professionalization, participation, and approval, as well as the relationship among professionalization, participation, and professionalism (an ideology consistent with a professionalized organization). The Madison department was most approving and showed the most professionalism, followed in order by Racine, Kenosha, and Green Bay. The Madison department was very different from the other three departments in regard to its manifestation of a *positive* relationship between professionalism and approval. Compared to the approvers in the other three cities, the approving officers in Madison also had much greater access to the most important state-wide advocate of this reform, the state attorney general. This is precisely the type of source that advocates of police professionalization would expect to be influential, and its influence was also in the expected direction. On the other hand, the reformers might not expect the other important difference between Madison and non-Madison approvers. The Madison training process generally placed much greater reliance on the FBI and not on outside non-law enforcement sources. The FBI training sessions were quite explicit in discussing the interrogation behavior still possible. Reflecting this influence, officers in the Madison department more frequently recognized these limits. Again the approvers in the other departments were more like the disapprovers in this regard.

In sum, the Madison department differs in degree of professionalism, degree of approval, correctness of its perceptions, and in the nature of some sources of information. We must be extremely cautious in interpreting these findings, especially in regard to attributing causality. Nonetheless, a relationship seems quite plausible among professionalization, participation, and the Madison response. Both the attorney general and the FBI seemed more accessible to the Madison department. The attorney general was more accessible to the approving, professionalized Madison officers because he viewed *Miranda* in terms of professionalization and professionalism (see Chapter 3). Thus his participation reinforced existing professional ideology in the department. The FBI, a far more important source for Madison, was influential because the more professionalized department consequently was more likely to use it as a reference group. Like the attorney general, the FBI discussed the need for professionalization, but the bureau was more interested in emphasizing the limits of *Miranda's* constraints.

The influence of these sources helps explain why the relationship among professionalization, professionalism, and approval is stronger in Madison. As the most professionalized department, Madison was more amenable to both sources of information although the amenability to each source was for a different reason. The importance of the FBI suggests that professionalization greatly increases the importance of law enforcement sources and that the professionalized and approving officers are amenable to outside sources like the attorney general when such sources reinforce a professional ideology.

Conclusion

Conclusions about the process by which professionalization affects police behavior must remain tentative and must await more thorough comparison of the attitudes and behavior of professionalized and non-professionalized police officers. The present analysis suggests at least that police professionalization is related to the milieu or the context of communications which departments use in their response to *Miranda*. In this chapter we have not discussed the changes effected by the *Miranda* decision as much as we have discussed the factors related to these changes. On the basis of the preceding analysis we can nevertheless conclude that responses to *Miranda* innovations are related to the extent to which a police organization contains a milieu and dominant ideology which sanctions professionalization. Participation levels are also important, because the success which groups have in communicating their norms about professionalization seemed to affect the extent to which further professionalization and bureaucratization were adopted as means of implementing *Miranda*.

Five factors limit the positive relationship between professionalization and response to innovation. First, only a minority of officers, even in the Madison department, approved. Second, inbred law enforcement sources increase in importance as a department becomes more professionalized. Although there was no strong conflict between the views of the dominant FBI and those of the attorney general, such conflict could readily occur. Indeed there is some evidence that serious conflict has developed in regard to FBI influence on police views of the civil rights movement.[8] Third, Madison, which stood out in its approval on professionalism, also stood out in its lack of anticipation. Perhaps the dominant sources of information in this department deemphasized the need to anticipate. This also could be troublesome in the future. Fourth, greater formal education—a favorite remedy for all sorts of police response to social change—was only weakly related to approval of *Miranda*. The data suggest that on-the-job influences were more important. Finally, as shall be emphasized in the next chapter, some important—perhaps most important—changes do not occur in any of the departments. When the goals of the Court as reflected in *Miranda's* majority opinion are used as standards of compliance, certain police behavior seems noncompliant, and professionalization, furthermore, did not increase compliance.

NOTES

1. H. M. Vollmer and D. G. Mills, "Introduction," in H. M. Vollmer and D. G. Mills, *Professionalization* (Englewood Cliffs, N.J.: Prentice-Hall, 1966), vii-viii.

2. The following shows by department each total response and the response to this question.

City	Percent of Total Response	Percent of Response on *General* Miranda open-ended Question	Difference
Green Bay	26	27	+1
Kenosha	24	24	0
Racine	22	20	−2
Madison	29	30	+1
Total	100	100	

3. See Jerome H. Skolnick, *Justice Without Trial* (New York: Wiley, 1966), 197.

4. Jerome Frank, *Law and the Modern Mind* (Garden City: Anchor, 1963), 3-13. For an interesting discussion of assumptions accompanying various models of constitutional change, see Glendon Schubert, "The Rhetoric of Constitutional Change," *Journal of Public Law* 16 (1967), 16-50.

5. Walter Murphy, *Congress and the Court* (Chicago: University of Chicago, 1962.)

6. In a discussion of compliance with the Supreme Court's school prayer decisions, Johnson also found that this argument was sometimes made on the part of persons who disagreed with the decision. "In this sense then," he goes on to say, "a dissenting opinion can—like a majority opinion—exist as a symbol to legitimate one's position, and it may be disfunctional as far as stimulation of complaint behavior and attitudinal change is concerned." Richard M. Johnson, *The Dynamics of Compliance* (Evanston: Northwestern, 1967), 56.

7. One former advocate of the usual police reforms, who has become disillusioned with their success, has specifically questioned the effectiveness of greater formal education in making better police forces. See Burton Levy, "Cops in the Ghetto: A Problem of the Police System," in Louis H. Masotti and Don R. Bowen, *Riots and Rebellion* (Beverly Hills:

Sage, 1968), 351. The data in this study suggest that Levy's view is worth attention. See also Jerome H. Skolnick, *The Politics of Protest* (New York: Ballantine, 1969).

8. This finding is potentially significant enough to be worth further investigation with better data. We can only speculate that this may result from at least two factors. First, there is now a greater difference between college and non-college men. Second, perhaps as job experience increases, other factors common to all policemen become more important determining attitudes. This would explain why attitudes become more homogeneous, but one must note that, among those with the greatest length of service, education again makes a difference. The latter conclusion is limited because of the small number of college-attending policemen with at least twenty years of experience.

Chapter 10

MIRANDA'S IMPACT
ON INTERROGATION BEHAVIOR

Finally, we must investigate what is perhaps the most important facet of the *Miranda* decision, its effect on police interrogation behavior. The importance of this question is reflected by the fact that virtually all of the other studies of the impact of *Miranda* have concentrated on this area, although none of them has really been comparative.[1] The data for this analysis come from four sources: observation of interrogations, additional interviews with detectives and other local informants, crime and guilty plea data, and, to a lesser extent, survey data from the questionnaire. The analysis is limited somewhat for lack of available statistics on the number of confessions obtained either prior to or after *Miranda* was handed down. Also, the techniques and resources used to observe interrogations limited the actual number of observed interrogations. Most of the observed interrogations occurred in the station house or in jail rather than in the field, and detectives did most of the observed interrogating.[2]

This chapter continues the investigation of the relationship among professionalization, participation, and impact. It should be emphasized again that the study is too preliminary in nature to test very explicit hypotheses. Instead, as in previous chapters, some general assumptions often associated with advocates of police professionalization are tested. They are as follows:

1. More professionalized departments more easily adjust to the formalization of procedures required by the *Miranda* innovation.

2. As a consequence of *Miranda*, more professionalized departments are more likely to refrain from using interrogation as means of obtaining evidence.

3. Because of their greater abilities to adjust to innovation, more professionalized departments should show relative stability in the number of crimes they clear by arrest. (See the discussion of clearance rates in Chapter 1.)

Assumption three might appear to contradict the other two. If more professionalized departments make greater adjustments, then it would seem likely that their clearance rates would be most affected. In the *Miranda* majority opinion, Chief Justice Warren seemed—at least implicitly—somewhat sanguine about this contradiction. He appeared to suggest that effective police work would not be hampered by the adoption of the new interrogation procedures.[3] This possible contradiction will also be considered in the subsequent analysis.

Formalization of Procedures—With Local Option

INTERROGATION TECHNIQUES

In all departments the *Miranda* decision led to the adoption of two new procedures which conceivably affected police interrogation behavior directly:

(1) The adoption of a statement of rules and procedures which all interrogators must present to their suspects;

(2) The requirement that attorneys must be allowed to be present at the interrogation.

According to virtually all informants, after *Miranda* the police in the four cities paid more attention to the need to regularize the first of these procedures. Prior to *Miranda*, the extent and frequency of warnings of the right to remain silent varied according to circumstances. They were often given in a very perfunctory manner. Interrogators are now much more likely to advise suspects of their rights without arbitrarily deciding whether it is necessary. There is now a greater awareness of the formalization required by the legal restraints on police behavior. A veteran detective aptly described the change typical in all departments:

You know, I learn something new after every interrogation. I now know that if I go get the suspect coffee, or leave the room, I should record the time. Otherwise the suspect can say we held him for many hours. I guess the *Miranda* decision has made me more concerned about this.

There are, nevertheless, some important differences among the departments regarding the degree of formalization of this advisement procedure. These differences are partially related to the degree of professionalization and partially related to the amount of serious crime in the cities. The Green Bay police department did not even adopt a formalized statement of the *Miranda* rules to be read verbatim to all suspects. Such statements were adopted in the other departments. The format of their guidelines and rules varies somewhat. For example, the Madison department form gives a more thorough description of the stage at which the *Miranda* warning should be given and the way the procedures must be presented.

The departments follow an expected pattern. Green Bay, the least professionalized department, responded by means of procedures which were less regular or formal than those of the other departments. Madison's new procedures seemed slightly more formalized than those of any of the other organizations. But there was also less pressure for formalization in Green Bay because the department's workload was lighter. The crime rate was considerably lower in Green Bay, and the police simply had fewer reasons for routinizing the new procedures.

Green Bay's procedures also show there are still local police differences concerning the ways in which *Miranda* actually was implemented in the interrogation room. These differences are further reflected in the ways the organizations used to advise a suspect of his rights—and to record waiver of these rights and the subsequent incriminating statements. Although the departments differ in these procedures, one important similarity remains. Interrogators in all departments continue to exercise much informal discretion over the ways in which the *Miranda* procedures are used. This combination of local differences and officer discretion is apparent in the following detailed analysis of the relationship between interrogator and suspect.

Because of the relative paucity of interrogation, Green Bay will not be considered here, although there is indirect evidence to suggest that its interrogations also include a great deal of discretionary behavior.[4] Kenosha's procedures, however, offer a good case in point.

These procedures center around the use of a tape recorder to record interrogations. Confessions had been recorded prior to *Miranda*, but neither before nor after *Miranda* were the tapes actually presented as evidence. Instead, a transcript was prepared on the basis of the taped statement. Before the *Miranda* decision, the detectives were inconsistent, prior to making the recorded confession, in advising a suspect of his rights. *Miranda* did lead to a change in this procedure. Now interrogators must and do regularly warn their suspects of their rights before the tape is taken. Indeed one of the successful motions to suppress a confession on *Miranda* grounds was based on an interrogator's failure to advise a suspect of his rights until after the recording. But interrogators still have leeway *before* the taping session has begun. In the interrogation rooms the detective first advises the suspect of his rights. This stage is most important because, if the interrogator can initially get the suspect to waive his rights, he can then continue interrogation and ultimately "get a good tape."

The means of obtaining an initial waiver, though by no means devious, were quite subtle and worked to the disadvantage of an ignorant suspect. The usual warning was given with the implicit assumption that the right to counsel will be waived. This observer neither saw nor heard of any interrogation where the detectives discussed with the suspect the disadvantage of counsel, but at the same time the advantages of having an attorney were similarly not discussed. Furthermore, the suspect was given no more than a few seconds to decide on the desirability of counsel. The *Miranda* stipulations were read to him, and he was immediately asked whether or not he will waive. One has only to observe many of these suspects in order to appreciate their truly low level of knowledge about the implications of such waivers.

If the suspect refused to waive, the interrogation ended. If not, the interrogation, still not on tape, proceeded much the way it always did. The initial interaction between officer and suspect was in fact a type of dress rehearsal for the final performance. However, the final performance recorded none of the methods used to obtain the confession. What emerged on tape was a cut-and-dried version of the detective's merely asking questions he wishes to have answered and the suspect responding in a manner at least informally determined by the earlier interrogation. The confession was later signed by the suspect. Instead of furnishing an accurate account of the interrogation process, the tape presents a *fait accompli*.[5]

The Madison and Racine methods were similar to each other except that the Madison department had procedures requiring that a suspect write out his incriminating statement in his own hand, while in Racine the suspect ultimately signed a typed copy of his confession. Both of these procedures are remnants of pre-*Miranda* methods. In fact, as suggested earlier, the requirement that waiver of rights be formalized by the suspect's signature was also occasionally used prior to *Miranda* in all four departments. After *Miranda* this waiver procedure was further routinized.

The Madison and Racine interrogators also manifested the same discretionary behavior as their Kenosha counterparts. They were able quite frequently to induce waiver, not by refusing to furnish the suspect with information about the *Miranda* rules, but by virtually requiring that, on the basis of meager information about ramifications, a suspect make a decision about waiving his rights. After waiver, interrogation proceeded with some of the same techniques which even prior to *Miranda* could have been judged coercive, under certain circumstances. All of these techniques were used after the waiver but *prior* to the formal recording of the confession. The formal statement was thus often simply a rather sterile record.

Some observed interrogation techniques are as follows:[6]

1. Encouraging the suspect to get information off his chest: "Take the big step forward and clear up anything else you have on your mind. Make a clean breast of it. I can't help but feel there are other things you should clear up." [a Racine detective]

2. Suggesting leniency if the suspect confesses: "I can't promise you anything but the judge often looks more leniently at those who come clean." [a Kenosha detective]

3. Denigrating the importance of the formalities: "Listen, Bill, I have some questions to ask you, but first let me state this to you. [He then presents the *Miranda* warning.] We have to say that before you can talk." [Madison detective—interrogation in squad car]

4. Ignoring the procedures entirely [less frequent] "The other day some kid asked me why I didn't tell him his rights. I said, '[If] you want to know your rights, go read them in a book.'"

I'd as soon as lose a case as have to worry about this [*Miranda*] warning in every situation." [Madison detective—to author]

There are local differences in formal patterns of response to the decision, but there is a similarity in discretionary behavior which in fact both blurs these local differences and limits the effectiveness of the *Miranda* rules. While resulting variations in *formal* procedures were consistent with the variations in professionalization, there were no variations in these important *informal* procedures.[7]

COUNSEL

We have already seen at least indirectly some signs of the resulting changes in procedures regarding counsel, and the limitations of the significance of these changes. As a result of *Miranda*, all departments were more likely to give formal recognition to the suspect's right to counsel during interrogation. In all four departments the effectiveness of this procedure was limited because many suspects continued to waive their right to counsel. In none of the cities was it possible for an indigent suspect to obtain an attorney at any hour of the night. If during a late-hour interrogation the suspect refuses to waive his rights and requests an attorney, questioning stops until morning when one can be appointed. There are various reasons why the availability of counsel was not more thoroughly institutionalized. These again relate to professionalization and participation.

In Green Bay, there is no formal procedure for appointing attorneys at the interrogation stage. The bar does not furnish the judiciary with a list of attorneys available for such cases, and no such action was contemplated. This would seem consistent with the lack of bureaucratization and the type of isolation from local groups characteristic of the Green Bay police.

The Kenosha procedures on the surface appear much more formalized. Because of *Miranda*, the local bar association prepared a list of attorneys who would represent indigent suspects at the interrogation stage. Presumably this list is furnished to any indigent suspect who can choose any attorney on the list. The officers are supposed to exercise no influence over an indigent's choice of attorneys, but certainly no bar association member is present to make certain that the police do not try. Indeed, two informants suggested that the Kenosha police exercise discretion in a very interesting manner. Instead of allowing the suspect to choose any lawyer on the list, the officer strongly recommends one of them. He avoids the best known or most effective criminal lawyers, and for this reason they are never chosen. One should be cautious in accepting this evidence because the author did not observe such behavior, and the police certainly did not discuss it. However, one of the informants is an attorney who claimed that a police officer told him of this procedure.

Such behavior again seems characteristic of a department like Kenosha's, relatively unprofessionalized yet operating in a milieu where participation is common but not pervasive. In the end the police are able to limit the effects of this participation.

In both Madison and Racine formal methods of furnishing counsel to an indigent existed prior to *Miranda*, and initially there was little change after *Miranda*. As previously mentioned in Chapter 7, there was some pressure in Racine for new procedures but they were never made formal. The relatively great amount of formalization in the Madison criminal justice process included the most well-developed means of furnishing counsel both prior to and after *Miranda*. Moreover, post-*Miranda* changes occurred in that city which not only further professionalized the process of assigning counsel, but also potentially increased the possibility that counsel could be assigned to an indigent at any hour (see Chapter 8).

LOCAL POLICE DISCRETION

Professionalization is considerably more related to the nature of formal changes than it is to the actual process of implementing these changes. Indeed, the actual interrogation behavior of detectives did not seem to be at all related to their department's professionalization or to the resulting milieu this professionalization creates.[8] Their operational discretion limits the range of compliance with the *Miranda* decision.

There seem to be several reasons for a difference between formal and actual compliance and, as a corollary, for professionalization having little of the assumed effect. Most interrogation is unsupervised, and despite the *Miranda* majority's claim that lawyers will participate in interrogation, this is simply not true in practice. If a lawyer wishes to supervise an interrogation, the questioning almost always stops immediately. The interrogation process involves activities with low visibility. The United States Supreme Court has always found this lack of visibility to be an obstacle in regulating police behavior. The low visibility increases the incidence of discretion, and its manifestations, *e.g.* getting suspects to waive their rights, in turn decreases the visibility.[9]

Furthermore, there are only limited institutionalized channels to confront police with their interrogation behavior. The local court seems to be the most effective institution, but its effectiveness is limited for two reasons. First, the tremendous pressure to plead guilty without counsel and to avoid a time-consuming trial reduces severely the number of cases where trials occur.[10] The number of confessions challenged in court is certainly much smaller than the number of coerced confessions. Propensity to challenge does vary from community to community and, as the earlier analysis of Racine suggested, it does not depend only on police behavior but also on the *standards* for police behavior which the local lawyers can get the local judge to adopt. But even if standards are formally adopted and trials raising this issue are more likely to be held, as they were in Kenosha, Racine, and Madison, the effectiveness of the local court decision as a pronouncement of general policy is also limited. The discussions of participation levels in the criminal justice process in four cities showed that in each of them there were some severe obstacles to communication among local court, local prosecutor, and police officer.[11] In fact this was quite explicitly the case in Madison, even though the police chief sought policy guidance from the local judiciary and even though that same judiciary's organization seemed most amenable toward giving such guidance.[12]

Impact on Interrogation Behavior: The Broader Perspective

So far this chapter has used a rather narrow focus in its analysis of changes in interrogation behavior. It has dwelt on the individual interrogation situation and the responses of the interrogating officer to the *Miranda* procedures. There is a danger that such an approach leads to an overemphasis on the isolation of the interrogation process. We must attempt to look more systematically at the departments' arrest activities.

One way to do this is to focus once again on the officers' perceptions of the changes and to take a more systematic look at the perceived changes in methods of obtaining evidence. In addition, data on the clearance rates can give some indication of the general trends resulting from the decision.

Table 10-1 gives a comparison of the officers' perception of the

Table 10-1. Perceived Changes in Evidence-Gathering Procedures (by Department), in Percentages

	Green Bay	Kenosha	Racine	Madison
General changes in methods of obtaining evidence	47.1	70.3	63.8	48.7
Greater sympathy for suspect	17.2	18.8	17.2	28.2
New methods adopted to obtain confessions	7.1	7.8	13.8	15.3

Each officer could make two choices.

resulting changes in methods of obtaining evidence. These perceptions were discussed in detail in Chapters 5-8. The more systematic presentation of the data in Table 10-1 suggests that in all departments the officers quite frequently thought that *Miranda* had effected changes in methods of obtaining evidence. Indeed, such changes were evident in all the departments. Surveillance, for example, became a more common technique of obtaining evidence than it had been prior to the *Miranda* decision. Officers claimed that they now must gather some evidence prior to interrogation because the interrogation is no longer as dependable a source of information. This seemed to be particularly true in more highly salient crimes where the suspect's lawyer prohibited interrogation. The investigation of the much publicized murder in Kenosha was such a case.

Neither greater sympathy for the suspect nor adoption of new methods to obtain confessions seem to be important results of *Miranda*. Given the police attitudes toward the decision and given the fact that old interrogation techniques are still frequently used, this should not be surprising.

The relationship between professionalization and *Miranda*-induced changes is again ambiguous. The Madison officers more frequently claimed increased sympathy for a suspect, but they also claimed more frequently that they have now adopted new means of obtaining a confession. The frequency of seeking such new methods is *directly* related to degree of professionalization. This is certainly contrary to one of the goals of *Miranda*, which involved discouraging the use of confessions. In fact, though the evidence is only impressionistic, all the departments continued to rely first on interrogations. If that failed, either because of lack of relevant information or because of a lawyer's refusal to allow questioning, only then were alternative methods relied upon.

In regard to perceptions of general changes in evidence procedures, the Madison department closely resembles the least professionalized Green Bay department. We might expect that change would be least likely in Green Bay because of its low professionalization, little pressure for change from other local forces, and the general lack of crime. But why is Madison so similar? Advocates of police professionalization would perhaps argue that fewer changes were necessary because Madison was more professionalized prior to *Miranda.*

A comparison of the 1966 and early 1967 clearance rates partially supports this argument.[13] Such a comparison of the clearance rates for the seven crimes used by the FBI to assess the degree of serious crime (see Chapter 1) shows that they dropped considerably less in the more professionalized departments. Green Bay's clearance rate decreased 51 percent, Kenosha's dropped 32 percent, Racine's lessened by 13 percent, while the Madison department's clearance rate went up 5 percent. The problems of establishing a causal relationship between *Miranda* and these changes are obvious, but the general trend follows the expected pattern.

Many have suggested that the *Miranda* decision hampers ability to obtain multiple clearance of crimes. That is, because *Miranda* limits the effectiveness of interrogation, the police cannot get an individual to admit to a whole series of crimes. Such multiple clearances are most common in burglary and theft cases. A 1966-67 comparison of the departments' clearance rates for theft over $50 and burglary suggests that more professionalized departments were again less affected although the pattern is not always consistent. The Green Bay department's rate for theft dropped 48 percent while the Kenosha rate dropped 42 percent. The rate also decreased in the two more professionalized departments, but the decline was smaller. Racine's rate dropped 23 percent, and Madison's, 28 percent. The pattern of

burglary rates is more ambiguous. Because of the paucity of burglaries Green Bay is not included in this comparison. Kenosha's rate
dropped 34 percent, but this was smaller than the Racine decline of
42 percent. Madison's rate *increased* by 22 percent.

The ultimate impact of *Miranda* might be reflected in changes
in conviction rates. Unfortunately, only the Madison and Racine
departments have information which allows such consideration. In
both communities the conviction rate remained quite stable during
late 1966 and early 1967. In 1964 the Racine adult conviction rate
was 76 percent; in 1965 it was 75 percent. For each half of 1966 the
rate was 74 percent. The rate increased slightly to 77 percent during
the first six months of 1967. There are signs that *Miranda* may give
the defendant's attorney another weapon to use in bargaining for a
lesser charge for his client. In 1966, during the six months prior to
Miranda, only 18.9 percent of the guilty parties were found guilty
of an offense less serious than the one with which they were originally charged. For the first six months after the decision, this number
increased to 47.9 percent, and in the first six months of 1967, the
percentage increased still further to 59.3 percent—over three times
the rate for the first half of 1966. This may reflect an increasing willingness by the prosecutor's staff to avoid *Miranda* constraints by
compromising.[14]

In Madison there was a small decrease in the percentage of arrested persons who were ultimately convicted. The 1966 rate of
convictions of all defendants, both juveniles and adults, was 90 percent, a decrease from the 96 percent conviction rate in 1965. (The
1966 adult rate was 92 percent; comparable figures for other years
are unavailable.) This 1965 rate was not unusually high; the rates in
1960 and 1961 equalled this rate, and the 1964 rate was 94 percent.
Since these figures include juveniles, not covered by the *Miranda*
procedures, we must somehow isolate the adult conviction rates. In
order to do this, however, we must, unfortunately, use data not completely comparable to the pre-1966 data. Prior to 1966, the department kept no separate conviction rates for adults and juveniles. For
the first half of 1966 the adult conviction rate was 93 percent. During
the latter half of that year the rate dropped slightly to 91 percent.
During the first half of 1967 the rate dropped a little more to 89
percent.

Earlier we noted that, although the conviction rate did not decline in Racine, the percentage of defendants found guilty of a lesser charge increased after *Miranda*. This pattern did not occur in Madison. In fact, there was a great *decrease* in the percentage of reduced charges. During the 1966 months prior to *Miranda*, 28 percent of those who were convicted or who pled guilty did so on a lesser charge. This declined to 23 percent for the post-*Miranda* part of 1966 and to only 8 percent for the first six months of 1967.

This decrease in successful plea bargaining suggests that officers now screen the cases more carefully prior to requesting a warrant. If they are now forced to make a better case prior to arrest, then, as a result, we would expect a smaller percentage of suspects released without charge after arrest. In 1966 13 percent of those arrested were released without charge. This is equal to the average for the years 1963-65 and is slightly higher than the 1965 rate. Thus we can tentatively conclude that on the whole the Madison officers are not forced to release more arrestees because of lack of evidence. These data do not tell us whether fewer arrests are made as a result of *Miranda*, but the general lack of decrease in clearance rates suggests that, except for certain crimes involving multiple clearance, the arrest rate did not decrease.

Conclusion

This necessary but often tortuous journey with police statistics is not without danger. Beside the more obvious difficulties in attributing causality, there is also a more subtle problem. Crime and arrest statistics do not measure perceptions, nor do they assess the qualitative difference between cases. Earlier chapters showed that, despite important differences related to professionalization, the police generally saw the *Miranda* decision as harmful and drastic. A change in procedure involving one highly visible case can have more important implications than the sum total of change as reflected in the total statistics. The Kenosha murder case seemed to be a far more important source of attitude change than any other single case or any series of cases. Thus, despite the lack of change in interrogation behavior, the decision may have resulted in important changes in police morale.[15] Further investigation of these changes is beyond the scope of the present study.

We can conclude that change in interrogation behavior seemed limited in all departments. The more professionalized departments did seem more likely to make their formal procedures consistent with *Miranda*, but in their informal procedures they were much like their less professionalized counterparts. They were not more likely to refrain from the use of interrogation, and their interrogation techniques were not only similar in all departments but also similarly reflected practices somewhat contrary to the goals of *Miranda*. The clearance rate changes suggest that professionalized departments may have been better able to "adjust" to *Miranda*, but not because they adopted innovations more consistent with procedural due process requirements. For the average case many aspects seemed similar and unchanged in all departments.

The reasons for this lack of change have already been detailed. They do not include outright, direct non-compliance, but rather involve techniques used by the lower levels of organizations partially to counteract procedures they find contrary to their own goals. The ability to continue old procedures is aided by the lack of supervision. It is also aided by the lack of sophistication of most suspects who, like those observed in another study of interrogation behavior, "may have had cognitive understanding of these rights but no appreciation of them and lacked the ability to apply them to their crisis-laden situation." [16] It may be that the combined lack of sophistication and the motives of police practices make the goals of *Miranda* unrealistic— even in an optimal situation where representation with well-trained counsel is possible.[17] The point is moot because representation is far from optimal at present.

NOTES

1. "Interrogations in New Haven: The Impact of *Miranda*." *Yale Law Journal* 76 (1967), 1521-1648; Albert J. Reiss, Jr. and Donald J. Black, "Interogations and the Criminal Process." *Annals* 374 (1967), 47-57; Richard J. Medalie, *et al.*, "Custodial Police Interrogation in Our Nation's Capital: The Attempt to Implement *Miranda*," in Theodore J. Becker, *The Impact of Supreme Court Decisions* (New York: Oxford, 1969), 165-175.

2. I received permission to observe both field and station-house interrogations. Because I did not spend all my field research time in the police station, I did not see all interrogations occurring during my period of research. Of course, this places limits on the reliability of my observations, but for two reasons I think I observed interrogation which seemed typical and not biased by my presence. First, the evidence to be presented in this chapter suggests that, despite my presence, the interrogators did not implement all of the goals of the *Miranda* decision. Second, thanks to the thin walls of the interrogation rooms, I was able to listen to some interrogations unbeknownst to the police. The ethics of such research deserve more consideration than they have received in the literature. As Skolnick pointed out, one's own conscience and moral standards are important factors in determining his ethical standards as a participant observer. The rub is, of course, that my standards and those of the interrogators sometimes varied. I chose not to inform the suspect that my standards were different. As a witness I did sign some confessions and would have testified in court about my views of the interrogation had I been so asked. Thus, while I did not aid the police directly, I also chose not to aid the suspect. My dilemma was eased somewhat, though by no means completely, because of my willingness to testify and my opinion that my presence did not make the interrogation any more coercive. Compare Jerome H. Skolnick, *Justice Without Trial* (New York: Wiley, 1966), 38-39.

3. *Miranda v. Arizona*, 384 U.S. 436, 477-78, 480-81.

4. These conclusions are based upon non-structural interviews with Green Bay detectives whom I asked to reconstruct a typical interrogation situation.

5. After one of the observed interrogations—but before the tape— a suspect changed his mind, and decided he wanted a lawyer at county expense. The detective told the eighteen-year-old with no previous record that, since the suspect was making a $100 a week, he would no doubt have to pay for his own attorney. The boy decided he would not pay for his own attorney and proceeded to record his confession.

6. Compare "Interrogations in New Haven," *op. cit.*, 1547-62.

7. A further note of caution is necessary. Again it must be empha-sized that the method limited the number of observed confessions. A more subtle but perhaps more serious limitation is the lack of any sensitive technique to observe behavior in a manner which would facilitate comparison. Indeed, social scientists generally have not paid enough attention to developing techniques of behavior observation in non-experimental settings. See Irwin Deutcher, "Words and Deeds: Social Science and Social Policy." *Social Problems* 13 (1966), 235-54; Lewis A. Froman, "The Categorization of Policy Content," in Austin Ranney (ed.), *Political Science and Public Policy* (Chicago: Markham, 1968), 43-44.

8. See note 7, above.

9. Although, according to Wilson, such policies dealing with law enforcement are easier to supervise than are policies concerning the maintenance of order, one should remember that this ease is relative. That is, nowhere does Wilson deny the difficulty of making law enforcement policies. See James Q. Wilson, *Varieties of Police Behavior* (Cambridge, Mass.: Harvard University, 1968).

10. Abraham S. Blumberg, *Criminal Justice* (Chicago: Quadrangle, 1967), 95-116.

11. Wayne R. La Fave and Frank J. Remington, "Controlling the Police: The Judge's Role in Making and Reviewing Law Enforcement Decisions." *Michigan Law Review* 62 (1965), 987-1012.

12. For a discusion of the reasons for non-compliance in regard to other Court decisions, see Kenneth M. Dolbeare and Phillip E. Hammond, "Local Elites, the Impact of Judicial Decisions, and the Process of Change." Paper presented to the American Political Science Association, New York, 1969. William K. Muir, in *Prayer in the Public Schools* (Chicago: University of Chicago, 1967) discusses non-compliance by using cognitive dissonance theory.

13. Because *Miranda* was decided in June 1966, it might seem more useful to compare separate clearance rates for the first six months of 1966 from those of the last six months of that year. This was not done because a compilation of monthly rates actually inclures clearances occurring some time earlier. Thus, the clearance rates reflecting post-*Miranda* procedures would not be included in these compilations until late in 1966. Thus, the early 1967 data should furnish a more accurate indication of post-*Miranda* procedures.

14. All data on disposition of the cases can be found in *Annual Report—1964*, 20; *Annual Report—1965,*, 27; and *Annual Report— 1966*, 20. The 1967 data are from the files of the Racine department's records bureau. In their study of Chicago and Cook County, Oaks and Lehman try to discover the reasons for a paradox involving a decline of convictions in Cook County courts accompanied by an increase in guilty pleas prior to trial. One would expect that a decline in court convictions would make a suspect less willing to plead guilty because

he could expect a better break in court. They suggest, with some evidence, that trial judges now convict less often because of their greater sensitivity to *Escobedo* and *Miranda* requirements. Perceiving this greater sensitivity, the prosecutor works harder to obtain a guilty plea by bargaining. Oaks and Lehman claim that such procedure partially neutralizes the *Miranda* requirements because in fact the individual suspect is now less likely to appear in court, allowing diminished judicial supervision of police-prosecutor interrogation behavior. Although the Racine evidence does not permit rigorous comparison to the Chicago and Cook County data, the increase in reduced sentences along with the slight 1967 increase in conviction rates suggests that the Racine prosecutor may be responding to *Miranda* in this manner. See Dallin H. Oaks and Warren Lehman, *A Criminal Justice System and the Indigent: A Study of Chicago and Cook County* (Chicago: University of Chicago, 1968), 64-81.

15. James Q. Wilson suggests this possibility. See his "Police Morale, Reform, and Citizen Respect: The Chicago Case," in David Bordua (ed.), *The Police: Six Sociological Essays* (New York: Wiley, 1966), 156.

16. Medalie, *et al.*, *op. cit.*, 174. An ex-prosecutor related to me an incident which also suggests the lack of sophistication of some suspects. A suspect confidently informed his interrogators that he knew the meaning of the Fifth Amendment. When he was asked to describe it, he replied, "Honor thy father and thy mother."

17. *Ibid.*, 175.

Chapter 11

POLICY, COMPLIANCE, AND REFORM:
SUMMARY AND IMPLICATIONS

Two general questions require final analysis. First, is the organizational context in which the Wisconsin police departments operated related to the impact of the *Miranda* decision? Second, using the majority opinion as a statement of the Supreme Court's goals, to what extent can we say that the departments complied with *Miranda*?

Table 11-1 shows more clearly what we had emphasized earlier. The degree of a department's professionalization and the level of group participation surrounding its activities is indeed related. The number of sources of information and the percentage who received information from training sessions vary directly with professionalization and participation. The relative importance of the training session for Madison officers suggests that despite the greater amount of information which they receive, internal sources of information were paramount. This is characteristic of a highly professionalized organization, more likely to have its own professionals as important reference groups. This observation contradicts the views of police reformers which assume that professionalization increases a police department's amenability to the influence of outside groups. Note that local groups are considered less important in Madison than in any other department.

Professionalization is also directly related to some basic attitudes toward and perceptions of the *Miranda* decision (see Table 11-2). The degree of *Miranda* approval varies in this manner as does the frequency with which the decision was conceptualized or discussed

Table 11-1. Comparison of *Miranda* Communications Process (by Department)

DEPARTMENT

Process	Green Bay	Kenosha	Racine	Madison
Number of sources of *Miranda* information	4.95	5.20	5.24	5.82
Learned about decision at conference, training session	61.4%	67.2%	69.0%	92.3%
Conference, training best source of *Miranda* information	37.1%	34.4%	24.1%	44.9%
Local officials best source of *Miranda* information	7.1%	12.6%	17.3%	3.8%
(N)	(70)	(64)	(58)	(78)

Table 11-2. Comparison of Attitudes and Perceptions about *Miranda* (by Department), in Percentages

DEPARTMENT

Attitude Perception	Green Bay	Kenosha	Racine	Madison
Approved of the decision	11.4	10.9	17.2	35.9
Correct response: can still ask person to come voluntarily to police station	40.0	37.5	34.5	62.8
Correct response: may no longer talk to anyone without advising him of his rights	21.4	34.4	32.8	53.8
"Professionalized" response	14.0[a]	23.0[a]	28.0[a]	33.0[a]
(N)	(70)	(64)	(58)	(78)

a. N for these responses are Green Bay (43), Kenosha (39), Racine (32), and Madison (48).

in ways consistent with a professional ideology. Madison, the most professionalized department, stands out by the frequency with which its members recognized the limits of the *Miranda* constraints. This can be attributed to the importance of the FBI-led training sessions in that department. Generally these findings would seem to be consistent with the expectations of police reform advocates. They would predict that approval of innovations such as *Miranda* would be related to professionalization, and, without supposing too much, we can also assume that they would expect professionalized departments to discuss the decision either in a positive manner or in a way compatible to views stressed by reformers. The success of the Madison department in communicating the limits of *Miranda's* constraint may be somewhat surprising. Because this success is so closely related to the FBI training, we can say that perhaps once again the previously discussed advocates of police professionalization overemphasized the amenability of more professionalized departments to the influence of outside groups.

As shown in the preceding chapter, *formal* changes in interrogation procedures also were generally consistent with the degree of professionalization. Thus we can summarize the consequences of *Miranda* and the effects of the two socio-political variables as follows:

1. The decision was less likely to be opposed in the more professionalized department and more completely understood in the most professionalized department.

2. The decision did not basically change the decentralized and often unsystematic communications processes used to inform police departments about innovation, although it did increase somewhat the activities of the prosecutors in Racine and Kenosha. The existing levels of participation and professionalization were generally unchanged; however, these levels seemed related to certain departments' attitudes, perceptions, and characteristics of the communications processes, all of which are summarized in Tables 11-1 and 11-2. The Madison department's adoption of new incentives for greater education was the most tangible evidence that *Miranda* may increase professionalization, but we must remember that this change occurred in a department that was already relatively highly professionalized.

3. On the surface, the decision generally led to greater standardization and routinization of interrogation procedures. The more

professionalized the department, the more bureaucratized and formalized these procedures appeared to be.

4. Multiple clearances lessened as a result of the decision.

The impact of the decision was limited because of the lack of change in the dynamics of the interrogation processes. This was discussed in Chapter 10. What we have not yet thoroughly discussed is the relationship between this behavior and the goals of the Court's interrogation policy. We must look at the degree of compliance, as measured by a comparison to the Court's policy preferences.

In Chapter 2 four goals were extrapolated from the *Miranda* opinion. First, the Court sought to discourage wherever possible the use of confessions, all of which are allegedly obtained under inherently coercive circumstances. Members of the four police departments generally felt that the decision had indeed effectively limited the use of confessions, but other data do not always support this contention. Interrogations were still regularly attempted and some of the circumstances under which these attempts took place could quite readily be interpreted as coercive.

Continuation of interrogation procedures also acted to limit the implementation of another goal of the *Miranda* majority. This goal involves the attempt to protect a suspect by requiring that police inform him of his rights and by requiring that they allow a lawyer to observe his client's interrogation. Both the lawyer's counsel and the information presented to the suspect were seen as ways of reducing coercion and giving the suspect a greater understanding of his situation. Again we find little before-and-after difference in the departments' behavior regarding this goal. Although formal procedures varied, informal routines were quite similar. Unquestionably, as a result of *Miranda* the police were much more likely to give the suspect information about his rights, and the procedure became much more standardized. Nonetheless, neither this information nor the potential protection of counsel seemed to guarantee that the suspect would grasp the significance of his position. The use of old interrogation techniques was often possible because the suspect waived his rights, including the right to counsel. It should be noted that the *Miranda* opinion gives no new guidance about the types of interrogation behavior that can be used *after* a suspect waives his rights. Thus, generally most interrogations continued to operate under rules formalized prior to the *Miranda* decision.

For several reason lawyers virtually never participated directly in the interrogation process. First, if a suspect asked for a lawyer, his attorney generally told him not to say anything. Thus there was no interrogation whatsoever.[1] Finally, the suspect himself regularly waived his right to counsel. Perhaps contrary to the Court's goals, the pressure of attorneys did not greatly increase the outside supervision of police interrogation procedures. They commonly either prevented such procedures from being used or were not an integral part of the process.

The other *Miranda* goals involved police organizational changes which would make police officers more amenable to innovations (like *Miranda*). The majority Justices seemed somewhat—but by no means thoroughly—aware of the police efficiency-due process dilemma and claimed rather sanguinely that the problem could be minimized by improving the quality of the police officer. The data for the present study were collected too early to establish whether much change actually increased amenability to the new Court-imposed innovations which further constrain and bureaucratize police procedures. We can, however, discuss the initial organizational changes that were made at least as a partial consequence of *Miranda*. These changes were related to the previously existing levels of participation. They ranged from virtually no change in Green Bay, to initial attempts to facilitate greater specialization and formal education in Racine and Kenosha, to Madison's most complete attempt at adopting pervasive organizational sanctions which would encourage such specialization and education. It must again be emphasized that no evidence supports the view that there is a clear and consistent relationship between such changes and the Court's goals involving amenability to reform.[2]

Finally, the majority attempted to ease police anxieties by stressing the limits of the *Miranda* constraints. They went so far as to admit that interrogations could at times still be a legitimate technique. It is perhaps not surprising that this goal was the one most implemented by the police. Conceivably it conflicts somewhat with the Court's attempt to discourage interrogation. The police departments' thorough implementation of the anxiety-reducing goal certainly limits the degree to which the use of interrogations was discouraged.

One reason for this stemmed from the officers' ability to continue old interrogation techniques. As previously mentioned, another reason for this limitation is that the Court itself was still unclear about what circumstances (other than failure to advise the suspect of his rights) necessarily resulted in a coerced confession.

On the basis of the Court's standards, it is clear that there was not a complete degree of compliance. It is equally clear that there was little evidence of direct, complete non-compliance. Instead, police behavior might be categorized as "formal, perfunctory or rhetorical" compliance.[3] We know very little about techniques of measuring compliance or non-compliance, and consequently have no refined typologies to which we can relate this behavior. Krislov, however, offers several general conditions amenable to compliance. These can be used to create a matrix of possible conditions which facilitate or limit compliance. These possibilities consider the advantages or disadvantages of compliance based on personal utilities, organizational utilities, and psychological utilities. Compliance is highest when personal advantages are highest, organizational sanctions against non-compliance are certain and severe, and the legitimacy of the issuing authority is acknowledged.[4]

There were important personal advantages to police officers for maintaining a relatively low degree of compliance with the *Miranda* decision. Police efficiency was still primarily measured by clearance rates, and officers were rewarded no less for solving a case by means of interrogation. Indeed such solutions were often quicker and thus more efficient. By encouraging the suspect to make a hasty decision on whether to request counsel or the right to remain silent, the interrogation facilitated a relatively quick solution to many cases. Perhaps greater police agreement with the policy would also mean a greater degree of compliance, but there were few positive attitudes toward the decision.[5] Given this low degree of approval, the personal utilities related to the existing police procedures were even more apparent.

Organizational sanctions against the low degree of compliance manifested by the interrogations were often uncertain or mild. The sanctions against non-compliance with formal rules were indeed quite clear, and this information was most thoroughly disseminated in the most professionalized department. But these sanctions were clear only in regard to requiring the police to inform a suspect of his rights.

There were no certain or clear sanctions which discouraged waiver. We must remember that despite the possibility of legal sanctions, the everyday interrogation situation is relatively free from direct sanction control. Upper-echelon police supervising personnel and other potentially important organizations such as judges and the bar have little opportunity for close, daily supervision of police interrogation activities.

This is a particularly interesting finding because others have suggested that organizational factors are of paramount importance in affecting police behavior.[6] Professionalization, a key variable in this analysis, is certainly an organizational factor which does seem to be important in explaining certain departmental differences in the response to *Miranda*. Yet professionalization does not seem to increase the clarity or certainty of sanctions involving much interrogation behavior. As suggested in Chapter 10, some real obstacles to organizational sanctions continued to exist despite *Miranda*.[7]

A higher degree of compliance is likely when implementers accept the legitimacy of the authority who issues the policy. In this case we refer only to the Court as an issuing authority. This study did not systematically investigate the relationship between questioners of the Court's legitimacy and response to *Miranda*. There is some evidence, nonetheless, to suggest that legitimacy was much in doubt. The comments of the officers in Chapter 9 reveal that a majority of those officers questioned the Court's competence in making the *Miranda* decision. They frequently emphasized the lack of Court understanding of police work. Others challenged the Court's goals and its own procedures. Other studies have shown that the police consider themselves more expert than judges in determining guilt or innocence.[8] We use the concept of legitimacy rather loosely here, and one might argue that this questioning of Court competence and goals does not necessarily limit the Court's legitimacy. Indeed the fact that there was some compliance despite objections to the rules suggests that the police to some extent have accepted this legitimacy. But by disputing the Court's competence to rule on interrogation behavior, by criticizing the Justices for changing the traditional interpretation of the privilege against self-incrimination, and by thus questioning the Justices' special abilities to interpret law, the police certainly limit the Court's legitimacy, at least in the area of interrogation policy.[9]

The preceding discussion suggests that there is more to the dynamics of compliance than merely individual attitudes or the clarity of organizational communication. An additional factor, the nature of the Court's information, must also be considered. In Chapter 2 we emphasized the obstacles which the Court faced in obtaining information about police interrogation. These obstacles were reflected in the *Miranda* majority opinion which used virtually no empirical evidence to support its contentions or assumptions about actual police behavior. In making its decisions involving police interrogation the Court paid only passing attention to the distinction between its goals and those of the policy implementers. It has never really confronted the due process-police efficiency dilemma, nor has it ever paid much attention to the means of achieving desired innovation in police administration, given the characteristics and goals of the implementing organizations.[10] This indifference on the part of the Court facilitates avoidance of achieving the Court's goals because it increases the likelihood that both personal and organizational goals will differ from Court goals, and it increases the likelihood that its competence will be questioned. It further increases the likelihood that other goals will form the standards of compliance. The importance of the FBI, whose goals regarding police interrogation were by no means completely contradictory to the Court's aims but whose emphasis was certainly different, shows how easily other standards of compliance can be adopted, especially in relatively highly professionalized departments.

There is a lesson in police reform to be learned from these observations. First and foremost, it seems essential that we question and investigate some of the basic assumptions made about police reform policies and their results. This suggestion applies to social scientists, who have for the most part ignored the subject, to police administrators, who often either fear change or refuse to accept the perspective of others, and to Supreme Court Justices, who ignore extensive consideration of the policy implementation process. More specifically, we must further inquire into the relationship among police professionalization, police amenability to group influences, and response to innovation.[11]

Ultimately we must understand what seems to be a simple but nevertheless ignored fact. Successful innovation depends to a great extent upon the goals and sanctions of the organizations which are asked to accept them. We cannot assume that innovations will automatically be accepted, nor can we assume that piecemeal change can be successful without making other basic organizational changes. The subject of police policy-making is obviously too vital to permit the existence of untested assumptions, shibboleths, and minds that are closed to basic reforms that may be necessary. Though the present study is limited in its consideration of such questions, it should at least suggest the need for further confrontation of the realities of police behavior.

NOTES

1. As suggested earlier, there was some evidence that plea bargaining increased in one department. Thus another reason lawyers did not participate more formally was the increase of informal decision-making.

2. Burton Levy, "Cops in the Ghetto: A Problem of the Police System," in Louis H. Masotti and Don R. Bowen, *Riots and Rebellion* (Beverly Hills: Sage, 1968), 347-58.

3. Kenneth B. Dolbeare and Phillip E. Hammond, "Local Elites, The Impact of Judicial Decisions and the Process of Change." Paper presented to the American Political Science Association, New York, 1969, 8.

4. Samuel Krislov, *The Supreme Court in the Political Process* (New York: Macmillan, 1965), 135-36. Another way of looking at this would be to consider conditions which increase resistance to change. See Alvin Zander, "Resistance to Change—Its Analysis and Prevention," in W.G. Bennis, K.D. Benne, and R. Chin, *The Planning of Change* (New York: Holt, Rinehart & Winston, 1964).

5. It should again be noted that there was no atempt to compare the interrogation behavior of those who approve and those who disapprove.

6. Jerome H. Skolnick, *Justice Without Trial* (New York: Wiley, 1966), 6. Arthur Niederhoffer, *Behind The Shield* (Garden City, N.Y.: Doubleday, 1967), especially Chapter 5; John H. McNamara, "Uncertainties in Police Work," in David Bordua (ed.), *The Police* (New York: Wiley, 1967), 194. These authors are cited and the point is discussed in Michael Lipsky, "Toward a Theory of Street-Level Bureaucracy." Paper presented to the American Political Science Association, New York, 1969.

7. Compare Niederhoffer, *op. cit.*, Chapter 3.

8. Skolnick, *op. cit.*

9. For a brief discusion of Supreme Court legitimacy, see Walter F. Murphy, *Elements of Judicial Strategy* (Chicago: University of Chicago, 1964), 12-18. Grossman and Wells also suggest that legitimacy is related to perceived conformity with technical procedures. See Richard S. Wells and Joel B. Grossman "The Concept of Judicial Policy Making," in Thomas B. Jahnige and Sheldon Goldman, *The Federal Judicial System* (New York: Holt, Rinehart & Winston, 1968), 302.

10. Abraham Blumberg, *Criminal Justice* (Chicago: Quadrangle, 1967), 183-84. James P. Levine and Theodore C. Becker, "Toward and

Beyond a Theory of Supreme Court Impact." Paper presented to the American Political Science Association, New York, 1969, 10-19.

11. There is some further evidence to suggest that police professionalization and amenability to group particpation are inversely related. In a national survey of police-community relations, Madison ranked third (among seventeen cities between 100,000 and 250,000) in the amount of police recruit training. The data for the two highest cities were estimates. This recruit training was one of our criteria of professionalization. The Madison department was second lowest in the percentage of recruit training devoted to police-community relations. The latter may be an indicator of amenability to participation. In any case, such correlations deserve further investigation. See "A National Survey of Police and Community Relations," in *Field Survey V*, a report submitted to the President's Commission on Law Enforcement and the Administration of Justice (Washington: U.S. Government Printing Office, 1967), Table V, 304-09.

INTERVIEWING POLICE OFFICERS
Techniques, Questionnaire, and Sample

The study of police organizations potentially poses some serious obstacles to systematic empirical research. First, the success of many police activities often depends upon maintaining secrecy. Secondly, despite the voluminous statistics kept by police departments, much of it is of little value to the social scientist. The discussion of crime statistics in Chapter 1 bears out this contention. Too often the aims of police statistics simply do not correspond to the aims of the social scientist interested in police behavior.

The lack of visibility of many important aspects of police behavior, combined with a lack of available data measuring such behavior, is certainly a serious obstacle. It becomes even more encumbering because police officials are not always inclined to trust a researcher who seeks to overcome the problems of police isolation and secrecy.[1] It is understandable that police officials desire to maintain this secrecy especially against the annoyance of a young, inexperienced investigator fresh from the university campus.

Thus, the researcher must take certain steps initially to convince top level police officers of his sincere interest in police behavior, his empathy with police problems, and his experience in investigating such problems. The following is a discussion of the strategies followed in order to get permission for a relatively free hand in investigating police behavior. It focuses primarily on the means used to obtain permission to administer a questionnaire, the adoption and administration of an interview schedule, and finally it describes the statistical characteristics of the questionnaire itself.

MEANS OF OBTAINING PERMISSION

Each police chief was initially contacted by a letter stating the general purposes of the study and its importance to the public's better understanding of police behavior. In this letter I also told each chief that he would receive a telephone call. During that call I requested an appointment to see him. All four chiefs responded favorably. No formal schedule was adopted for the interview with them. The chiefs were asked general questions about their opinion of *Miranda* and about the changes it made. The nature of the response to these questions set the tone for the rest of each interview.

Basically the purpose of the interview was twofold: first, to get some idea of the nature of the police organization, and, second, to allay any anxieties the police chief might have. I attempted to convince the chief that I had no intention of doing an exposé of police activities, but rather that I was sincerely concerned with an analysis of police problems. Though I did not so explicitly state my purpose, through my questions, which allowed the chief to emphasize the police view, I hoped to leave the impression of a sympathetic— though not necessarily agreeing—observer. During the interviews no mention was made of the desire to administer a questionnaire to all police officers in each of the four cities. But each chief expressed willingness to my general request for further contact with other members of the department.

In order to obtain permission to use the questionnaire, another appointment was made with each chief. At these meetings I presented a copy of the questionnaire to the chiefs and asked for permission to give a copy to every officer. I stressed that this was the only way to discover what the "police officer really thinks."

CONSTRUCTION AND ADMINISTRATION
OF THE QUESTIONNAIRE

The questionnaire is composed almost entirely of close-ended questions. I chose this type of question not because it facilitated reliable coding, but rather because I decided that the questionnaire must remain brief and easy to answer. (In retrospect I believe that I could have asked a greater number of more complex questions.) The brevity was particularly important because the questionnaires were not administered to the police directly by the interviewer.

Instead, the following procedure was adopted. In the two departments where each officer had his own mail box, a copy of the questionnaire and a return envelope was placed in each box along with a memorandum from the chief stating his approval. Special problems arose in the departments where no such individual mailing facilities were available. In these departments I had to rely upon a superior officer, usually a sergeant, to distribute the questionnaire and the return envelope. At both of these departments I personally distributed the questionnaire to at least one of three shifts (for response rates see table, p. 247). The chiefs informed the men of their permission to respond to my request. Thus one methodological weakness certainly can be attributed to the lack of any consistent means of distributing the interview schedule. My method, however, seemed to be the best compromise between a mailed questionnaire, a method more consistent in distribution but probably less likely to result in completion, and the impractical method of administering the questionnaire in person either to a group or to individual officers. The questionnaire, along with the cover letter, is reprinted here.

Dear Police Officer:

Many people are well aware of the increasingly more important and complex functions the police are being asked to perform in our society. As part of a research project in the University of Wisconsin's Graduate School's Department of Political Science, I hope to find out more about your own views on this subject. You certainly are the most qualified-- but often the least asked--person to state your views on this important matter.

Consequently I am asking you to answer these few short questions or the following questionnaire. Let me emphasize two very important asp of this questionnaire:

1. Your answers will be completely anonymous. Neither I nor anyone else will know which man filled out any particular questionnaire.

2. This is Not a test. There are no right or wrong answers. Just answer on the basis of your own knowledge and opinions.

Please complete this questionnaire as soon as possible. The questions are geared for quick answers. When you finish, please place it i the attached stamped envelope and mail it.

Thank you very much for interrupting your busy schedule to furnish this information.

Sincerely yours,

NEAL MILNER

<u>WISCONSIN PO LICE</u> SURVEY

PLEASE NOTE

I HAVE CONSULTED WITH YOUR CHIEF ABOUT THIS
QUESTIONNAIRE. HE HAS NO OBJECTIONS TO ITS
COMPLETION BY ANY MEMBERS OF THIS DEPARTMENT.

WISCONSIN POLICE SURVEY

1. In your opinion, which of the following are the greatest problems
    facing you as a police officer? Rank them by putting a "1" in
    front of the greatest problem, "2" in front of the second greatest,
    etc., until you have ranked what you consider to be the four (4)
    greatest problems.

    ____ an increasing crime rate
    ____ bad working hours
    ____ limitations on your job imposed by court decisions
    ____ low moral standards in your community
    ____ the dangers of your job
    ____ temptations for dishonesty among police
    ____ lack of cooperation from people in your community
    ____ insufficient salary
    ____ other; please specify:_____

2. Recently the U.S. Supreme Court decided the case Miranda v.
    Arizona. This case resulted in a rule about police interrogation
    procedures. Describe this rule as best as you can by putting an
    "x" next to all of the following statements which you think apply
    to the rule.

    ____ A person in custody must be advised of his right to
    remain silent.
    ____ A person in custody must have an attorney whether he
    wants one or not.
    ____ Confessions may no longer be used as evidence.
    ____ A person in custody must be advised that anything he
    says may be held against him in court.
    ____ A policeman may no longer talk to a person about a
    crime without first informing the person of his right
    to remain silent.
    ____ Wiretapping will no longer be tolerated.
    ____ Any person in custody has the right to an attorney if
    he wants one.
    ____ A person in custody who cannot afford to hire his own
    attorney has the right to have one appointed at county
    expense.
    ____ Voluntary confessions are no longer legal source of
    information.
    ____ A police officer can still ask a person to come volun-
    tarily to the police station without first advising him
    of his constitutional rights.

3. Which of the following are the most important effects the Miranda rule has on your own individual job? Check only the two most important.

    ___I must learn new methods of gathering evidence.

    ___I must now have more advanced education and training.

    ___I must become more sympathetic toward the rights of a suspect in custody.

    ___I spend more time explaining police activities and problems to people in my community.

    ___I pay more attention to other people whose work also deals with the problems of crime and the criminal.

    ___I try to find new methods to obtain a confession.

    ___I am more closely observed by people outside my police department.

    ___I am not affected by this rule.

    ___I don't know.

4. Some police officers may be affected more than others by the Miranda rule. From the list below, choose the one which best describe the most important effect the Miranda rule has on your department in general.

    ___More responsibilities for the detectives.

    ___More education and training becomes necessary.

    ___New techniques are used to gather evidence.

    ___More sympathy is given to the rights of a person in custody.

    ___Department members spend more time explaining police activities and problems to the community.

    ___The department pays more attention to other people whose work deals with the problems of crime and the criminal.

    ___The department spends more time trying to find new ways to use confessions.

    ___It did not affect the department's activities.

    ___I don't know.

5. To what extent do you think the Miranda rule changed your own job?

    ___a very great extent

    ___a great but not very great extent

    ___to some extent

    ___no change at all

    ___I don't know

6. To what extent do you think the Miranda rule changed police work in your own police department in general? Choose one of the following:

___ a very great extent
___ a great but not a very great extent
___ to some extent
___ no change at all
___ I don't know

7. To what extent do you think the Miranda rule changed police work in other police departments? Choose one of the following:

___ a very great extent
___ a great but not very great extent
___ to some extent
___ no change at all
___ I don't know

8. From whom or from where did you FIRST hear of the Miranda decision? Choose one of the following:

___ television or radio
___ a fellow police officer but NOT a superior officer
___ a fellow police officer who IS a superior officer
___ newspaper
___ magazines which do not specialize in police activities
___ District Attorney's office
___ magazines which do specialize in police activities
___ reading the opinion written by the U.S. Supreme Court
___ Attorney General's office
___ local judge
___ other; please specify:_____
___ no sources of information

9. From whom and from where did you receive ANY OTHER information about the Miranda rule? Choose ALL of the appropriate categories.

___ television or radio
___ District Attorney's office
___ a fellow officer but NOT a superior officer
___ a fellow police officer who IS a superior officer
___ newspapers
___ magazines which do NOT specialize in police activities
___ magazines which DO specialize in police activities
___ conference and/or training sessions
___ Attorney General's office
___ reading the opinion written by the U.S. Supreme Court
___ local judge
___ no sources of information

10. Which of these would you say was the best single source of information about the Miranda rule? Choose one.

___television or radio
___District Attorney's office
___a fellow police officer but NOT a superior officer
___a fellow police officer who IS a superior officer
___newspapers
___magazines which do Not specialize in police activity
___magazines which Do specialize in police activities
___conferences or training sessions
___reading the opinion written by the U.S. Supreme Court
___Attorney General's office
___local judge
___received no information

11. Would you say that generally these sources of information thought the Miranda rule was a good idea, were neutral toward the rule, or were critical toward the rule? Choose One of the following:

___thought it was a good idea
___neutral
___critical toward it
___no information
___I don't know

12. How, if at all, were these sources different from your usual sources of information about police activities?

___The sources were completely new.
___Some of the sources were new.
___None of the sources were new.
___I don't know.
___There were no sources of information.

12a. Name some of the new sources:_____

13. In your opinion how clear is the Miranda rule?

___very clear
___clear
___unclear
___very unclear
___I don't know

14. Before the Miranda case was decided did you expect the Supreme Court to make such a decision regarding police interrogation procedures?

___Yes
___No
___I don't know

15. Some people say that Supreme Court decisions which hamper
    police department procedures should not be followed by police
    departments. Others say that these decisions must be followed.
    Choose one of the following which best sums up your own position.

    ____Such court decisions should not be followed by police
        departments.
    ____Such decisions should be followed because otherwise the
        courts will undo the police work anyway.
    ____Such decisions should be followed because the Supreme
        Court knows more about those problems than the police do.
    ____Such decisions should be followed because only the Court
        has the right to decide what the law is.
    ____I don't know.

16. What is your personal opinion of the Miranda rule?

    ____I strongly approve of the rule
    ____I approve of the rule
    ____I disapprove of the rule
    ____I strongly disapprove of the rule
    ____I don't know

17. In your opinion, what do the people in your community generally
    think of the Miranda rule? Choose one of the following:

    ____They strongly disapprove of the rule
    ____They disapprove of the rule
    ____They approve of the rule
    ____They strongly approve of the rule
    ____They are generally unaware of the rule
    ____They are generally aware of the rule but don't care about
        its effects
    ____I don't know

    The following questions are included to furnish some general
    THOUGH STILL ANONYMOUS information.

18. For what city are you employed?

19. What is your rank? Please also tell whether or not you are a
    detective.

20. How long have you been on the police force?

21.   Extent of education. Choose the most appropriate category.

_____some high school but no high school diploma.
_____some high school and some specialized police training
          (for example the FBI Academy).
_____high school graduate with no additional schooling.
_____high school graduate with some specialized police training
          (for example, FBI Academy)--but no college.
_____some college but no specialized police training.
_____some college and some specialized police training.
_____college degree but No specialized police training.
_____college degree and some specialized police training.

This last question offers you a chance to express your own
opinions more fully:

22.   If you so desire, please make any other comments about the
Miranda rule. Why, for example, do you think the Supreme
Court decided the Miranda case the way it did?

Thank you for your cooperation.

Statistical Tests

Because the questionnaire was not distributed to a random sample, no tests of statistical significance can be used. I do know the number of officers who should have received questionnaires, and I know the distribution of the population by rank. Since much of the analysis involves comparison of ranks, we can compare rank breakdown of the respondents with the rank breakdown of the total population of their respective departments. We can thus get some idea of the "representativeness" of the sample.

In all of the tables, totals may not equal 100 percent because of rounding.

Generally detectives are most over-represented in our sample. Supervisors are slightly over-represented. Thus the final—perhaps inevitable—caveats are in order: One must be extremely careful about generalizing from the attitude and behavior patterns found in this study. Some caution must be used in employing the activities of the respondents to describe representative behavior even in their own departments.

A Comparison of Respondents to Population by Rank, in Percentages

Rank	Green Bay		Kenosha		Racine		Madison	
	Department	Sample	Department	Sample	Department	Sample	Department	Sample
Patrolman	65.0	58.6	66.1	62.5	73.4	53.4	70.3	52.6
Superior	24.2	25.7	16.9	15.6	17.1	27.6	15.9	16.7
Detective	10.8	14.4	16.9	20.3	9.5	15.5	14.9	29.5
Unknown	0.0	1.4	0.0	1.6	0.0	3.4	0.0	1.3
Total	100.0	100.0	100.0	100.0	100.0	100.0	100.0	100.0
(N)	(120)	(70)	(120)	(64)	(158)	(58)	(202)	(78)
Response Rates, in Percentages	58.3[a]		54.2		37.2		38.6[a]	

a. Men had individual mail boxes.

NOTE

1. Compare Jerome H. Skolnick, *Justice Without Trial* (New York: Wiley, 1966), chapter 2.

THE INDEX
OF PROFESSIONALIZATION

The choice of criteria for any index requires arbitrary decisions, and the validity of the criteria thus depend on how adequately these choices are defended. The following is a brief defense of the choices of criteria.

The first two of the eight items listed on p. 250 obviously attempt to compare departments on the salary criteria. As previously shown, good salaries are considered one essential prerequisite for professionalized law enforcement. Detectives' salaries were chosen as a criterion because the detective is the most important individual officer in the interrogation process.

A comparison of the numbers of civilian employees was made as a measure of specialization. According to the President's Commission, civilian employees should replace police officers in jobs which require no formal police training. This allows the officer to concentrate on more specialized law enforcement activities. The percentage of detectives and other investigators was chosen as a further measure of specialization because of their importance in the interrogation process.

To measure the extent of education, two extremes were chosen. On the one hand, the percentage of men with highschool diplomas was chosen as an indicator of the number of officers who lack the education requirements now considered the very minimal for police agencies. Indeed, all four departments presently require highschool diplomas as one of the prerequisites of eligibility. A measure of college education was used because of the increasing emphasis on the need for post-highschool education.

Data and Alternative Comparative Profesionalization Index: Four Cities

Item	Green Bay		Kenosha		Racine		Madison	
	Amount	Rank	Amount	Rank	Amount	Rank	Amount	Rank
Patrolman's Monthly Salary[a]	$530	(4)	$586	(3)	$588	(1)	$575	(2)
Detective's Monthly Salary[a]	$530	(4)	$648	(3)	$655	(1)	$651	(2)
Full-time civilian employees[b]	9.6%	(3.5)	10.7%	(2)	9.6%	(3.5)	23.8%	(1)
Investigators in Department	13.5%	(3.5)	15.4%	(2)	13.6%	(3.5)	18.3%	(1)

Officers with at least highschool diploma	89.0% (3)	94.3% (1)	83.0% (4)	89.7% (2)
Officers with some college	26.5% (3)	17.1% (4)	34.5% (2)	37.2% (1)
Weeks of required recruit training	10 (3)	8 (4)	12 (2)	14 (1)
Annual in-service training hours per officer	55 (4)	61 (3)	100 (1)	90 (2)
Total rank score	28	22	18	12
Average rank	3.50	2.75	2.25	1.50

a. Average based on annual salary ranges.
b. Includes stenographers, janitors, police cadets, radio operators, dog pound, and meter officials.
c. Includes detectives, juvenile investigators, and special non-traffic investigators.

Because of the paucity of college graduates in any department, the college graduate criterion was not used. The education measurements were not obtained from department records. They were taken from the questionnaire sent to all police officers in the four cities (see Appendix A).

The final criterion of police professionalization is the amount of specialized police training. There are, of course, many types of specialized programs. For example, traffic law institutes, narcotics institutes, and riot control programs are periodically offered by many law enforcement agencies. In constructing this index a decision was made to measure the most encompassing special education programs. All individual officers were most likely to be exposed at least to a recruit and general in-service training program. The reader should be particularly cautious in his interpretation of the in-service training indicators. In later analysis, it becomes apparent that the quality and methods of training vary greatly. The measurement includes everything from fifteen-minute roll-call refresher lectures to extensively organized in-service programs. For example, Racine's apparently great number of hours mostly consist of roll-call programs. Madison, on the other hand, is the only department with a training program required of all officers every year. Each Madison officer must annually complete a formal forty-hour training course.

The preceding table presents the data from which the index of professionalization was constructed. It also presents an alternative method of constructing the index. The numbers in parentheses represent the rank order of the departments on each variable. Because an index constructed in this manner did not take into consideration the extent of departmental differences on any single variable, I used the other index. Note that according to the alternative index Kenosha is more professionalized than Green Bay.

I used an analysis of variance to test the null hypothesis that all the data used to construct the index were drawn from the same sample. The formula is as follows:

$$F = \frac{m\Sigma\,(\bar{X}i - \bar{X})^2/n - 1}{\Sigma\,(Xij - Xj)^2/n\,(m-1)}$$

where Xij = individual deviation for ith role jth column; $\bar{X}j$ = column mean of column j; $\bar{X}$ = mean of all observations; m = number of rows; n = number of columns. $F = 6.13473$, which means that the null hypothesis is disproven; the statistic is significant at the .01 level.

BIBLIOGRAPHY

BOOKS

Alford, Robert R., with the collaboration of Harry M. Scoble, *Bureaucracy and Participation: Political Culture in Four Wisconsin Cities.* Chicago: Rand McNally, 1969.

Bauer, Raymond A. (ed.), *Social Indicators.* Cambridge, Mass.: MIT, 1966.

Becker, Theodore C. (ed.), *The Impact of A Supreme Court Decision.* New York: Oxford, 1969.

Bell, Daniel, *The End of Ideology.* Glencoe, Ill.: Free Press, 1960.

Bennis, W.G., K.D. Benne, and R. Chin, *The Planning of Change.* New York: Holt, Rinehart, & Winston, 1964.

Blau, Peter M., and W.R. Scott, *Formal Organizations: A Comparative Approach.* San Francisco: Chandler, 1962.

Bordua, David (ed.), *The Police: Six Sociological Essays.* New York: Wiley, 1967.

Cartwright, Dorwin, and Alvin Zander, *Group Dynamics: Research and Theory.* New York: Harper & Row, 1960.

Chevigny, Paul, *Police Power.* New York: Vintage, 1969.

Easton, David, *A Systems Analysis of Political Life.* New York: Wiley, 1965.

Edelman, Murray, *The Symbolic Uses of Politics.* Urbana: University of Illinois, 1964.

Gardiner, John A., *Traffic and the Police.* Cambridge, Mass.: Harvard University, 1969.

Germann, A.C., *Police Personnel Management.* Springfield, Ill.: Charles C. Thomas, 1958.

Holgren, R. Bruce, *Primary Police Functions.* New York: William C. Copp, 1960.

Johnson, Richard M., *The Dynamics of Compliance: Supreme Court Decision-Making from a New Perspective.* Evanston: Northwestern University, 1967.

Kenney, John P., and John B. Williams, *Police Operations.* Springfield, Ill.: Charles C. Thomas, 1960.

Kephart, William H., *Racial Factors and Urban Law Enforcement.* Philadelphia: University of Pennsylvania, 1957.

Klapper, Joseph T., *The Effects of Mass Communication.* Glencoe, Ill.: Free Press, 1963.

Krislov, Samuel, *The Supreme Court in the Political Process*. New York: Macmillan, 1965.

LaFave, Wayne R., *Arrest: The Decision to Take the Suspect into Custody*. Boston: Little, Brown, 1965.

Leonard, V. A., *Police Organization and Management*. New York: The Foundation Press, 1964.

Muir, William ., *Prayer in the Public Schools: Law and Attitude Change*. Chicago: University of Chicago, 1967.

Murphy, Walter F., *Congress and the Court*. Chicago: University of Chicago, 1965.

—, *Elements of Judicial Strategy*. Chicago: University of Chicago, 1964.

Newman, Donald J., *Conviction: The Determination of Guilt or Innocence Without Trial*. Boston: Little, Brown, 1966.

Niederhoffer, Arthur, *Behind the Shield*. Garden City, New York: Doubleday, 1967.

Oaks, Dallin H., and Warren Lehman. *A Criminal Justice System and the Indigent: A Study of Chicago and Cook County*. Chicago: University of Chicago, 1968.

Parker, W.H., *Daily Training Bulletin of the Los Angeles Police Department*. Springfield, Ill.: Charles C. Thomas, 1954.

Perkins, Rollin M., *Elements of Police Science*. Chicago: The Foundation Press, 1942.

Schaefer, Walter E., *The Suspect and Society*. Evanston, Ill.: Northwestern, 1967.

Simon, Herbert A., *Administration Behavior: A Study of Decision-Making Processes in Administrative Organizations*. New York: Macmillan, 1957.

Skolnick, Jerome H., *Justice Without Trial: Law Enforcement in Democratic Society*. New York: Wiley, 1966.

Smith, Bruce, *Police Systems in the United States*. New York: Harper & Brothers, 1949.

Trebach, Arnold, *The Rationing of Justice*. New Brunswick: Rutgers University, 1964.

Wilson, Orlando W., *Police Administration*. New York: McGraw-Hill, 1960.

ARTICLES

Abernathy, M. Glenn, "Police Discretion and Equal Protection." *South Carolina Law Quarterly* 14 (1962), pp. 472-86.

Alltman, Michael L., "The Effect of the Miranda Case on Confessions in the Juvenile Court." *American Criminal Law Quarterly* 5 (Winter, 1967), pp. 79-83.

Barrett, Edward L., "Police Practices and the Law—From Arrest to Release or Charge." *California Law Review* 50 (March, 1962), pp. 11-55.

Baylor Law Review, Note. 17 (Summer-Fall, 1965), pp. 376-98.

Beattie, Ronald H., "Criminal Statistics in the United States." *Journal of Criminal Law, Criminology and Police Science* 51 (May-June, 1960), pp. 49-65.

Birkby, Robert H., "The Supreme Court and the Bible Belt: Tennessee Reaction to the 'Schempp' Decision." *Midwest Journal of Political Science* 10 (1966), pp. 304-19.

Boggs, Sarah L., "Urban Crime Patterns." *American Sociological Review* 71 (1965), pp. 899-908.

Bordua, David J., and Albert J. Reiss, Jr., "Command, Control, and Charisma: Reflections on Police Bureaucracy." *American Journal of Sociology* 72 (1966), pp. 68-76.

Boston University Law Review, Comment. 42 (1962), pp. 129-34.

Breitel, Charles D., "Controls in Criminal Law Enforcement." *University of Chicago Law Review* 27 (Spring, 1960), pp. 427-37.

Brooklyn Law Review, Note. 31 (Dec., 1964), pp. 162-66.

Brown, Lawrence E., "Police Interrogation Dilemma." *Police* (Jan.-Feb., 1964), pp. 75-77.

California Law Review, Comment. 53 (March, 1965), pp. 337-63.

Caputo, Rudolph R., "The Confession." *Police* 9 (May-June, 1965), pp. 85-86.

—, "Interrogation Is Still a Valuable Technique." *Police* 11 (Nov.-Dec., 1966), pp. 20-21.

Casper, Joseph J., "A Great Dilemma for Police." *The Wisconsin Police Chief* 3 (Oct.-Nov., 1965), pp. 2, 4-5, 19-22.

Chapman, Samuel G., "Functional Problems Facing Law Enforcement Stemming from Supreme Court Decisions." *Police* 11 (Sept.-Oct., 1966), pp. 44-48.

—, "The Chief Salutes the NA Man." *The Wisconsin Police Chief* 1 (Sept.-Oct., 1963), pp. 24-28.

Chwast, Joseph, "Value Conflicts in Law Enforcement." *Crime and Delinquency* 11 (March, 1965), pp. 151-161.

Cipes, Robert M., "Crime, Confession and the Court." *Atlantic* 218 (September, 1966), pp. 51-58.

Connecticut Bar Journal, Note. 40 (March, 1966), pp. 118-132.

Dahl, Robert, "Decision-Making in a Democracy: The Supreme Court as a National Policy-Maker." *Journal of Public Law* 6 (1958), pp. 279-95.

Dolbeare, Kenneth M., and Phillip E. Hammond, "Local Elites, The Impact of Judicial Decisions and the Process of Change." Paper delivered at meeting of American Political Science Association, New York, September, 1969.

Dow, Thomas E., Jr., "The Role of Identification in Conditioning the Public Attitude Toward the Offender." *Journal of Criminal Law, Criminology and Police Science* 58 (March, 1967), pp. 75-79.

Edwards, George, "Due Process of Law in Criminal Cases." *Journal of Criminal Law, Criminology and Police Science* 57 (June, 1966), pp. 130-135.

Edwards, H. Lynn, "Law Enforcement Training in the United States." *American Criminal Law Quarterly* 3 (Winter, 1965), pp. 89-96.

"FBI Training Assistance for Local Police." *FBI Law Enforcement Bulletin* 34 (April, 1965), pp. 22-23.

Feld, M. D., "Political Policy and Persuasion: the Role of Communications from Political Leaders." *Journal of Conflict Resolution* 2 (1958), pp. 78-89.

Fox, Vernon, "Sociological and Political Aspects of Police Administration." *Sociology and Social Research* 51 (October, 1966), pp. 39-48.

Griffin, John I., "The Future of Police Statistics." *Police* 5 (Nov.-Dec., 1960), pp. 68-71.

"Here's How Crime Problems Look to Law Enforcement Officials." *FBI Law Enforcement Bulletin* 35 (Dec., 1966), pp. 16-29.

Hoover, J. Edgar, "Message from the Director." *FBI Law Enforcement Bulletin* 35 (Sept., 1966), p. 1.

Ibele, Oscar H., "Law Enforcement and the Permissive Society." *Police* 10 (Sept.-Oct., 1965), pp. 15-17.

Inbau, Fred E., "Popular Misconceptions Regarding Police Interrogation of Criminal Suspects." *Buffalo Law Review* 14 (Winter, 1968), pp. 274-77.

"Interrogations in New Haven: The Impact of *Miranda*." *Yale Law Journal* 76 (July, 1967), pp. 1521-1648.

Kadish, Sanford H., "Legal Norms and Sentencing Discretion in the Police and Sentencing Process." *Harvard Law Review* 75 (1962), pp. 904-931.

Kamisar, Yale, "On the Tactics of Police-Prosecution Oriented Critics of the Courts." *Cornell Law Quarterly* 49 (Spring, 1964), pp. 436-77.

Katzenbach, Nicholas deB., Letter to Judge David C. Bazelon. *Kentucky Law Journal* 54 (1966), pp. 490-494.

Kommers, Donald P., "Professor Kurland, The Supreme Court, and Political Science." *Journal of Public Law* 15 (1966), pp. 230-250.

Kuh, Richard H., "Interrogating Criminal Defenders." *NDAA*, 3 (Jan.-Feb., 1967), pp. 4-8.

LaFave, Wayne R., and Frank J. Remington, "Controlling the Police: The Judge's Role in Making and Reviewing Law Enforcement Decisions." *Michigan Law Review* 63 (April, 1965), pp. 987-1012.

LaFave, Wayne R., "Improving Police Performance Through the Exclusion Rule—Part I: Current Police and Local Court Practices." *Missouri Law Review* 30 (Summer, 1965), pp. 391-458.

—, "Improving Police Performance Through the Exclusionary Rule—Part II: Defining Norms and Training the Police." *Missouri Law Review* 30 (Fall, 1965), pp. 566-610.

—, "The Police and Non-Enforcement of the Law—Part I." *Wisconsin Law Review* (January, 1962), pp. 104-37.

—, "The Police and Non-Enforcement of the Law—Part II." *Wisconsin Law Review* (March 1962), pp. 179-239.

Lafollette, Bronson C., "Police and the Law." *The Wisconsin Police Chief* 3 (July-August, 1965), pp. 5-7.

Levine, James P., and Theodore L. Becker, "Toward and Beyond a Theory of Supreme Court Impact." Paper delivered at meeting of American Political Science Association, New York, September, 1969.

MacKenzie, John P., "The Compromise Report on Crime." *New Republic* 156 (Feb. 4, 1967), pp. 15-16.

McCormick, Charles T., "Some Problems and Developments in the Admissibility of Confessions." *Texas Law Review* (April, 1940), pp. 238-78.

Mechanic, David, "Sources of Power of Lower Participants in Complex Organizations." *Administrative Science Quarterly* 7 (1962), pp. 349-64.

Melia, Aloysius J., "The Admissibility of Confessions in Evidence in Criminal Courts." *Police* 3 (Nov.-Dec., 1958), pp. 12-15.

Moenssens, Andre A., "Police-Law Review." *Police* 11 (Jan.-Feb., 1967), pp. 112-45.

More, Henry (ed)., "Professional Periodical Reviews," *Police* 11 (Mar.-April, 1967), pp. 51-54.

Murphy, Michael J., "The Problem of Compliance by Police Departments." *Texas Law Review* 44 (April, 1966), pp. 939-53.

Newman, Donald J., "The Effect of Accommodations in Justice Administration on Criminal Statistics." *Sociology and Social Research* 46 (January, 1962), pp. 144-55.

—, "Pleading Guilty for Considerations: A Study of Bargain Justice." *Journal of Criminal Law, Criminology and Police Science* 46 (Mar.-April, 1956), pp. 780-790.

Norris, Fred F., "Accepting Crime Statistics." *Police* 6 (July-August, 1962), pp. 40-41.

Patric, Gordon, "The Impact of a Court Decision: Aftermath of the McCullom Case." *Journal of Public Law* 6 (1957), pp. 455-63.

Pittman, David J., and William F. Hardy, "Uniform Crime Reporting: Suggested Improvements." *Sociology and Social Research* 46 (January, 1962), pp. 135-44.

Pope, Walter L., "Escobedo, Then Miranda, and Now Johnson v. New Jersey." *American Criminal Law Quarterly* 5 (Winter, 1967), pp. 72-78.

"Professionalism and Good Public Relations Give Madison Police Department Excellent Image." *Wisconsin Police Chief* 2 (November, 1964), pp. 11, 13-14.

Reiss, Albert J., and Donald J. Black, "Interrogation and the Criminal Process." *Annals of the American Academy of Political and Social Science* 374 (November, 1967), pp. 47-57.

Ritz, Wilfred J., "State Criminal Confession Cases: Subsequent Developments in Cases Reversed by U.S. Supreme Court and Some Current Problems." *Washington and Lee Law Review* 19 (Fall, 1962), pp. 202-236.

—, "Twenty-five Years of State Criminal Confession Cases in the U.S. Supreme Court." *Washington and Lee Law Review* 19 (Spring, 1962), pp. 35-70.

Rodgers, Jack W., "Civil Liberties and Law Enforcement." *Police* 5 (July-August, 1961), pp. 10-14.

Rothblatt, Henry B., and Robert M. Pitler, "Police Interrogation: Warnings and Waiver—Where Do We Go From Here?" *Notre Dame Lawyer* 42 (April, 1967), pp. 479-98.

Rothblatt, Henry B., and Emma Alden Rothblatt, "Police Interrogation: The Right to Counsel and to Prompt Arraignment." *Brooklyn Law Review* 27 (December, 1960), pp. 24-68.

Schroetel, Stanley R., "Police Community Relations: My Impressions." *Police* 11 (Sept.-Oct., 1966), 52-54.

Schubert, Glendon, "The Rhetoric of Constitutional Change." *Journal of Public Law* 16 (1967), pp. 16-50.

Schuessler, Karl, "Components of Variation in City Crime Rates." *Social Problems* 9 (Spring, 1962), pp. 314-24.

Scott, Edgar E., "The Mallory Decision and the Vanishing Rights of Crime Victims." *Police* 4 (May-June, 1960), pp. 61-64.

Sellin, Thorsten, "Crime and Delinquency in the United States: An Over-All View." *Annals of the American Academy of Political and Social Science* 339 (January, 1962), pp. 11-23.

Shapiro, Martin, "Stability and Change in Judicial Decision-Making: Incrementalism or State Decisis?" *Law in Transition Quarterly* 2 (Summer, 1965), pp. 134-157.

Shulman, Harry M., "The Measurement of Crime in the United States." *Journal of Criminal Law, Criminology and Police Science* 57 (1966), pp. 483-92.

Smith, Alexander B., Bernard Locke, and William F. Walker, "Authoritarianism in College and Non-College Oriented Police." *Journal of Criminal Law, Criminology and Police Science* 58 (March, 1967), pp. 128-132.

Sorauf, Frank J., "Zorach v. Clauson: The Impact of a Supreme Court Decision." *American Political Science Review* 53 (1958), pp. 777-91.

Steamer, Robert J., "The Court and the Criminal." *William and Mary Law Review* 8 (Spring, 1967), pp. 319-42.

Sterling, David L., "Police Interrogation and the Psychology of Confession." *Journal of Public Law* 14 (1965), pp. 25-65.

Sullivan, F.C., "Know Your Law." *Police* 3 (Jan.-Feb., 1954), pp. 53-57.

"The Supreme Court: 1963 Term." *Harvard Law Review* 78 (November, 1964), pp. 143-320.

"Symposium." *Kentucky Law Journal* 54 (1966), pp. 463-527.

UCLA Law Review, Comment. 14 (1967), pp. 604-30.

University of Chicago Law Review, Comment. 32 (Sept., 1965), pp. 560-80.

Villanova Law Review, Comment. 7 (Summer, 1962), pp. 656-673.

Vines, Kenneth N., and Herbert Jacob, "Studies in Judicial Politics." *Tulane Studies in Political Science* 8 (1962).

Vorenberg, James, "Police Detention and Interrogation of Uncounselled Suspects: The Supreme Court and the States." *Boston University Law Review* 44 (Fall, 1964), pp. 423-434.

Warden, Karl F., "Miranda: Some History, Some Observations, and Some Questions." *Vanderbilt Law Review* 20 (1966), pp. 39-60.

Way, H. Frank, Jr., "The Supreme Court and State Coerced Confessions." *Journal of Public Law* 12 (1963), pp. 52-67.

Weisberg, Bernard, "Police Interrogation of Arrested Persons: A Skeptical View." *Journal of Criminal Law, Criminology and Police Science* 52 (May-June, 1961), pp. 21-46.

Wells, Richard S., and Joel B. Grossman, "The Concept of Judicial Policy Making: A Critique." *Journal of Public Law* 15 (1966), pp. 286-310.

Westley, William A., "Violence and the Police." *American Journal of Sociology* 59 (July, 1953), pp. 34-41.

Wilson, O. W., "Crime, the Courts, and the Police." *Journal of Criminal Law, Criminology and Police Science* 57 (1966), pp. 291-300.

Yale Law Journal, Comment. 73 (May, 1964), pp. 1025-58.

Younger, Evelle J., "Results of a Survey Conducted in the District Attorney's Office of Los Angeles County Regarding the Effect of the Miranda Decision Upon Prosecution of Felony Cases." *American Criminal Law Quarterly* 5 (Fall, 1966), pp. 32-39.

—, "Interrogating Criminal Defendants." *NDAA* 3 (Jan.-Feb., 1967), pp. 9-12.

CASES

Ashdown v. Utah, 357 U.S. 426 (1958).

Bianchi v. State, 169 Wis. 75, 171 N.W. 639 (1919).

Blackburn v. Alabama, 361 U.S. 199 (1960).

Bram v. U.S., 168 U.S. 532 (1897).

Bronston v. State, 17 Wis. 2d 627, 97 N.W. 504 (1959).

Brown v. Allen, 344 U.S. 443 (1952).

Brown v. Mississippi, 297 U.S. 278 (1936).

Brown v. Walker, 161 U.S. 591 (1896).

Browne v. State, 24 Wis. 2d 491, 129 N.W. 2d 175, 131 N.W. 2d 169 (1964).

Canty v. Alabama, 309 U.S. 629 (1939).

Chambers v. Florida, 309 U.S. 227 (1939).

Cicenia v. Lagay, 357 U.S. 501 (1957).

Conners v. State, 95 Wis. 77, 69 N.W. 981 (1897).

Counselman v. Hitchcock, 142 U.S. 547 (1892).

Crooker v. California, 357 U.S. 433 (1958).

Culombe v. Connecticut, 367 U.S. 568 (1961).

Davis v. North Carolina, 384 U.S. 719 (1966).
Escobedo v. Illinois, 378 U.S. 478 (1964).
Farino v. State, 203 Wis. 374, 234 N.W. 366 (1931).
Fikes v. Alabama, 352 U.S. 191 (1957).
Flamme v. State, 171 Wis. 501, 177 N.W. 596 (1920).
Gallegos v. Colorado, 370 U.S. 49 (1962).
Gallegos v. Nebraska, 342 U.S. 55 (1951).
In re Gault, 387 U.S. 1 (1967).
Haley v. Ohio, 332 U.S. 546 (1963).
Haynes v. Washington, 373 U.S. 503 (1963).
Hintz v. State, 125 Wis. 405, 104 N.W. 110 (1905).
Hoft v. Utah, 110 U.S. 574 (1884).
Holt v. State, 17 Wis. 2d 468, 117 N.W. 2d 626 (1962).
Johnson v. New Jersey, 384 U.S. 719 (1966).
Keenan v. State, 8 Wis. 132 (1858).
Kiefer v. State, 258 Wis. 47, 44 N.W. 2d 537 (1950).
Lang v. State, 178 Wis. 114, 189 N.W. 558 (1922).
Lee v. Mississippi, 332 U.S. 742 (1948).
Leyra v. Denno, 347 U.S. 556 (1954).
Link v. State, 217 Wis. 582, 259 N.W. 428, 261 N.W. 416 (1935).
Lisenba v. California, 314 U.S. 219 (1941).
Lyons v. Oklahoma, 322 U.S. 596 (1944).
Malinski v. New York, 324 U.S. 401 (1945).
Mallory v. U.S., 354 U.S. 449 (1947).
Malloy v. Hogan, 378 U.S. 1 (1964).
Massiah v. U.S., 377 U.S. 201 (1964).
McNabb v. U.S., 518 U.S. 332 (1943).
Miranda v. Arizona, 384 U.S. 436 (1966).
Neuenfeldt v. State, 29 Wis. 2d 20, 138 N.W. 2d 252 (1965).
Payne v. Arkansas, 356 U.S. 560 (1958).
Phillips v. State, 29 Wis. 2d 521, 139 N.W. 2d 41 (1966).
Pointer v. Texas, 380 U.S. 400 (1965).
Pulaski v. State, 24 Wis. 2d 450, 129 N.W. 2d 204 (1964).
Reck v. Pate, 367 U.S. 433 (1961).
Reimers v. State, 31 Wis. 2d 457, 143 N.W. 2d 525 (1966).
Rogers v. Richmond, 365 U.S. 534 (1961).
Spano v. New York, 360 U.S. 315 (1959).
Schoeffler v. State, 3 Wis. 823 (1854).
State ex rel. Goodchild v. Burke, 27 Wis. 2d 244, 137 N.W. 2d 244, 137 N.W. 2d 753 (1965).
State ex rel. LaFollette v. Raskin, 30 Wis. 2d 39, 139 N.W. 2d 667 (1966).
State ex rel. Van Ermen v. Burke, 30 Wis. 2d 324, 140 N.W. 2d 737 (1966).
State v. Carter, 33 Wis. 2d 80, 146 N.W. 2d 466 (1961).
State v. Francisco, 257 Wis. 247, 43 N.W. 2d 38 (1950).
State v. Glass, 50 Wis. 218, 6 N.W. 500 (1880).

State v. Goodchild, 272 Wis. 181, 74 N.W. 2d 624 (1956).
State v. Hoyt, 21 Wis. 2d 284, 124 N.W. 2d 47 (1963).
State v. LaPean, 247 Wis. 302, 19 N.W. 2d 289 (1945).
State v. Miller, 35 Wis. 2d 454, 151 N.W. 2d 157 (1967).
State v. Smith, 201 Wis. 8, 229 N.W. 51 (1930).
State v. Stortecky, 273 Wis. 362, 77 N.W. 2d 721 (1950).
State v. Whatley, 210 Wis. 157, 245 N.W. 93 (1933).
Stein v. New York, 346 U.S. 156 (1953).
Stroble v. California, 343 U.S. 181 (1952).
Tarasinki v. State, 146 Wis. 508, 131 N.W. 889 (1911).
Thomas v. Arizona, 356 U.S. 340 (1958).
Vernon v. Alabama, 313 U.S. 547 (1940).
Wan v. U.S., 266 U.S. 1 (1924).
Ward v. Texas, 316 U.S. 547 (1941).
Watts v. Indiana, 338 U.S. 49 (1949).
White v. Texas, 310 U.S. 530 (1940).
Williams v. U.S., 341 U.S. 97 (1951).
Yanke v. State, 51 Wis. 464, 8 N.W. 276 (1881).

GOVERNMENT DOCUMENTS

"Annual Report of the Attorney General of the United States for the Fiscal Year Ended June 30, 1966." Washington: U.S. Government Printing Office, 1966.
"Message from the President of the United States Transmitting a Summarization of the Report of the National Crime Commission Together with Recommendations for Measures to Be Taken for the Prevention of Crime." House of Representatives, Document No. 53, 90th Congress, 1st Session.
"Police and Fire Protection Services in Wisconsin—Trends and Opportunities." Madison: Public Expenditure Survey of Wisconsin, 1966.
President's Commission on Law Enforcement and Administration of Justice, *The Challenge of Crime in a Free Society.* Washington: U.S. Government Printing Office, 1967.
—, *Field Survey III, Vol. 2.* Washington: U.S. Government Printing Office, 1967.
—, *Task Force Report: Crime and Its Impact—An Assessment.* Washington: U.S. Government Printing Office, 1967.
—, *Task Force Report: The Police.* Washington: U.S. Government Printing Office, 1967.
—, *Task Force Report: Organized Crime.* Washington: U.S. Government Printing Office, 1967.
Proceedings Fifty-Ninth Annual Meeting National Association of Attorneys General. Chicago: National Association of Attorneys General, 1964.

U.S. Department of Justice, Federal Bureau of Investigation, "Uniform Crime Reporting—Preliminary Reports 1965-66."

U.S. Department of Health, Education, and Welfare, *Toward A Social Report*. Washington: U.S. Government Printing Office, 1969.

Wisconsin Attorney General, "Organized Crime in Wisconsin: Letter Transmitting Basic Facts on the State of Organized Crime in Wisconsin." Madison: Office of the Attorney General, 1966.

MISCELLANEOUS

Clarke, F. W., Clerk of Wisconsin State Supreme Court. Letter to author, November 10, 1967.

Courtney, Janet, Wisconsin State Judicial Council. Letter to author, October 6, 1967.

Frank, John P., Attorney for Ernesto Miranda. Letter to author, March 21, 1967.

Milner, Neal A., "The Impact of *Gideon*—A Study of the State and Local Judicial Process." Unpublished M.A. Thesis, University of Wisconsin, 1965.

Nelson, Gary K., Assistant Attorney General, State of Arizona. Letter to author, May 16, 1967.

Robbins, Patricia V., "State Criminal Investigation Agencies." 1962. Legislative Reference Library, Madison, Wisconsin.

Sachse, Earl Gustave, "Cost of the Administration of Justice in American Cities: Racine and Madison, Wisconsin." Unpublished B.A. Thesis, 1931. Legislative Reference Library, Madison, Wisconsin.

Wisconsin Taxpayer's Alliance, "Crime Detection." Madison: Wisconsin Taxpayer's Alliance, 1954.

—, "Police Costs and Other Data, Selected Cities and Villages, 1960." Typed manuscript, 1961. Legislative Reference Library, Madison, Wisconsin.

—, "What is the Judicial Council?" Madison: Wisconsin Taxpayer's Alliance, 1954.

INDEX

Alford, Robert R., 20, 75, 106, 131, 132, 158
American Civil Liberties Union, 38-39
American Law Institute, 62
American Motors, 108
Amicus curiae briefs, 30, 38
Arrests, 17, 20
Ashcraft v. Tennessee, 31-32
Attitudes toward *Miranda;* see Miranda, attitudes
Attorneys; *see* Counsel; Fees, attorneys'; Criminal law practitioners
Attorney General (Wisconsin); approval of *Miranda* decision, 62; control over local police, 61; criminal investigator unit, 60; decision-making strategies, 61ff; memoranda to police, 62-63, 101; source of information to local police, 51, 61-63, 119, 123, 145, 175, 201
Attorney General's Conference on Law Enforcement, 51

Bar associations, conflict, 162-164; Green Bay, 84ff; involvement in criminal justice administration, 111, 135, 164ff; Kenosha 110ff; Madison, 160ff; Racine, 133ff.
Barrett, Edward, 18, 24
Bauer, Raymond, 23
Becker, Theodore J., 23, 25, 221, 233
Benne, K. D., 233
Bennis, W., 233
Biderman, Albert, 24
Bill of Rights, 26
Black, Donald J., 221
Black, Hugo (Justice), 31, 32, 34
Blumberg, Abraham, 222
Bowen, Don R., 206, 233
Bureaucratization, 68, 129; *see also* Professionalization

Brown County Bar Association, 76
Brutality, police officers' views of, 192

Carlin, Jerome, 158
Capital Times (Madison), 72, 169-170, 187
Chicago, 109, 132
Chin, R., 233
Clearance rates, 16, 17, 217, 229
Communism, relationship to response to Supreme Court interrogation decision, 32
Communications process, emphasis on law enforcement sources of information, 93, 95; impact of *Miranda*, 95-97, 179; local criminal justice, 117ff, 122, 145ff, 156, 157, 171ff, 201-203; obstacles, 95-97; state-wide criminal justice administrations, 91ff; U.S. Supreme Court, 27-29, 35, 48; *see also* District attorney; Local judges; Police; U.S. Supreme Court
Compliance, 14, 220; indicators and measures of, 17-18, 227-229; organizational sanctions against, 229-230; personal disadvantages to, 229; *see also* Impact; *Miranda v. Arizona*, impact
Confessions; *see* Interrogation process
Conflict, between police and legal perspectives, 29, 32, 38, 41-43, 88, 114-115, 190-191, 194-196; political, 160; police-prosecutor, 88, 113, 140, 168-169; prosecutor-criminal law practitioner, 136
Congress, response to Supreme Court, 32-33
Constitution, 194
Conviction rates, 218
Cosa Nostra, 109

DATE DUE